Papillon—". . . a figu⌖ P9-DTQ-889
a blend of François Villon and the early
Errol Flynn . . . a talented storyteller of the
gee-whiz variety."   —*San Francisco Chronicle*

"BANCO is an inventive, romping adventure
story. . . . The voice of Charrière's escaped
con rings hard, true, and lusty, even as it sur-
faces with the coda of an underground morality."   —*Chicago Tribune Book World*

"The colors are lush. The gambles are crazy,
sinister, deadly. . . . A tale of bizarre adventure, danger, courage, passion and iron
nerve."   —*Philadelphia Bulletin*

"BANCO is an intriguing book, beguil-
ing . . . tantalizing . . . charming. . . ."
                              —King Features Syndicate

"PAPILLON was the adventure of a man.
BANCO is [about] a man of adventures."
                              —Dudley Lehew, Associated Press

BANCO
was originally published by
William Morrow and Company, Inc.

BANCO

The Further Adventures of
PAPILLON

by
HENRI CHARRIÈRE

Translated from the French by
PATRICK O'BRIAN

A POCKET BOOK EDITION published by
Simon & Schuster of Canada, Ltd. • Richmond Hill, Ontario, Canada
Registered User of the Trademark

BANCO

William Morrow edition published 1973

POCKET BOOK edition published September, 1974
2nd printing...............July, 1974

This POCKET BOOK edition includes every word contained
in the original, higher-priced edition. It is printed from brand-
new plates made from completely reset, clear, easy-to-read type.
POCKET BOOK editions are published by POCKET BOOKS,
a division of Simon & Schuster of Canada, Ltd.,
330 Steelcase Road, Markham, Ontario L3R 2M1.
Trademarks registered in Canada and other countries.

Standard Book Number: 671-78688-1.
Library of Congress Catalog Card Number: 73-13897.

Front cover illustration by Bob Maguire.

Printed in Canada.

To the memory of Dr. Alex Guibert-Germain,
to Madame Alex Guibert-Germain,
to my countrymen, the Venezuelans,
to my French, Spanish, Swiss, Belgian, Italian, Yugoslav,
German, English, Greek, American, Turkish, Finnish,
Japanese, Israeli, Swedish, Czechoslovak, Danish,
Argentine, Colombian, and Brazilian friends, and all those
friends who are faceless but who have done me the honor
of writing to me.

Contents

Translator's Introduction

Middle-aged, impoverished by an earthquake and worried about his future, Henri Charrière sat down to write a book to restore his fortunes: it was his first, and he called it *Papillon,* the name by which he had been known in the underworld of Paris and in the French penal settlements. He had no great opinion of himself as an author and he was quite willing to have it improved, cut about and put into "good French"; but the first publisher he sent it to happened to employ a brilliant editor who at once realized the exceptional quality of the manuscript and who delivered it to an astonished public in its original state, merely tidying up the punctuation, the spelling and a very few points of style.

That was in 1970, the year of the *phénomène Papillon,* a phenomenon almost unparalleled in the annals of publishing: it was not only that an extraordinary number of people read the book (850.000 copies were sold in the first few months), but that the readers embraced the whole spectrum of literary opinion, from the Académie Française to those whose lips moved slowly as they made their fascinated way through the strange adventures of an indomitable man struggling against the society that had sent him to rot in the infamous tropical prisons of Guiana with a life sentence for a murder that he had never committed.

They were all deeply moved by the burning sense of injustice that runs right through the book and that gives it its coherence and validity, but even more by Papillon's sheer narrative power, his innate genius for telling a story. "This is a literary prodigy," said François Mauriac. "It is utterly fascinating reading. . . . This new colleague of ours is a master!" And he pointed out that it was not enough to have been a transported convict and to have escaped again and again; extraordinary talent was required to give the book its ring of truth and to make its value "exactly proportional to its immense success."

The soundness of Mauriac's words can be seen not only from the immense quantities of hopeless manuscripts by other ex-prisoners (purple characters, but untouched by genius) that flow into publishers' offices every week, but also by the baldness of the following summary that is intended to put the reader of this second volume into the picture: the main facts are here, but I am the first to admit that the heart of the matter is lacking.

The facts, then: in 1931 Henri Charrière, alias Papillon, was sentenced to hard labor for life, and in 1933 he was taken away with some hundreds of others in a prison ship bound for South America, for French Guiana. Here he found himself in an appallingly tough and savage world where corruption, terrorism, sodomy and murder were commonplace; he was well equipped for survival in this world, being as tough as any man there, perfectly loyal to his friends and perfectly uncompromising in his hatred of the official establishment, and in time he could have carved out a respectable place for himself. But he had no intention of staying; he had sworn not to serve his unjust sentence, and forty-two days after his arrival he made a break. With two companions (one broke his leg in escaping) he made his way down the Maroni River in a crazy boat; at a remote lepers' island they changed boats and so rode out to sea, sailing under the broiling sun day after day until at last they reached Trinidad. On and on to Curaçao, where the boat was wrecked; on to Río

Hacha in Colombia, where the wind failed them and they were taken prisoner. Another break, this time with a Colombian friend, and eventually Papillon reached hostile Indian territory, alone and on foot. They took him in, gave him two wives, and then, when at last he would stay no longer, a bag of pearls. Back to Colombia, only to be arrested and imprisoned once more, and, after several abortive breaks, handed over to the French authorities. Then solitary confinement on the Ile Saint-Joseph—a deeply moving account of the silence, the heat and the utter loneliness of that dim, timeless, underground cage— two years of it. When at last it was over and he was out in the light again, he began to make a raft for another break; but a fellow convict informed upon him, and having killed the informer he went back to solitary—an eight years' sentence cut to nineteen months for rescuing a little girl from the sharks. Another attempt at escape; transfer to Devil's Island; and then the final break at last, riding two sacks of coconuts through the shark-infested sea to the mainland. A new boat and a new series of adventures brought him to Venezuela and to the Venezuelan penal settlement at El Dorado, where he was held on the charge of being a rogue and a vagabond. But a coup d'état in Caracas brought the promise of release, and the last pages of the book show Papillon, equipped with genuine papers at last, and dressed in good civilian clothes, ready to walk out into freedom after fourteen years of being in prison or on the run. That is where the present volume starts, and from now on his story is told in his own infinitely more living words.

                                        Patrick O'Brian

What you think of yourself matters more than what others think of you.

(author unknown to Papillon)

First Steps into Freedom

"Good luck, Frenchman! From this moment, you're free. *Adios!*"

The officer of the El Dorado penal settlement waved and turned his back.

And it was no harder than that to get rid of the chains I had been dragging for fourteen years. I held Picolino by the arm, and we took a few steps up the steep path from the riverbank, where the officer had left us, to the village of El Dorado. Now, sitting here in my old Spanish house on the night of August 18, 1971, to be exact, I can see myself on that pebbly track with unbelievable clarity; and not only does the officer's voice now ring in my ears in just the same way, deep and clear, but I make the same movement that I made twenty-six years ago—I turn my head.

It is midnight: outside the night is dark. But for me, for me alone, the sun is shining: it's ten o'clock in the morning, and I stare at the loveliest back I have ever seen in my life—the back of my jailer as he moves farther and farther away, symbolizing the end of the watching, the eavesdropping, the prying that I endured every day, night, minute and second for fourteen years.

I turn my head for a last look at the river, a last look, beyond the guard, at the island with its Venezuelan penal settlement, a last look at a hideous past when I was trampled upon, degraded and ground down.

Abruptly, I catch Picolino by the arm, turn my back on

the picture and lead him quickly up the path, first giving myself a shake to get rid of the filth of the past for good and all.

Freedom? Yes, but where? At the far end of the world, way back in the plateaus of Venezuelan Guiana, in a little village deep in the most luxuriant virgin forest you can imagine. I was at the southeastern tip of Venezuela, close to Brazilian frontier: an enormous sea of green, broken only here and there by the waterfalls of the rivers and streams that run through it—a green ocean dotted with little communities, each gathered around a chapel. Often these *pueblitos* are linked to others by only a truck or two, and looking at the trucks, you wonder how they ever got so far. In their isolation these simple, poetic people live just as people did hundreds and hundreds of years ago, free from all the taints of civilization.

When we had climbed up to the edge of the plateau where the village of El Dorado begins, we almost stopped; and then slowly, very slowly, we went on. I heard Picolino draw his breath, and, like him, I breathed in very deeply, forcing the air right down into the bottom of my lungs and letting it out gently, as though I were afraid of living these wonderful minutes too fast, these *first minutes of freedom*.

The broad plateau opened in front of us; to the right and left were houses, all bright and clean and surrounded by flowers. Some children had caught sight of us, and even though they knew where we came from, they approached us, not unfriendly at all; no, they were kind, and they walked beside us without a word. They seemed to understand how grave this moment was, and they respected it.

In front of the first house there was a little wooden table where a fat black woman was selling coffee and *arepas,* corn muffins.

"Good morning, lady."

"Buenas dias, hombres!"

"Two coffees, please."

"Sí, señores." And the good fat creature poured us two cups of delicious coffee; we drank standing, there being no chairs.

"What do I owe you?"

"Nothing."

"How come?"

"It's a pleasure for me to give you the first coffee of your freedom."

"Thank you. When's the next bus?"

"Today's a holiday, so there's no bus; but there's a truck at eleven."

"Okay. Thanks."

A black-eyed, light-skinned girl came out of a house. "Come in and sit down," she said with a lovely smile.

We walked in and sat down with a dozen people who were drinking rum.

"Why does your friend loll out his tongue?"

"He's sick."

"Can we do anything for him?"

"No, nothing: he's paralyzed. He's got to go to the hospital."

"Who's going to feed him?"

"Me."

"Is he your brother?"

"No, my friend."

"You got money, Frenchman?"

"Very little. How did you know I was French?"

"Everything gets known here in no time. We knew you were going to be let out yesterday and that you escaped from Devil's Island, and that the French police are trying to catch you to put you back there again. But they won't look for you here; they don't give orders in this country. We are the ones who are going to look after you."

"Why?"

"Because . . ."

"What do you mean?"

"Here, drink a shot of rum and give one to your friend."

Now a woman of about thirty was taking over. She was almost black. She asked me whether I was married. No. If my parents were still alive. Only my father.

"He'll be glad to hear you are in Venezuela."

"That's right."

A tall dried-up white man spoke up—he had big, staring eyes, but they were kind—"My relative didn't know how to tell you why we are going to look after you. Well, I'll tell you. Because unless he's mad—and in that case there's nothing to be done about it—a man can be sorry for what he's done, and he can turn into a good man if he's helped. That's why you'll be looked after in Venezuela. Because we love other men, and, with God's help, we believe in them."

"Why do you think I was a prisoner on Devil's Island?"

"Something very serious, for sure. Maybe for having killed someone, or for a really big theft. What did you get?"

"Life."

"The top sentence here is thirty years. How many did you do?"

"Fourteen. But now I am free."

"Forget all that, *hombre*. As quick as you can, forget everything you suffered in the French prisons and here in El Dorado. Forget it, because if you think about it too much you'll feel ill will toward other men and maybe even hate them. Only forgetting will let you love them again and live among them. Marry as soon as you can. The women in this country are hot-blooded, and the love of the woman you choose will give you happiness and children, and help you forget whatever you have suffered in the past."

The truck arrived. I thanked these kind, good people and went out. holding Picolino by the arm. There were about ten passengers sitting on benches in the back of the truck. They left us the best seats, next to the driver.

As we lurched along the potholed track, I thought about this strange Venezuelan nation. Neither the fishermen of the Gulf of Paria, nor the ordinary soldiers of El Dorado, nor the humble workingman who talked to me in that thatched mud hut had had any education. They could hardly read and write. So how did they come to have the charity and nobility to forgive men who had done wrong? How did it come about that the heads of the penal settlement of El Dorado, both the officers and the governor—educated men, those—had the same ideas as the simple people, the belief in giving every man a second chance, whoever he is and whatever he's done? That generosity could not have come from Europeans; so the Venezuelans must have got it from the Indians.

We arrived in El Callao. A big square, music. Of course: it was July 5, the national holiday. All the people in their best clothes made up a motley crowd, typical of tropical countries where so many colors are mixed— black, yellow, white and the copper of the Indians, whose race always shows in the slightly slanting eyes and the lighter skin. Picolino and I got out, along with some passengers from the back of the truck. One of them, a girl, came up to me and said, "Don't pay: that has been looked after." The driver wished us good luck, and the truck set off again. Holding my little bundle in one hand while Picolino gripped the other with the three fingers he had left, I stood there wondering what to do. I had some English pounds from the West Indies, a few hundred

bolívars* given me by my math pupils at the penal settlement, and some raw diamonds found among the tomatoes
in the vegetable garden I had made.

The girl who had told us not to pay asked me where we
were going, and I told her my idea was to find a little
boardinghouse.

"Come to my place first; then you can look around."

We crossed the square with her, and in a couple hundred yards we reached an unpaved street lined with low
houses; they were all made of baked clay, and their roofs
were thatch or corrugated iron. At one of them we
stopped.

"Walk in. This house is yours," the girl said. She must
have been about eighteen.

She made us go in first. A clean room with a floor of
pounded earth; a round table; a few chairs. A man of
about forty, medium height, with smooth black hair, Indian eyes, and the same light reddish-brown skin as his
daughter. And three girls of about fourteen, fifteen and
sixteen.

"My father and my sisters," she said, "here are some
strangers I have brought home. They've come from the El
Dorado prison, and they don't know where to go. I ask
you to take them in."

"You're welcome," the father said. And he repeated
the ritual words, "This house is yours. Sit down here,
around the table. Are you hungry? Would you like coffee
or rum?"

I didn't want to offend them by refusing, so I said I'd
like some coffee. I could see from the simple furniture
that they were poor.

"My daughter Maria, who brought you here, is the
oldest. She takes the place of her mother, who left us five

* A bolívar is worth about a quarter in U.S. money.

years ago with a gold prospector. I'd just as soon tell you that myself, before you hear it from someone else."

Maria poured coffee for us. Now I could look at her more closely, because she had taken a seat next to her father, right opposite me. The three sisters stood behind her. They looked closely at me, too. Maria was a girl of the tropics, with big, black, almond-shaped eyes. Her jet-black curling hair, parted in the middle, fell to her shoulders. She had fine features, and although you could detect the drop of Indian blood from the color of her skin, there was nothing Mongolian about her face. She had a sensuous mouth and splendid teeth. Every now and then she revealed the tip of a very pink tongue. She was wearing a white, flowered, wide-open blouse that showed her shoulders and the beginning of her breasts, covered by a brassiere that was visible under the blouse. This blouse, a little black skirt, and flat-heeled shoes were what she had put on for the holiday—her best. Her lips were painted bright red, and she had penciled two lines at the corners of her huge eyes to make them seem even larger.

"This is Esmeralda [Emerald]," she said, introducing her youngest sister. "We call her that because of her green eyes. This is Conchita; and the other is Rosita, because she looks like a rose. She is much lighter than the rest of us, and she blushes at the least thing. Now you know the whole family. My father's name is José. The five of us are the same as one, because our hearts beat all together. And what's your name?"

"Enrique."*

"Were you in prison long?"

"Fourteen years."

"Poor thing. How you must have suffered."

"Yes, a great deal."

* Enrique is the Spanish form of Henri.

"Papa, what do you think Enrique can do here?"

"I don't know. Do you have a trade?"

"No."

"Well then, go to the gold mine. They'll give you a job."

"And what about you, José? What do you do?"

"Me? Nothing. I don't work—they pay you very little."

Well, well, well. They were poor, sure enough; yet they were quite well dressed. Still, I couldn't very well ask him what he used for money—whether he stole instead of working. Wait and see, I said to myself.

"Enrique, you'll sleep here tonight," Maria said. "There's a room where my father's brother used to sleep. He's gone, so you can have his place. We'll look after the sick man while you go to work. Don't thank us; we're giving you nothing—the room's empty in any case."

I didn't know what to say. I let them take my little bundle. Maria got up and the other girls followed her. She had been lying: I could tell the room was in use, because they brought out women's things and put them somewhere else, but I pretended not to notice anything. In the room there was no bed, but something better, something you often see in the tropics—two fine wool hammocks. A big window with just shutters—no glass—opened onto a garden full of banana palms.

As I swung there in the hammock I could hardly believe what had happened to me. How easy this first day of freedom had been! Too easy. I had a free room and four sweet girls to look after Picolino. Why was I letting myself be led by the hand like a child? I was at the world's end, to be sure; but I think the real reason I let myself be managed was that obeying was the only thing I understood after being a prisoner for so long. I was just like a bird that, when you open the door of its cage, doesn't know how to fly anymore. It has to learn all over again.

I went to sleep without thinking about the past, exactly as the humble man of El Dorado had advised me.

I had just breakfasted off two fried eggs, two fried bananas covered with margarine, and black bread. Maria was in the bedroom, washing Picolino. A man appeared in the doorway; he was wearing a machete in his belt.

"Gente de paz," he said. Men of peace, which is their way of saying, I'm a friend.

"What do you want?" asked José, who had had breakfast with me.

"The chief of police wants to see the men from Devil's Island."

"You don't want to call them that. Call them by their names."

"Okay, José. What are their names?"

"Enrique and Picolino."

"Señor Enrique, come with me. I am a policeman, sent by the chief."

"What do they want with him?" Maria asked, coming out of the bedroom. "I'll come, too. Wait while I dress."

In a few minutes she was ready. As soon as we were in the street she took my arm. I looked at her, surprised, and she smiled at me. When we reached the little administrative building, there were more police, all in plain clothes except for two in uniform with machetes hanging from their belts. A black man with a gold-braided cap presided over a roomful of rifles. He said to me, "You're the Frenchman?"

"Yes."

"Where's the other?"

"He's sick," Maria said.

"I command the police. I'm here to help you if you

need it. My name's Alfonso." And he held out his hand.

"Thanks. Mine's Enrique."

"Enrique, the chief administrator wants to see you. You can't go in, Maria," he added, seeing she was about to follow me. I went into the next room.

"Good morning, Frenchman. I am the chief administrator. Sit down. Since you're in compulsory residence here in El Callao, I sent for you so that I could get to know you. I'm responsible for you." He asked me what I was going to do—where I wanted to work. After we had talked a while he said, "If there's anything at all, come and see me. I'll help you work out as good a life as we can manage."

"Thank you very much."

"Oh, there's one thing. I must warn you that you're living with very good, honest girls; but their father, José— he's a pirate."

Maria was outside, at the station door, settled into that attitude Indians adopt when they are waiting, neither moving nor talking to anyone at all. She was not an Indian, but because of that little drop of Indian blood she had, the race came out. We took another way back to the house and walked through the whole village, her arm in mine.

"What did the chief want with you?" Maria asked, calling me by the familiar pronoun for the first time.

"Nothing. He told me I could count on him to help me find a job or in case I was in a hole."

"Enrique, you don't need anyone now. Nor does your friend."

"Thanks, Maria."

We passed a peddler's stall, full of women's trinkets— necklaces, bracelets, earrings, brooches, etc.

I took her over and picked out the best necklace with matching earrings, and three other, smaller sets for her sisters. I gave thirty bolívars for these tinselly little things, paying with a hundred note. Maria put the necklace and the earrings on right away. Her big black eyes sparkled and she thanked me as though the jewels were really valuable.

When we got back to the house the three girls shrieked with delight over their presents. I went to my room, leaving them. I had to be alone to think. This family had offered me their hospitality with a splendid generosity; but should I accept it? I had some money, after all, not to mention the diamonds. Reckoning it all together, I could live four months and more without worrying, and I could have Picolino looked after.

All these girls were lovely, and like tropical flowers they were surely all warm, sexy, ready to give themselves only too easily, almost without thinking. I had seen Maria looking at me today almost as if she were in love. Could I resist so much temptation? It would be better for me to leave this too welcoming house before my weakness brought trouble and suffering. I was thirty-nine, although I looked younger, and Maria was not quite eighteen, her sisters younger still. I ought to go, I thought. The best thing would be to leave Picolino in their care, paying for his board, of course.

"Señor José, I'd like to talk to you alone. Shall we go and have a rum at the café in the square?"

"All right. But don't call me señor. You call me José and I'll call you Enrique. Let's go. Maria, we're going out to the square for a minute."

"Enrique, change your shirt," Maria said. "The one you've got on is dirty."

I went and changed in the bedroom. Before we left, Maria said, "Don't stay long, Enrique; and above all, don't drink too much!" And before I had time to step back she kissed me on the cheek.

Her father burst out laughing. "That Maria," he said, "she's in love with you already."

As we walked toward the bar I began, "José, you're a man, so you will understand that if I lived among your daughters it would be hard for me not to fall in love with one of them. But I'm twice as old as the eldest, and I'm legally married in France. So let's go and have a drink or two together, and then you take me to some cheap little boardinghouse. I can pay."

"Frenchman, you're a real man," José said, looking me straight in the eye. "Let me shake your hand like a brother for what you've just said to a poor guy like me. In this country, you see, almost nobody's married legally. You like one another, you make love, and if there's a child, you set up house together. You join up as easily as you leave one another. It's very hot here, and on account of the heat the women are very full-blooded. They mature early. Maria's an exception; she's never had an affair although she's nearly eighteen. I think your country's morality is better than ours, because here many women have children without a father, and that's a very serious problem. But what can you do about it? The good Lord says you must love one another and have children. So although I see you are surrounded by temptation all the time, I ask you again to stay with us. I'm glad to have a man like you in the house."

We were in the bar before I answered. A dozen men were sitting around. We drank a few rum-and-Cokes. Several people came up to shake my hand and bid me welcome to their village, and each time José introduced me as a friend who was living at his house. We had a good many drinks. When I asked what they came to, José became almost annoyed; he wanted to pay for everything. Still, I finally managed to persuade the bartender to take my money instead.

Someone touched me on the shoulder. It was Maria.

"Come home. It's lunchtime. Don't drink anymore; you promised me not to drink too much."

José was arguing with another man; she said nothing to him, but took me by the arm and led me out.

"What about your father?"

"Let him be. I can never say anything to him when he's drinking and I never come to fetch him from the café. He wouldn't have it, anyway."

"Why did you come and fetch me, then?"

"You're different. Be good, Enrique, and come along." Her eyes were so brilliant, and she said it so simply, I went back to the house with her.

"You deserve a kiss," she said when we got there. And she put her lips to my cheek, too near my mouth.

José came back after we had had lunch together at the round table. The youngest sister helped Picolino eat, giving him his food little by little.

José sat down by himself. He was high, so he spoke without thinking. "Enrique is frightened of you, my girls," he said, "so frightened he wants to go away. I told him that in my opinion he could stay, and that my girls were old enough to know what they were doing."

Maria gazed at me. She looked astonished, perhaps disappointed. "If he wants to go, Papa, let him. But I don't think he'd be better off anywhere else than he is here, where everyone likes him." And turning to me she added, "Enrique, don't be a coward. If you like one of us, and she likes you, why should you run away?"

"On account of he's married in France," her father said.

"How long since you saw your wife?"

"Fourteen years."

"The way we see it, if you love a man you don't necessarily marry him. If you give yourself to a man, it's to love him, nothing more. But it was quite right of you to tell our father you were married, because like that you can't promise any of us anything at all, aside from just loving her." And she asked me to stay with them without committing myself. They would look after Picolino and I would be more free to work. She even said I could pay a little, as if I were a boarder, to ease my mind. Did I agree?

I had no time to think properly. It was all so new and so quick after my years as a convict. I agreed.

"Would you like me to go with you to the gold mine this afternoon to ask for a job? We could go at five, when the sun is lower. It's a mile and a half from the village."

"Fine."

Picolino's movements and his expression showed how pleased he was that we were going to stay. The girls' kindness and their care had won his heart. My staying was chiefly on account of him. Because here I was pretty sure I'd have an affair before long, and I wasn't sure it would suit me.

With all that had been going on inside my head these last fourteen years, with all that had kept me from sleeping all those nights in prison, I was not going to drop everything as quickly as all this and settle down in a village at the far end of the world just because of a girl's pretty face. I had a long road in front of me, and any stops must be short. Just long enough to catch my breath. Because there was a reason why I had been fighting for my liberty these fourteen years and there was a reason why I had won the fight; and that reason was *revenge*. The prosecuting counsel, the false witness, the cop: I had a score to settle with them. And that was something I was never to forget. Never.

I wandered out to the village square. I noticed a shop with the name Prospéri over it and figured the owner must be a Corsican or an Italian. Indeed, the little shop did belong to the descendant of a Corsican. Monsieur Prospéri spoke very good French. He kindly suggested writing a letter for me to the manager of La Mocupia, the French company that worked the Caratal gold mine. This splendid man even offered to help me with money. I thanked him for everything and went out.

"What are you doing here, Papillon? Where the hell have you come from, man? From the moon? Dropped by parachute? Come and let me kiss you!" A big guy, deeply sunburned, with a huge straw hat on his head, jumped to his feet. "You don't recognize me?" And he took off his hat.

"Big Charlot! I'll be damned!" Big Charlot, the man who knocked off the safe at the Place Clichy Gaumont in Paris, and the safe in the Batignolles station! We embraced like two brothers. Tears came into our eyes, we were so moved. We gazed at one another.

"A far cry from the Place Blanche and the clink, pal, huh? But where the hell have you come from? You're dressed like an English lord: and you've aged much less than me."

"I'm just out of El Dorado."

"How long were you there?"

"Over a year."

"Why didn't you let me know? I'd have got you out right away, signed a paper saying I was responsible for you. Christ above! I knew there were some hard cases in El Dorado, but I never for a moment imagined you were there, you, a buddy!"

"It's a miracle we should meet."

"Don't you believe it, Papi. The whole of Venezuelan Guiana is stuffed with convicts making a break. And as this is the first bit of Venezuelan territory you come across when you escape, there's no miracle in meeting anyone at all between the Gulf of Paria and here—every last son of a bitch comes this way. All those who don't come apart on the road, I mean. Where are you staying?"

"With a decent fellow named José. He has four daughters."

"Yes, I know him. He's a good man, a pirate. Let's go and get your things: you are staying with me, of course."

"I'm not alone. I've got a paralyzed friend and I have to look after him."

"That doesn't matter. I'll send a donkey for him. It's a big house and there's a Negrita who'll look after him like a mother."

When we had found the donkey we went to the girls' house. Leaving these kind people was very painful. It was only when we promised to come and see them, and said they could come and see us at Caratal, that they calmed down a little.

Two hours later we were at Charlot's "chateau," as he called it. A big, light, roomy house on a headland looking out over the whole of the valley running down from the hamlet of Caratal almost to El Callao. On the right of this virgin forest was the Mocupia gold mine. Charlot's house was built entirely of hardwood logs from the bush: three bedrooms, a fine dining room and a kitchen; two showers inside and one outside, in a perfectly kept garden. All the vegetables we had at home were growing there, and growing well. Besides a chicken run with more than five hundred hens, there were rabbits, guinea pigs, two goats and a pig. All this was the fortune and the present happiness of Charlot, the former crook and safecracker, specialist in very delicate operations worked out to the second.

"Well, Papi, how do you like my shack? I've been here seven years. As I was saying in El Callao, it's a far cry from Montmartre and the clink! Who'd ever have believed that one day I'd be happy with such a quiet, peaceful life? What do you say, pal?"

"I don't know, Charlot. I'm too lately out of stir to have

a clear idea. It sets me back a little, seeing you quiet and happy here at the back of beyond. As far as I'm concerned, you see, I don't feel up to it yet."

When we were sitting around the table in the dining room and drinking Martinique punch, Big Charlot went on, "Yes, Papillon, I can see you're amazed that I live by my own work. Eighteen bolívars a day means a modest life, but one not without its pleasures. A hen that hatches me a good brood of chicks, a rabbit that brings off a big litter, a kid being born, tomatoes doing well . . . all these little things we despised for so long add up to something that gives me a lot. Hey, here's my black girl. Conchita! Here are some friends of mine. That one's sick; you'll have to look after him. This one's called Enrique, or Papillon. He's a friend from France, an old-time friend."

"Welcome to this house," the black girl said. "Don't you worry, Charlot, your friends will be properly looked after. I'll go and see to their room."

Charlot told me about his break—an easy one. When he first got to the penal colony he was kept at Saint-Laurent-du-Maroni, and after six months he escaped from there with another Corsican called Simon and a detainee. "We were lucky enough to reach Venezuela a few months after the dictator Gomez died. These open-handed people helped us make a new life for ourselves. I had two years of compulsory residence at El Callao, and I stayed on. Little by little, I took to liking this simple life, you know? I lost one wife when she was having a baby, and the daughter, too. Then this black girl you've just seen, Conchita, she managed to comfort me with her real love and understanding, and she's made me happy. But what about you, Papi? You must have had a cruelly hard time of it; fourteen years is a hell of a stretch. Tell me about it."

I talked to this old friend for more than two hours, spilling out everything these last years had left rankling in

me. It was wonderful for us both to be able to talk about
our memories. But, oddly, there was not a single word
about Montmartre, not a word about the underworld, no
reminders of jobs that were pulled off or misfired, nothing
about crooks still at large. It was as though for us life had
begun when we stepped aboard *La Martinière,* me in
1933, Charlot in 1935.

Good Chianti, excellent salad, a grilled chicken, goat
cheese and a delicious mango, all put on the table by the
cheerful Conchita, meant that Charlot could welcome me
properly in his house, and that pleased him. He suggested
going down to the village for a drink. I said it was so
pleasant where we were I didn't want to go out.

"Thanks, my friend," my Corsican said—he often put
on a Paris accent. "You're dead right: we are comfortable
here. Conchita, you'll have to find a girl friend for Enrique."

"All right: Enrique, I'll introduce you to friends prettier
than me."

"You're the prettiest of them all," Charlot said.

"Yes, but I'm black."

"That's the very reason why you're so pretty, poppet.
Because you're a thoroughbred."

Conchita's big eyes sparkled with love and pleasure; it
was easy to see she worshipped Charlot.

Lying quietly in a fine big bed I listened to the BBC
news from London on Charlot's radio: but being plunged
back into the life of the outside world worried me a
little—I was not used to it anymore. I turned the knob.
Now it was Caribbean music that came through: Caracas
in song. I didn't want to hear the great cities urging me to
live their life. Not this evening, anyway. I switched off
quickly and began to think over the last few hours.

Had we purposely avoided talking about the years
when we both lived in Paris? No. Had we purposely not
mentioned the men of our world who had been lucky

enough not to be picked up? No again. So did what had happened before the trial no longer matter?

I tossed and turned in the big bed. It was hot; I couldn't bear the heat anymore and walked out into the garden. I sat down on a big stone, from where I could look out over the valley and the gold mine. Everything was lit up down there. I could see trucks, empty or loaded, coming and going.

Gold: the gold that came out of the depths of that mine. A lot of it, either in bars or turned into bills, would give you anything on earth. This prime mover of the world, which cost so little to mine, since the workers had such miserable wages. was the one thing you had to have to live well. Charlot had lost his freedom because he had wanted a lot of it, yet today he hadn't even mentioned the stuff. He hadn't told me whether the mine had much gold in it or not. These days his happiness was his back girl, his house, his animals and his garden. He had never even referred to money. He had become a philosopher. I was puzzled.

They caught Charlot because a guy by the name of Little Louis tipped off the police; and during our short meetings in the Santé Charlot never stopped swearing he would get Louis the first chance he had. Yet this evening he had not so much as breathed Louis's name. And as for me—Christ!—I had not said a word about my cops, or Goldstein, or the prosecuting counsel, either. I should have talked about them! I hadn't escaped just to end up a cross between a gardener and a day laborer.

I had promised to go straight in this country, and I'd keep my word. But that didn't mean I had given up my plans for revenge. You mustn't forget, Papi, that the reason you're here today is that the idea of revenge kept you going for fourteen years.

His little black girl was very pretty, all right; but still I wondered whether Big Charlot wouldn't be better off in a city than in this hole at the far end of creation. Or maybe I was the square, not seeing that my friend's life had its charm? That was something to chew over.

Charlot was forty-five, not an old man. Very tall, very strong, built like a Corsican peasant fed on plenty of good, healthy food all his young days. He was deeply burned by the sun of this country, and with his huge straw hat on his head, its brim turned up at the sides, he looked terrific. He was a perfect example of the pioneer in these virgin lands, and he was so much one of the people and the country he did not stand out at all. Far from it: he really belonged.

Seven years he'd been here, this still young Montmartre safecracker! He must certainly have worked more than two years to clear this stretch of plateau and build his house. He had to go out into the bush, choose the trees, cut them down, bring them back, fit them together. Every beam in his house was made of the hardest and heaviest timber in the world, the kind they call ironwood. I was sure all he earned at the mine had gone into it, because he must have had help and must have paid for the labor, the cement (the house was concreted), the well, and the windmill for pumping the water up to the tank.

That well-rounded young Negrita with her big loving eyes: she must be a perfect companion for this old sea dog on shore. I'd seen a sewing machine in the big room. She must make those little dresses that suited her so well.

Maybe the reason Charlot hadn't gone to the city was that he wasn't sure of himself, whereas here he enjoyed a life with no problems at all. You're a great guy, Charlot! You're the very picture of what a crook can be turned into. I congratulate you. And I also congratulate the people who changed your way of seeing what a life can or ought to be.

But still these Venezuelans are dangerous, with their generous hospitality. Kindness and goodwill turn you into a prisoner if you let yourself be caught. I'm free, and I mean to stay that way forever.

I'd better watch it. Above all, no setting up house with a girl. A man needs love when he's been cut off from it for a long time, but fortunately I'd had a girl in Georgetown two years before my Hindu, Indara. So I was not so vulnerable as if I'd come straight from jail, as Charlot had. Indara was lovely and I was happy with her; but it wasn't for that I had settled in Georgetown, living there in clover. If the quiet life is too quiet, even though it's happy, it's not for me· that I know very well.

Adventure! A man needs adventure to feel alive, alive all through! That was why I left Georgetown and why I ended up at El Dorado. And that was why I was where I was today.

Okay. The girls were pretty, full-blooded and charming, and I certainly could not live without love. It was up to me to avoid complications. I must promise myself to stay there a year, since I was forced to do so anyway. The less I owned, the easier I'd be able to leave this country and its enchanting people. I was an adventurer, but an adventurer with a shift of gear—I must get my money honestly, or at least without hurting anyone. Paris, that was my aim: Paris one day, to present my bill to the people who put me through so much suffering.

I was calmer now, and my eyes took in the setting moon as it dipped toward the virgin forest, a sea of black treetops with waves of different heights—but waves that never stirred. I went back to my room and stretched out on the bed.

Paris was still a great way off, but not so far that I wouldn't be there again one day, walking the asphalt of her streets.

2

The Mine

A week later, thanks to the letter that Prospéri, the Corsican grocer, wrote for me, I was taken on at the Mocupia mine. There I was, looking after the working of the pumps that sucked up the water from the shafts.

The mine looked like a coal pit, with its underground galleries. There were no veins of gold and very few nuggets. The gold was found in very hard rock; they blasted this rock with dynamite and then broke the oversized lumps with a sledgehammer. The pieces were put into trucks, and the trucks brought to the surface in elevators; then crushers reduced the rock to a powder finer than sand. This was mixed with water, making a liquid mud that was pumped up into tanks as big as the reservoirs in an oil refinery. These tanks had cyanide in them. The gold dissolved into a liquid heavier than the rest and sank to the bottom. Under heat, the cyanide evaporated, carrying off the particles of gold; they solidified and were caught by filters very like combs as they went past. Then the gold was collected, melted into bars, carefully checked for 24-carat purity and put into a strictly guarded store. But who did the guarding? I still can't get over it. Simon, no less, the crook who had made his break from the penal colony with Big Charlot.

When my work was over, I went to gaze at the sight. I went to the store and stared at the huge pile of gold ingots neatly lined up by Simon, the ex-convict. Not even a strongroom, just a concrete storehouse with walls no thicker than usual, and a wooden door.

"Everything okay, Simon?"

"Okay. And what about you, Papi? Happy at Charlot's?"

"Yes, I'm fine."

"I never knew you were in El Dorado. Otherwise I'd have come to get you out."

"That's a good guy. Are you happy here?"

"Well, you know, I have a house: it's not as big as Charlot's but it's made of bricks and mortar. I built it myself. And I've got a young wife, very sweet. And two little girls. Come and see me whenever you like—my house is yours. Charlot tells me your friend is sick; my wife knows how to give injections, so if you need her don't hesitate."

We talked. He, too, was thoroughly happy. He, too, never spoke of France, of Montmartre, though he had lived there. Just like Charlot. The only thing that mattered was the present—wife, children, the house. He told me he earned twenty bolívars a day. Fortunately their hens gave them eggs for their omelettes, and the chickens were on the house; otherwise they wouldn't have gone far on twenty bolívars, Simon and his brood.

I gazed at that mass of gold lying there, so carelessly stored behind a wooden door, and the four walls only a foot thick. A door that two heaves on a jimmy would open without a sound. This heap of gold, at three bolívars fifty a gram or thirty-five dollars an ounce, would easily add up to three million five hundred thousand bolívars, or almost a million dollars. And this unbelievable fortune was within hand's reach! Knocking it off would be almost child's play.

"Elegant, my neat pile of ingots? Eh, Papillon?"

"It'd be more elegant still well salted away. Christ, what a fortune!"

"Maybe, but it's not ours. It's holy, on account of they've entrusted it to me."

"Entrusted it to you, sure; but not to me. You must admit it's tempting to see something like that just lying about."

"It's not just lying about, because I'm looking after it."

"Maybe. But you aren't here twenty-four hours a day."

"No. Only from six at night to six in the morning. But during the day there's another guard: maybe you know him—Alexandre, of the forged postal orders."

"Yes, I know him. Well, I'll see you later, Simon. Say hello to your family for me."

"You'll come and visit us?"

"Sure. I'd like to. *Ciao*."

I left quickly, as quickly as I could to get away from this scene of temptation. It was unbelievable! Anyone would say they were yearning to be robbed, the guys in charge of this mine. A store that could hardly hold itself upright, and two onetime high-ranking crooks taking care of all that treasure! In all my life on the loose I'd never seen anything like it!

Slowly I walked up the winding path to the village. I had to go right through it to reach the headland where Charlot's chateau was. I dawdled; the eight hour day had been tough. In the second gallery there had been precious little air, and even that was hot and wet, in spite of the ventilators. My pumps had stopped sucking three or four times and I had had to set them right again. It was half past eight now, and I had gone down the mine at noon. I'd earned eighteen bolívars. If I had had a workingman's mind, that wouldn't have been so bad. Meat was 2.50 bolívars per kilo; sugar 0.70; coffee 2. Vegetables weren't dear either: 0.50 for a kilo of rice and the same for dried beans. You could live cheaply, that was true. But did I have the sense to put up with this kind of life?

In spite of myself, as I climbed the stony path, walking

easily in the heavy nailed boots they had given me at the mine—in spite of myself. and although I did my best not to think about it, I kept seeing that million dollars in gold bars just calling out for some enterprising hand to grab it. At night, it wouldn't be hard to jump Simon and chloroform him without being recognized. And then the whole thing was in the bag. because they carried their fecklessness to the point of leaving him the key to the store so he could take shelter if it rained. Criminal irresponsibility! All I'd have to do then was carry the two hundred ingots out of the mine and load them into something—a truck or a cart. I'd have to prepare several caches in the forest, all along the road, to salt the ingots away in little bundles of a hundred kilos each. If it was a truck, then once it was unloaded I'd have to carry on as far as possible, pick the deepest place in the river and toss it in. A cart? There were plenty in the village square. The horse? That would be harder to find, but not impossible. A night of very heavy rain would give me all the time I needed for the job, and it might even let me get back to the house and go to bed meek as a monk.

By the time I reached the lights of the village square, I had already brought the heist off in my mind, and was slipping into the sheets of Big Charlot's bed.

"Buenas noches," called a group of men sitting at the village bar.

"Hello there, one and all. Good night, *hombres.*"

"Come and join us for a while. Have an iced beer."

It would have been rude to refuse, so there I was sitting among those good souls, most of them miners, who wanted to know whether I was all right, whether I'd found a woman, whether Conchita was looking after Picolino properly, and whether I needed money for medicine or anything else. These generous, spontaneous offers brought me back to earth. A gold prospector said that if I didn't care for the mine and if I only wanted to work when I felt like it I could go off with him. "It's tough going, but you make more. And then there's always the possibility you'll be rich in a single day." I thanked them all and offered to stand a round.

"No, Frenchman, you're our guest. Another time, when you're rich. God be with you."

I went on toward the chateau. Yes, it would be easy enough to turn into a humble, honest man among all these people who lived on so little, who were happy with almost nothing, and who adopted a man without worrying where he came from or what he had been.

Conchita welcomed me back. She was alone. Charlot was at the mine—so when I left for work he'd be coming back. Conchita was full of fun and kindness: she gave me a pair of slippers so I could rest my feet after the heavy boots.

"Your friend's asleep. He ate well and I've sent off a letter asking them to take him into the hospital at Tumereno, a little town not far off, bigger than this."

I thanked her and ate the hot meal that was waiting for me. This welcome, so homely, simple and happy, made me relax; it gave me the peace of mind I needed after the temptation of that ton of gold. The door opened.

"Good evening, everybody." Two girls came into the room, just as if they were at home.

"Good evening," Conchita said. "Here are two friends of mine, Papillon."

One was dark, tall and slim; she was called Graciela and was very much the gypsy type, her father being a Spaniard. The other girl's name was Mercedes. Her grandfather was a German, which explained her fair skin and very fine blond hair. Graciela had black Andalusian eyes with a touch of tropical fire; Mercedes' were green and suddenly reminded me of Lali, the Goajira Indian. Lali . . . Lali and her sister Zoraïma: what had become of them? It was 1946 now, and twelve years had gone by, but in spite of all those years I felt a pain in my heart when I remembered those two lovely creatures. Since those days they must have made themselves a fresh life with men of their own race, and honestly I had no right to disturb their new existence.

"Your friends are terrific, Conchita! Thank you very much for introducing me to them."

I gathered they were both free and neither had a fiancé. In such good company the evening went by in a flash. Conchita and I walked them back to the edge of the village, and it seemed to me they leaned very heavily on my arms. On the way back Conchita told me both the girls liked me, the one as much as the other. "Which do you like best?" she asked.

"They are both charming, Conchita; but I don't want any complications."

"You call making love complications? Love, it's the same as eating and drinking. You think you can live without eating and drinking? When I don't make love I feel really ill, although I'm already twenty-two. They are only sixteen and seventeen, so just think what it must be for them. If they don't take pleasure in their bodies, they'll die."

"And what about their parents?"

She told me, just as José had done, that the daughters of the ordinary people loved just to be loved. They gave themselves to the man they liked spontaneously, wholly, without asking anything in exchange except the thrill.

"I understand you, poppet. I'm willing as the next man to make love for love's sake. Only you tell your friends that an affair doesn't bind me in any way at all. Once they're warned, it's another matter."

Dear Lord above! It wasn't going to be easy to get away from an atmosphere like this. Charlot, Simon, Alexandre and no doubt a good many others had been positively bewitched. I saw why they were so thoroughly happy among these cheerful people, so different from ours. I went to bed.

"Get up, Papi! It's ten o'clock. And there's someone to see you."

"Good morning, Monsieur." A graying man of about fifty; no hat; candid eyes; bushy eyebrows. He held out his hand. "I'm Dr. Bougrat.* I came because they told me one of you is sick. I've had a look at your friend, and there's nothing to be done unless he goes into the hospital at Caracas. It'll be a tough job to cure him."

"You'll have supper with us, Doctor?" Charlot asked.

"I'd like to. Thanks."

Anisette was poured out, and as he drank Bougrat said to me, "Well, Papillon, and how are you getting along?"

"As a matter of fact, Doctor, I'm taking my first steps in life. I feel as if I'd just been born. Or rather as if I'd lost my way like a boy. I can't make out the road I ought to follow."

"The road's clear enough. Look around and you'll see. Except for one or two exceptions, all our old companions have gone straight. I've been in Venezuela since 1928. Not one of the convicts I've known has committed a crime since being in this country. They are almost all married, with children, and they live honestly, accepted by the community. They've forgotten the past so completely that some of them couldn't tell you the details of the job that sent them down. It's all very far away, buried in a misty past that doesn't matter."

"Maybe it's different for me, Doctor. I have a pretty

---

* The hero of a well-known criminal affair in Marseille during the twenties. A dead man was found in a cupboard in his consulting room. Bougrat pleaded professional error in the amount of an injection. The court said it was murder. They gave him a life sentence, but he soon escaped from Devil's Island and made himself a new life in Venezuela.

long bill to present to the people who sent me down
against all justice—fourteen years of struggle and suffering. To see the bill is paid, I have to go back to France;
and for that I need a lot of money. It's not by working as
a laborer that I'm going to save up enough for the voyage
out and back—if there *is* any return."

"And do you think you're the only one of us with an
account to settle? Just you listen to the story of a boy I
know. George Dubois is his name. A kid from the slums
of La Villette—alcoholic father, often locked up with the
dt's, the mother with six children: she was so poor she
went around the North African bars looking for customers. Jojo, they called him; and he'd been going from one
reformatory to the next since he was eight. He started by
knocking off fruit outside shops—did it several times.
First a few terms in the Abbé Rollet's homes, then, when
he was twelve, he got a tough stretch in a really hard
reformatory. I don't have to tell you that the fourteen-
year-old Jojo, surrounded by young fellows of eighteen,
had to look out for his ass. He was a puny kid, so there
was only one way of defending himself—a knife. One of
these perverted little thugs got a stab in the belly, and the
authorities sent Jojo to Esse, the toughest reformatory of
the lot, the one for hopeless cases. Until the age of twenty-one. Then they gave him his marching orders for the
African disciplinary battalions, because with a past like
his, he wasn't allowed into the ordinary army. They
handed him the few francs he had earned and farewell,
adieu! The trouble was that this boy had a heart.
Maybe it had hardened, but it still had some sensitive
corners. At the station he saw a train destined for Paris.
It was as if a switch had been triggered inside him. He
jumped in double quick, and there he was in Paris. It was
raining when he walked out of the station. He stood under
a shelter, figuring out how he would get to La Villette.
Under this same shelter there was a girl who was also

keeping out of the rain. She gave him a pleasant sort of look. All he knew about women was the chief warden's fat wife at Esse and what the bigger boys at the reformatory had told him—more or less true. No one had ever looked at him like this girl. They began to talk.

" 'Where do you come from?'

" 'The country.'

" 'I like you, boy. Why don't we go to a hotel? I'll be nice to you and we'll be warm.'

"Jojo was all stirred up. To him this chick seemed something wonderful—and what's more her gentle hand touched his. Discovering love was a fantastic, shattering experience for him. The girl was young and very amorous. When they had made love until they could no more, thay sat on the bed to smoke. and the chick said to him, 'Is this the first time you've been to bed with a girl?'

" 'Yes,' he confessed.

" 'Why did you wait so long?'

" 'I was in a reformatory.'

" 'A long time?'

" 'Very long.'

" 'I was in one too. I escaped.'

" 'How old are you?' Jojo asked.

" 'Sixteen.'

" 'Where are you from?'

" 'La Villette.'

" 'What street?'

" 'Rue de Rouen.'

"So was Jojo. He was afraid to understand. 'What's your name?' he cried.

" 'Ginette Dubois.'

"It was his sister. They were completely overwhelmed and they both began to cry with shame and wretchedness. Then each described the road they had traveled. Ginette and her other sisters had had the same kind of life as Jojo—homes and reformatories. Their mother had just come out of a sanatorium. The eldest sister was working in a brothel for North Africans in La Villette—hard labor. They decided to go and see her.

"They had scarcely left the hotel before a pig in uniform called out to the chick, 'Now you little tart, didn't I tell you not to come soliciting on my beat?' And he came toward them. 'This time I'll run you in, you dirty little whore.'

"It was too much for Jojo. After everything that had just happened, he no longer really knew what he was doing. He brought out a switchblade he had bought for the army and shoved it into the pig's chest. He was arrested, and twelve 'qualified' jurymen condemned him to death. He was reprieved by the President of the Republic and sent to the penal settlement.

"Well now, Papillon, he escaped and at present he's living at Cumaná, a fair-sized port. He's a shoemaker, he's married, and he has nine children, all well cared for and all going to school. Indeed, one of the elder children has been at the university this last year. Every time I'm in Cumaná I go and see them. That's a pretty good example, eh? Yet believe you me, he, too, had a long bill to present to society. You're no exception, Papillon. Plenty of us have reasons for revenge. But as far as I know, not one of us has left this country to take it. I trust you, Papillon. Since you like the idea of Caracas, go there; but I hope you'll have the sense to live the city life without falling into any of its traps."

Bougrat left very late that afternoon. My ideas were in a turmoil afterward. Why had he made such an impression on me? Easy to see why. During these first days of freedom I had met convicts who were happy and readjusted but leading lives that weren't the least bit extraordinary. It was a prudent, very modest kind of life. Their position was lowly—they were workmen or peasants. Bougrat was different. For the first time I had seen an ex-con who was now a monsieur, a gentleman. That was what had made my heart thump. Would I be a monsieur, too? Could I become one? For him, as a doctor, it had been comparatively easy. It would be harder for me, maybe; but even if I didn't yet know how to set about it, I was sure that one day I was going to be a monsieur, too.

Sitting on my bench at the bottom of the second gallery the next day, I watched my pumps; they had run without a hitch. The thoughts ran pell-mell through my head. "Papillon, I trust you." But could I put up with living like my companions? I didn't think so. After all, there were plenty of other ways of getting enough money honestly. I wasn't forced to accept a life that was too small for me. I could carry on as an adventurer—I could prospect for gold or diamonds, vanish into the bush and come out some day with enough to set me up in the kind of position I was after.

At eight o'clock the hoist brought me up to the surface. I took the long way around so as not to go by the storehouse. The less I saw of it, the better. I passed quickly through the village. greeting people and saying sorry to the ones who wanted me to stop—I was in a hurry, and I climbed fast to the house. Conchita was waiting for me, as black and cheerful as ever.

"Well, Papillon, and how are you doing? Charlot told me to pour you out a stiff anisette before dinner. He said you looked as though you had problems. What's wrong, Papi? You can tell me, your friend's wife. Would you like me to fetch Graciela for you, or maybe Mercedes if you like her better? Don't you think that would be a good idea?"

"Conchita, you're my little black pearl of El Callao, you're wonderful, and I see why Charlot worships you.

Maybe you're right: maybe to set me up I need a girl beside me."

"That's for sure. Unless it's Charlot who was right."

"How do you mean?"

"Well, I was saying what you needed was to love and be loved. And he told me to hold on before I put a girl in your bed—perhaps it was something else."

"How do you mean, something else?"

She hesitated for a moment and then blurted, "I don't care if you do tell Charlot; but he'll box my ears."

"I won't tell him anything. I promise."

"Well, Charlot says you aren't built for the same kind of life as he and the other Frenchmen here."

"What else? Come on, Conchita, tell me the lot."

"And he said you must be thinking that there's too much useless gold lying about at the mine and that you'd find something better to do with it. There! And he went on that you aren't the sort that can live without spending a lot; and that you had a revenge you couldn't give up and for that you wanted a great deal of money."

I looked her straight in the eye. "Well, Conchita, your Charlot got it wrong, wrong, wrong. You're the one who was right. As for my future—no problem at all. You guessed it: what I want is a woman to love. I didn't like to say so, on account of I'm rather shy."

"That I don't believe, Papillon."

"Okay. Go and fetch the blonde, and just you see if I'm not happy when I have a girl of my own."

"I'm on my way," she said, going into the bedroom to change her dress. "Oh, that Mercedes, how happy she will be!" she called. Before she had time to come back there was a knock at the door. "Come in," Conchita said. The door opened and there was Maria, looking a trifle confused.

"You, Maria, at this time of night? What a marvelous

surprise! Conchita, this is Maria, the girl who took me in when Picolino and I first landed up in El Callao."

"Let me kiss you," Conchita said. "You're as pretty as Papillon said you were."

"Who's Papillon?"

"That's me. Enrique or Papillon, it's all one. Sit down by me on the divan and tell me everything."

Conchita gave a knowing laugh. "I don't think it's worth my while going out now," she said.

Maria stayed all night. As a lover she was shy, but she reacted to the slightest caress. I was her first man. Now she was sleeping. The two candles I had lit instead of the raw electric light were guttering. Their faint glow showed the beauty of her young body even better, and her breasts still marked by our embrace. Gently I got up to make myself some coffee and to see what time it was. Four o'clock. I knocked over a saucepan and woke Conchita. She came out of her room, wearing a dressing gown.

"You want some coffee?"

"Yes."

"Only for you, I'm sure. Because she must be sleeping with those angels you've introduced her to."

"You know all about it, Conchita."

"My people have fire in their veins. You must have noticed it tonight. Maria has one touch of Negro, two touches of Indian and the rest Spanish. If you're not happy with a mixture like that, go hang yourself," she said, laughing.

The splendid sun was high in the sky when it saw Maria wake up. I brought her coffee in bed. There was a question already on my lips. "Aren't they going to worry, not finding you at home?"

"My sisters knew I was coming here, so my father must have known an hour later. You aren't going to send me away today?"

"No, dear. I told you I didn't want to set up house, but

sending you away is something else again. If you can stay without any trouble, stay as long as you like."

It was close to twelve and I had to leave for the mine. Maria decided to hitch a lift home in a truck and come back in the evening.

"Hey there," Charlot said. He was standing in the door of his room, wearing pajamas; and he spoke to me in French. "So you've found the chick you needed all by yourself. A luscious one, too: I congratulate you." He added that, as the next day was Sunday, we might drink to the occasion.

"Maria, tell your father and sisters to come and spend Sunday with us to celebrate this. And you come back whenever you like—the house is yours. Have a good day, Papi; watch out for the number three pump. And when you quit work, you don't have to drop in on Simon. If you don't see the stuff he is looking after so badly, you'll feel it less."

"You dirty old crook. No, I won't go see Simon. Don't worry, man. *Ciao.*"

Maria and I walked through the village arm in arm, close together, to show the girls she was my woman.

The pumps ran sweetly, even number three. But neither the hot, wet air nor the beat of the motor kept me from thinking about Charlot. He had grasped why I was so thoughtful, all right. It hadn't taken long for him, an old crook, to see that the heap of gold was at the bottom of it all. Nor for Simon either; and Simon must certainly have told him about our conversation. Those were the sort of friends a man should have—real friends, aglow with joy because I'd got myself a woman. They were hoping that this black-haired godsend would make me forget the blazing heap of loot.

I turned all this over and over in my head, and in time I began to see the position more clearly. These good guys were now as straight as so many rulers; they were leading blameless lives. But in spite of living like squares they had kept the underworld outlook and they were utterly incapable of tipping off the police about anyone whatsoever, even if they guessed what he was up to and knew for sure it would mean bad trouble for them. The two who would be taken in right away if the thing came off were Simon and Alexandre, the men who guarded the treasure. Charlot would come in for his share of the hornets' nest, too, because every single one of the ex-convicts would be trundled off to jail. And then farewell peace and quiet, farewell house, vegetable garden, wife, kids, hens, goats and pigs. So I began to see how these former crooks must have quaked not for themselves but for their homes, when they thought how my caper was going to ruin everything. "How I hope he doesn't go and screw it all," they must have said. I could see them holding a council of war.

I had made up my mind. I'd go and see Simon that evening and ask him and his family to the party tomorrow, and I'd tell him to invite Alexandre, too, if he could come. I must make them all think that having a girl like Maria was all I could ever want.

The hoist brought me up to the open air. I met Charlot on his way down, and I asked, "The party still on?"

"Of course it is, Papillon. More than ever."

"I'm going to ask Simon and his family. And Alexandre, too, if he can come."

Old Charlot was a deep one. He looked me straight in the eye and then in a rather flip tone he said, "Why, that's a sweet idea, my friend." Without another word he stepped into the hoist, and it took him down to where I had just come from. I went around by the store and found Simon.

The party was a marvelous success. José congratulated us on loving one another, and Maria's sister whispered questions in her ear—full of curiosity. Simon and his fine family were there, and Alexandre, too, since he had found someone to fill in for him guarding the treasure. He had a charming wife, and a well-dressed little boy and girl came with them. The rabbits were delicious, and the huge cake, shaped like a heart, lasted no time at all. We even danced to the radio and the Victrola, and an old convict played the accordion.

After a good many liqueurs I laid into my old crooks, in French. "Well, and what have you guys been thinking? Did you really believe I was going to pull something off?"

"Yes, friend," said Charlot. "We wouldn't have said a word if you hadn't brought it up yourself. But it's dead certain you had the notion of knocking off that ton of gold, right? Give the straight answer, Papillon."

"You know I've been chewing over my revenge these fourteen years. Multiply fourteen years by three hundred and sixty-five days and then by twenty-four hours and each hour by sixty minutes and you still won't have the number of times I've sworn to make them pay for what I went through. So when I saw that heap of gold in such a place, why true enough, I did think of working out a job."

"What then?" said Simon.

"Then I looked at the position from every side and I was ashamed. I was running the risk of destroying the happiness of you all. I came to see that this happiness of yours—a happiness I hope to have myself one day—was worth much more than being rich. So the temptation of knocking off the gold quite disappeared. You can take my word for it: I won't do anything here."

"There you are, then," said Charlot, grinning from ear to ear. "So now we can all sleep easy. Long live Papillon! Long live Maria! Long live love and freedom! And long live decency! Hard guys we were, hard guys we are still, but only toward the pigs. Now we're all of the same mind, including Papillon."

Six months I'd been here. Charlot was right. On the day of the party I had won the first battle against my longing to pull something off. I had been drifting away from the "road down the drain" ever since I had escaped. Now thanks to my friends' example I had gained an important victory over myself: I had given up the idea of grabbing that million dollars. One thing was sure: it would not be easy for any other job to tempt me, now that I'd given up a fortune like that. Yet I wasn't entirely at peace with myself. I had to make my money some other way than stealing it, fair enough; but still I had to get enough to go to Paris and hand in my bill. And that was going to cost me a pretty penny.

Boom-bom, boom-bom, boom-bom: all the time my pumps sucked up the water that flowed into the galleries. It was hotter than ever. Every day I spent eight hours down there in the bowels of the mine. At this time I was on duty from four in the morning until noon. When I knocked off I'd have to go to Maria's house in El Callao. Picolino had been there for a month, because in El Callao the doctor could see him every day. He was being given therapy, and Maria and her sisters looked after him wonderfully. So I was going to see him and to make love to Maria: it was a week since I'd seen her, and I wanted her, physically and mentally. I found a truck that gave me a lift. The rain was pouring down when I opened the door at about one o'clock. They were all sitting around the table, apart from Maria, who seemed to be waiting near the door. "Why didn't you come before? A week's a long, long time. You're all wet. Come and change right away."

She pulled me into the bedroom, took my clothes off and dried me with a big towel. "Lie down on the bed," she said. And there we made love, not caring about the others who were waiting for us on the other side of the door. We dropped off to sleep, and it was Esmeralda, the green-eyed sister, who gently woke us late that afternoon, when night was already coming on.

When we had all had dinner together, José the Pirate suggested going for a stroll.

"Enrique, you wrote to the chief administrator asking him to get Caracas to put an end to your *confinamiento* [compulsory residence], is that right?"

"Yes, José."

"He's had the reply for Caracas."

"Good or bad?"

"Good. Your *confinamiento* is over."

"Does Maria know?"

"Yes."

"What did she say?"

"That you'd always said you wouldn't stay in El Callao." After a short pause he asked me, "When do you think you'll leave?"

Although I was bowled over by this news, I answered right away. "Tomorrow. The truck driver who brought me said he was going on to Cuidad Bolívar tomorrow." José bowed his head. "*Amigo mio,* are you sore at me?"

"No, Enrique. You've always said you'd never stay. But it's sad for Maria—and for me, too."

"I'll go and talk to the driver if I can find him."

I did find him: we were to leave the next day at nine. As he already had one passenger, Picolino would travel in the cab and myself on the empty iron barrels behind. I hurried to the chief administrator; he handed over my papers and, like the good man he was, gave me some advice and wished me good luck. Then I went around seeing everybody who had given me friendship and help.

First to Caratal, where I picked up the few things I possessed. Charlot and I embraced one another, deeply moved. His black girl wept. I thanked them both for their wonderful hospitality.

"It's nothing, pal. You would have done the same for me. Good luck. And if you go to Paris, say hello to Montmartre from me."

"I'll write."

Then the ex-cons, Simon, Alexandre, Marcel, André. I hurried back to El Callao and said good-bye to all the miners and the gold and diamond prospectors and my fellow workers. All of them, men and women, said something from the heart to wish me good luck. It touched me a great deal and I saw even more clearly that if I had set up with Maria I should have been like Charlot and the others—I should never have been able to tear myself away from this paradise.

The hardest of all my farewells was to Maria. Our last night, a mixture of love and tears, was more violent than anything we had ever known. Even our caresses broke our hearts. The horrible thing was that I had to make her understand there would be no hope of my coming back. Who could tell what my fate would be when I carried out my plans?

A shaft of sunlight woke me. My watch said eight o'clock already. I hadn't the heart to stay in the big room, not even the few moments for a cup of coffee. Picolino was sitting in a chair, tears running down his face. Esmeralda had washed and dressed him. I looked for Maria's sisters, but I couldn't find them. They'd hidden so as not to see me go. There was only José standing there in the doorway. He grasped me in the Venezuelan *abrazo* (one hand holds yours and the other is round your shoulders), as moved as I was myself. I couldn't speak, and he said only this one thing: "Don't forget us; we'll never, never forget you. Good-bye: God go with you."

With all his clean things carefully folded into a bundle, Picolino wept bitterly, and his movements and the hoarse sounds he uttered conveyed his wretchedness at not being able to bring out the millions of thanks he had in his heart. I led him away.

Carrying our baggage, we reached the driver's place. A splendid exit from the town, all right: his truck had broken down; no leaving today. We had to wait for a new carburetor. There was no way out of it—I returned to Maria's with Picolino. You can imagine the shrieks when they saw us coming back.

"God was kind to have broken the truck, Enrique! Leave Picolino here and walk around the village while I get the meal ready. It's an odd thing," Maria added. "But it could be you're not fated to go to Caracas."

While I was strolling about I thought over this remark of Maria's. It worried me. I did not know Caracas, a big city, but people had talked about it and I could imagine what it was like. The idea certainly attracted me; but once I was there, what should I do, and how could I do it?

I walked slowly across the square of El Callao with my hands behind my back. The sun was blazing down. I went over to an almendro, a huge, very leafy tree, to take shelter from the furious heat. Under the shade there stood two mules, and a little old man was loading them. I noticed the diamond prospector's sieve and the gold prospector's trough, a kind of Chinese hat they use to wash the gold-bearing mud in. As I gazed at these things—they were still new to me—I went on pondering. In front of me there was this biblical picture of a quiet, peaceful life with no sounds apart from those of nature and the patriarchal way of living; and I thought of what it must be like at that very moment in Caracas, the busy, teeming capital that drew me on. All the descriptions I had heard turned into exact images. After all, it was fourteen years since I had seen a big town! Since I could now do as I liked, there was no doubt about it—I was going to get there, and as quick as I could.

3

Jojo La Passe

Jesus, the song was in French! And it was the little old prospector singing. I listened.

> *The old sharks are there already*
> *They've smelled the body of a man.*
> *One of them chews an arm like an apple,*
> *Another eats his trunk and tra-la-la*
> *The quickest gets it, the rest have none.*
> *Convict farewell; long live the law!*

I was thunderstruck. He sang it slowly, like a requiem. The "tra-la-la" had an ironic merriment, and the "long live the law" was full of the mockery of the Paris underworld: it sounded like an indisputable truth. But to feel the full irony of it you had to have been there.

I looked closely at the man: barely five feet tall. One of the most picturesque ex-convicts I had ever come across. Snowy white hair with long, gray whiskers cut on the slant. Blue jeans; a big, broad leather belt; on the right, a long sheath with a curved handle coming out of it at the height of his groin. I walked over to him. He had no hat on—it was lying on the ground—so I could see his broad forehead, speckled with a red even darker than his old sunbaked pirate's tan. His eyebrows were so long and thick he surely had to comb them. Beneath them, steely gray-green eyes like gimlets bored through me. I hadn't taken four steps before he said to me, "You come from the clink, as sure as my name's La Passe."

"Right. My name's Papillon."

"I'm Jojo La Passe." He held out his hand and took mine frankly, just as it should be between men, not so hard it crushes your fingers the way the show offs do, nor too flabby, like hypocrites and fairies. I said, "Let's go to the bar and have a drink. It's on me."

"No. Come to my place over the way, the white house. It's called Belleville, where I lived when I was a kid. We can talk there in peace."

Indoors it was swept and clean—his wife's field of action. She was young, very young; perhaps twenty-five. He—God knows—sixty at least. She was called Lola, a dusky Venezuelan.

"You're welcome," she said to me, with a pleasant smile.

"Thanks."

"Two anisettes," said Jojo. "A Corsican brought me two hundred bottles from France. You'll see whether it's good or not."

Lola poured it out and Jojo tossed back three-quarters of his glass in one gulp. "Well?" he said, fixing me with his eye.

"Well what? You don't think I'm going to tell you the story of my life, do you?"

"Okay, mac. But Jojo La Passe, doesn't that ring any bells?"

"No."

"How quickly they forget you! Yet I was a big shot in the clink. No one came within miles of me for throwing the seven and eleven with dice just touched with a file—not loaded, of course. That wasn't yesterday, to be sure; but after all, men like us, we leave traces—we leave legends. And now according to what you tell me, in a few years it's all forgotten. Didn't one single bastard ever tell you about me?" He seemed deeply outraged.

"Frankly, no."

Once again the gimlets bored right into my guts. "You weren't in stir for long; you've scarcely got the face at all."

"Fourteen years altogether, counting El Dorado. You think that's nothing?"

"It's not possible. You're scarcely marked, and only another con could tell that's where you come from. And even then, a con who was not a diabolically clever face reader might get it wrong. You had it easy, right?"

"It wasn't as easy as all that: the islands; solitary."

"Balls, man, balls! The islands—it's a holiday camp! All it lacks is a casino. For you, penal colony meant the sea breeze, crayfish, no mosquitoes, fishing, and now and then a real treat—the pussy or the ass of some screw's wife kept too short of it by her cunt of a husband."

"Still, you know . . ."

"Blah-blah-blah: don't you try to fool me. I know all about it. I wasn't on the islands, but I've been told about them." This man, maybe he was picturesque, but things were likely to turn nasty for him: I felt my temper rising fast. He went on, "Jail, the real jail, was Kilometer Twenty-four. That doesn't say anything to you? No, it doesn't, and that's for sure. With your mug, you've certainly never pissed in those parts. Well, mate, I have. A hundred men, every one of them with diseased guts. Some standing, some lying down, some groaning like dogs. There's the bush in front of them, like a wall. But it's not them that are going to cut the bush down: the jungle is going to do the cutting. Kilometer Twenty-four is not a working camp. As the prison administration puts it, it's a conveniently hidden little dell in the Guiana forest—you toss men into it and they never bother you again. Come, Papillon, don't try and impress me with your islands and your solitary. It won't wash with me. You've got nothing of the look of a dog with all the spirit beaten out of it, nor the hollow face of a skin-and-bones lag with a life sen-

tence, nor the dial you see on all those poor buggers who
escaped from that hell by some miracle—unfortunate sods
who look as if they'd been worked over with a chisel to
give them an old man's face on a young man's head.
There's nothing like that about you at all. So there's no
possible mistake about my diagnosis: For you, prison
meant a holiday in the sun."

How he did nag on and on, this little old bastard. I
wondered how our meeting was going to end.

"For me, as I've been telling you, it meant the hollow
nobody ever comes out of alive—amoebic dysentery, a
place where you gradually shit your guts out. Poor old
Papillon: you didn't even know what the clink was all
about."

I looked closely at this terribly energetic little man,
working out just where to plant my fist on his face, and
then all at once I shifted into reverse and decided to make
friends. No point in getting worked up: I might need him.
"You're right, Jojo. My stint didn't amount to much, since
I'm so fit it takes someone in the know, like you, to tell
where I come from."

"Okay, we're in agreement, then. What are you doing
now?"

"I'm working at the Mocupia gold mine. Eighteen bolívars a day. But I've got a permit to go wherever I like;
my *confinamiento* is over."

"I bet you want to head for Caracas and take up your
old life again."

"You're right: that's just what I want to do."

"But Caracas, it's the big city; so trying to pull off
anything there means a hell of a risk. You're scarcely out,
and you want to go back inside again?"

"I've got a long bill for the bastards who sent me
down—the pigs, the witnesses, the prosecutor. A fourteen-
year stretch for a crime I never committed: the islands,
whatever you may think of them, and solitary at Saint-

Joseph, where I went through the most horrible tortures
the system could think up. And don't forget I was only
twenty-three when they framed me."

"Hell: so they stole the whole of your youth. Innocent,
really innocent, cross your heart, or are you still pleading
before the judge?"

"Innocent, Jojo. I swear by my dead mother."

"Christ. Well, I see that must lie heavy on your chest.
But you don't have to go to Caracas if you want dough to
straighten out your accounts—come with me."

"What for?"

"Diamonds, man, diamonds! Here the government is
generous: this is the only country in the world where you
can burrow wherever you like for gold or diamonds.
There's only one thing: no machinery allowed. All they
let you use is shovel, pickax and sieve."

"And where's this genuine El Dorado? Not the one I've
just left, I hope?"

"A good way off. A good way off in the bush. A good
many days on a mule and then in a canoe and then on
foot, carrying your gear."

"It's not what you'd call in the bag; hardly child's
play."

"Well, Papillon, it's the only way of getting hold of a
fat sack of dough. You find just one bomb and there you
are, a wealthy man—a man who has women that smoke
and fart in silk. Or, if you like it that way, a man who can
afford to go and present his bill."

Now he was going full steam, his eyes blazed; he was
all worked up and full of fire. A bomb, he told me—and
I'd already heard it at the mine—was a little mound no
bigger than a peasant's handkerchief, a mound where by
some mystery of nature a hundred, two hundred, five
hundred, even a thousand carats of diamonds were clus-
tered together. If a prospector found a bomb in some
far-off hole, it didn't take long before men started coming

from north, south, east and west, as if they'd been told by
some grapevine. A dozen, then a hundred, then a thousand. They smelled the gold or the diamonds the way a
starving dog smells a bone or an old bit of neat. They
came flooding in from every point of the compass. Rough
types with no trade who'd had enough of battering away
with a pick at twelve bolívars a day for some employer.
They got sick of it, and then they heard the call of the
jungle. They didn't want their family to go on living in a
rabbit hutch, so they went off, knowing very well what
they were in for—they were going to work from one sun
to the next in a wicked climate and a wicked atmosphere,
condemning themselves to several years of hell. But with
what they sent home, their wives would have light, roomy
little houses, the children would be properly fed and
clothed and they'd go to school—even go on with their
own schooling, perhaps.

"So that's what a bomb gives?"

"Don't be such a dope, Papillon. The guy that finds a
bomb never goes back to mining. He's rich for the rest of
his life, unless he goes so crazy with joy that he feeds his
mule with hundred-bolívar notes soaked in kümmel or
anisette. No, the man I'm talking about, the ordinary guy,
he finds a few little diamonds every day, even though they
may be very, very small. Even that means ten or fifteen
times what he gets in the town. Then again, he lives as
hard as possible, right down to bedrock; because out there
you pay for everything in gold or diamonds. But if he
lives hard, he can still keep his family better than before."

"What about the others?"

"They come in every shape and size. Brazilians, guys
from British Guiana and Trinidad: they all escape from
exploitation in the factories or cotton plantations or whatever. And then there are the real adventurers, the ones
who can only breathe when they're not hemmed in by the

horizon, the ones who will always stake everything for the
jackpot—Italians, Englishmen, Spaniards, Frenchmen,
Portuguese—men from all over. Christ, you can't imagine
the types that come rushing into this promised land! The
Lord above may have filled it with piranhas and anacon-
das and mosquitoes and malaria and yellow fever, but
He's also scattered gold, diamonds, topazes and emeralds
and such all over its surface. There's a swarm of adventurers from everywhere in the world, and they stand there
in holes up to their bellies in the water, working so hard
they never feel the sun or the mosquitoes or hunger or
thirst, digging, tossing out the slimy earth and washing it
over and over again, straining it through the sieve to find
the diamonds. Then again, Venezuela has enormous
frontiers, and there you won't meet anyone who asks
you for your papers. So there's not only the charm of
the diamonds, but you can be sure of the pigs leaving you
in peace. A perfect place to hole up and get your breath if
you're on the run."

Jojo stopped. There was nothing he had forgotten: now
I knew the whole story. I thought quickly and then said,
"You go off alone, Jojo. I can't see myself working like a
Trojan. You'd have to be possessed—you'd have to be-
lieve in your bomb like you believe in God Almighty to
stand it in that kind of a hell. Yes, you go off by yourself.
I'll look for my bomb in Caracas."

Once again his hard eyes pierced me through and
through. "I get it; you haven't changed. Do you want to
know what I really think?"

"Go ahead."

"You're quitting El Callao because it makes you sick,
knowing there's an unprotected heap of gold at La Mocupia. Right or wrong?"

"Right."

"You're leaving it alone because you don't want to

muck things up for the ex-cons who are living here in retirement. Right or wrong?"

"Right."

"And you think that when it comes to finding the bomb there where I said, it's a matter of many are called and few are chosen? Right or wrong?"

"Right."

"And you'd rather find the bomb in Caracas, wrapped up and prepared, the diamonds already cut—find it in a jeweler's shop or a gem wholesaler's?"

"Maybe: but that's not certain. Remains to be seen."

"I swear, you're a true adventurer; nothing will cure you."

"That's as it may be. But don't you forget this thing that keeps eating me all the time—this revenge. For that I really think I'd do anything at all."

"Adventure or revenge, you still need dough. So come along into the bush with me. It's terrific. You'll see."

"With a pickax and a shovel? Not for me."

"You got a fever, Papillon? Or has it turned you into a lemon, knowing that you can go where you like since yesterday?"

"I don't feel that way."

"You've forgotten the main thing—my name. Jojo *La Passe:* Jojo the Craps."

"Okay, so you're a professional gambler; I don't see what that's got to do with this notion of laboring away like brutes."

"Nor do I," he said, doubling up with laughter.

"How come? We aren't going to the mines to dig up diamonds? Where do we get them from, then?"

"Out of the miners' pockets."

"How?"

"By shooting craps every night, and by sometimes losing."

"I get it, mac. When do we leave?"

"Wait a minute." He was very pleased with the effect of his words. Slowly he stood up, pulled a table into the middle of the room, spread a blanket over it and brought out six pairs of dice. "Have a good look." Very carefully I examined them. They were not loaded.

"No one could say those dice were loaded, could they?"

"Nobody."

He took a gauge out of a felt case, gave it to me and said, "Measure." One of the sides had been carefully filed and polished, reducing it less than a tenth of a millimeter. All you could see was shine. "Try and throw seven or eleven." I rolled the dice. Neither seven nor eleven. "My turn now." Jojo deliberately made a little wrinkle in the blanket. He held the dice with the tips of his fingers. "That's the trick," he observed. "Here we go! And there's seven! And there's eleven! And eleven! And seven! You want six? Boom, there's six! Six with four and two or five and one? There you are. Is the gentleman satisfied?"

I was fascinated, utterly fascinated. I'd never seen such a thing: it was extraordinary. You couldn't make out the slightest false move.

"Listen, mac. I've been shooting craps forever. I started on the Butte when I was eight. I've risked shooting them with dice like that, and you know where? On the crap table at the Gare de l'Est, in the days of Roger Sole and Company."

"I remember. There were some very tough customers there."

"You don't have to tell me. And among the regulars, as well as the tough guys and the pimps and the burglars, there were cops as famous as Jojo-le-Beau, the pimp cop from La Madeleine, and specialists from the gambling squad. And I took them as well as the rest. So you see there's no way to lose if you shoot these craps in a miners' camp."

"True enough."

"But get this: the one place is as dangerous as the other. At the Gare de l'Est the crooks were as quick on the draw as the miners. Just one difference: in Paris you shoot and you light out as quick as you can. At the mine, you shoot and stay put. There are no pigs; the miners make their own laws." He paused, slowly emptied his glass and went on, "Well now, Papillon, are you coming with me?"

I reflected for a moment; but not for long. The adventure tempted me. It was risky, without doubt; those miners would not be choirboys—far from it; but there might be big money to be picked up. Come on, Papillon, banco on Jojo! And again I asked, "When do we leave?"

"Tomorrow afternoon, if you like: at five, after the heat of the day. That'll give us time to get things together. We'll travel by night at first. You got a gun?"

"No."

"A good knife?"

"No knife."

"Never mind. I'll look after that. *Ciao.*"

I went back to the house, thinking about Maria. She'd certainly rather I went into the bush than to Caracas. I'd leave Picolino with her. And then tomorrow, on my way for the diamonds! And seven! And eleven! *Once, siete! Et sept, et onze!* I was there already; all I had to do was learn the numbers in Spanish, English, Brazilian and Italian.

I found José at home. I told him I'd changed my mind. Caracas would be for another time; at present I was going off with an old white-haired Frenchman called Jojo to the diamond mines.

"What are you going with him as?"

"As his partner, of course."

"He always gives his partners half his winnings."

"That's the rule. Do you know men who've worked with him?"

"Three."

"Did they make plenty of money?"

"I don't know. I dare say they did. Each one of them made three or four trips."

"And what about after those three or four trips?"

"After? They never came back."

"Why not? Did they settle down there at the mines?"

"No. They were dead."

"Is that right? Fever?"

"No. Killed by the miners."

"Oh. Jojo must be a lucky guy, if he always got out of it."

"Yes. But Jojo, he's very clever. He never wins much himself: *he works it so that his partner wins.*"

"I see. So it's the other man who's in danger; not him. It's good to know. Thanks, José."

"You're not going, now that I've told you that?"

"One last question, and give me the straight answer: Is there a chance of coming back with a lot of dough after two or three trips?"

"Sure."

"So Jojo is rich. Why does he go back there, then? I saw him loading the mules."

"To begin with Jojo doesn't risk anything, as I said. Secondly, he was certainly not going off. Those mules belong to his father-in-law. He made up his mind to go because he met you."

"But what about the stuff he was loading, or getting ready to load?"

"How do you know it was for him?"

"Oh-ho. What other advice have you got?"

"Don't go."

"Not that. I've made up my mind to go. What else?"

José bent his head as if to think. A long pause. When

he looked up again his face was bright. His eyes shone with intelligence, and slowly, drawing out his words, he said, "Listen to the advice of a man who knows that world through and through. Every time there's a big game, a real big game—when there's a heap of diamonds in front of you and everything is at the boiling point, get up unexpectedly and don't sit there with your winnings. Say you've got a bellyache and go straight to the john. You don't come back, of course; and that night you sleep somewhere else, not in your own place."

"Pretty good, José. And what else?"

"Although the buyers at the mine pay a good deal less than the ones in El Callao or Ciudad Bolívar, you want to sell them all the diamonds you win—sell them every day. And *don't ever take the cash*. Make them give you receipts in your name so as to cash them at El Callao or Ciudad Bolívar. Do the same with foreign banknotes. You say you're afraid of losing everything you've won in a single day and so you avoid the risk by never having much on you. And you tell everybody just what you're doing, so it becomes well known."

"So that way I'll have a chance of coming back?"

"Yes. You'll have a chance of coming back alive, if God wills."

"Thanks, José. *Buenas noches.*"

Lying in Maria's arms, exhausted with love, my head in the hollow of her shoulders, I felt her breath on my cheek. In the darkness, before I closed my eyes, I saw a heap of diamonds in front of me. Gently I picked them up, as though I was playing with them, and put them into the little canvas bag that all miners carry; then I got up right away and having looked round I said to Jojo, "Keep my place. I'm going to the john. I'll be back in a minute." And as I dropped off, there were José's knowing eyes, shining full of light—only people who live very close to nature have eyes like that.

The morning passed quickly. Everything was settled. Picolino was to stay there; he would be well cared for. I kissed everybody. Maria shone with delight. She knew that if I went to the mines I'd have to come back this way, whereas Caracas never gave back the men who went to live there. She went with me as far as the meeting place. Five o'clock; Jojo was there, and in great form. "Hello there, man! Okay? You're prompt—fine, fine! The sun will be down in an hour. It's better that way. No one can follow you at night."

A dozen kisses for my true love and I climbed into the saddle. Jojo fixed the stirrups for me and just as we were setting off Maria said to me, "And above all, *mi amor,* don't forget to go to the lavatory at the right moment."

I burst out laughing as I dug my heels into the mule. "You were listening behind the door, you Judas!"

"When you love, it's natural."

Now we were away, Jojo on a horse and me on a mule. The virgin forest has its roads called *piques.* A *pique* is a passage about two yards wide that has gradually been cut through the trees; and the men who pass along keep it clear with their machetes. On either side, a wall of green: above, a roof of millions of plants, but too high to be reached with a machete even if you stand in your stirrups. This is the selva, the tropical forest. It is made up of an impenetrable tangle of two kinds of vegetation: a layer of creepers, trees, and plants that do not rise much above twenty feet, and over that mounting to seventy-five or a hundred feet, the splendid great tops of the huge trees that climb higher and higher to reach the sun. Although their tops are in the sunlight the foliage of their wide, leafy branches makes a thick screen, keeping off all but a dim, filtered day. In a tropical forest you are in a wonderful landscape that bursts into growth all over, so as you ride along a *pique* you have to hold the reins in one hand and keep slashing at everything that gets in your way. A *pique* where a certain number of people keep coming and going always looks like a well-kept corridor.

There's nothing that gives a man such a sense of freedom as being in the bush and well armed. He has the feeling of being as much part of the landscape as the wild animals. He moves cautiously, but with unbounded self-confidence. He seems to be in the most natural of all possible elements, and all his senses are on the alert—hearing, sight and smell. His eyes dart perpetually from point to point, sizing up everything that moves. In the bush there is only one enemy that matters, the beast of beasts, the most intelligent, the cruelest, the wickedest, the greediest, the vilest and also the most wonderful—man.

We traveled all that night, going fairly well. But in the morning, after we had drunk a little coffee from the Thermos flask, my whore of a mule started dragging its feet, dawdling along sometimes as much as a hundred yards behind Jojo. I stabbed its ass with all kinds of thorns, but nothing did any good. And to aggravate matters, Jojo started bawling out, "Why, you know nothing about riding, man. It's easy enough. Watch me." And he would just touch his creature with his heel and set off at a gallop. And he'd stand in his stirrups and bellow, "I'm Captain Cook," or "Hey there, Sancho! Are you coming? Can't you keep up with your master, Don Quixote?"

This riled me, and I tried everything I could think of to make the mule get along. At last I hit on a terrific idea and right away it broke into a gallop. I'd dropped a lighted cigar-end into its ear. It tore along like a thoroughbred, and I rejoiced, full of glee; I even passed the Captain, waving as I went flashing by. But a mule is such a vicious brute the wild ride lasted only the length of the gallop. The animal rammed me up against a tree, nearly crushing my leg, and there I was on the ground, my ass filled with the prickles of some plant. And there was old Jojo, screeching with laughter like a child.

I won't tell the whole story of chasing the mule (two hours!), or of its kicking and farting and all the rest. But at last, out of breath. full of thorns, perishing with heat and weariness, I did manage to hoist myself onto the back of that cross-grained, obstinate bastard. This time it could go just as it chose: I was not going to be the one to cross it. The first mile I rode not sitting but lying on its back, with my ass in the air, trying to get the fiery thorns out of it.

The next day we left the pigheaded brute at a *posada,* an inn. Then two days in a canoe, followed by a long day's walk with packs on our back, brought us to the diamond mine.

I dumped my load on the log table of an open-air eating house. I was at the end of my rope, and I could have strangled old Jojo—he stood there with no more than a few drops of sweat on his forehead, looking at me with a knowing grin. "Well, pal, and how are you feeling? Okay?"

"Fine, fine! Is there any reason why I shouldn't be feeling fine? But just you tell me this: why have you made me carry a shovel, a pickax and a sieve all day long when we aren't going to do any digging at all?"

Jojo put on a sorrowful air. "Papillon, you disappoint me. Use your noggin. If a guy turned up here, not carrying these tools, what would he have come for? That's the question everybody would ask—all these eyes that watched you coming into the village through the holes in the walls and the tin roofs With you loaded as you were, no questions. Do you get it?"

"I get it, man."

"It's the same for me, since I'm carrying nothing. Suppose I turn up with my hands in my pockets and I set up my table without doing anything else: what are the miners and their girls going to say. eh, Papi? This old French type is a professional gambler, that's what they're going to say. Well now, you'll see what I'm going to do. If I can, I'll try and find a secondhand motor pump here in the village; otherwise I'll send for one. And twenty yards of big piping and two or three sluices. A sluice is a long wooden box with divisions, and these divisions have holes in them. You pump the mud into it, and a team of seven men can wash fifty times more earth than a dozen working the old-fashioned way. And it's still not looked upon as machinery. Then as the owner of the pump I get twenty-five percent of the diamonds; and what's more, I have a reason for being here. No one can say I live off gambling, because I live off my pump. But since I'm a gambler *as well,* I don't stop gambling at night. That's natural, because I don't take part in the actual work. You get it?"

"It's as clear as gin."

"There's a bright boy. Two *frescos,* Señora."

A fat, friendly old light-skinned woman brought us glasses full of chocolate-colored liquid with an ice cube and a bit of lemon swimming in it.

"That'll be eight bolívars, *hombres.*"

"More than two dollars! Hell, life is not cheap here."

Jojo paid. "How are things going?" he asked.

"So-so."

"Is there any loot or not?"

"Men in plenty. But very, very few diamonds. They found this place three months ago, and since then four thousand men have come rushing in. Too may men for so few diamonds. And what about him?" she said, jerking her chin toward me. "German or French?"

"French. He's with me."

"Poor soul."

"How come, poor soul?" I asked.

"Because you're too young and too good-looking to die. The men who come with Jojo never have any luck."

"You shut your trap, you old fool. Come on, Papi, let's go."

As we stood up, the fat woman said to me by way of good-bye, "Look out for yourself."

Of course, I'd said nothing about what José had told me, and Jojo was amazed that I did not try to find out what there was behind her words. I could feel him waiting for the questions that didn't come. He seemed upset and he kept glancing at me sideways.

Pretty soon, after he had talked to various people, Jojo found a shack. Three small rooms; rings to hang our hammocks; and some cartons. On one of them, empty beer and rum bottles; on another, a battered enamel bowl and a full watering can. Strings stretched across to hang up our clothes. The floor was pounded earth, very clean. The walls of this hutch were made of planks from packing cases—you could still read Savon Camay, Aceite Branca, Nestlé's Milk. Each room was about ten feet by ten. No windows. I felt stifled and took off my shirt.

Jojo turned, deeply shocked. "Are you crazy? Suppose somebody came in? You've got a wicked face already, and now if you go and show your tattooed hide, man, it's as if you were advertising the fact that you're a crook. Behave yourself."

"But I'm stifling, Jojo."

"You'll get used to it—it's all a matter of habit. But behave yourself, almighty God: above all, behave yourself."

I managed to keep myself from laughing: he was a priceless old fart, that Jojo.

We knocked two rooms into one. "This will be the casino," said Jojo, with a grin. It made a room twenty feet by ten. We swept the floor, went out to buy three big wooden crates, some rum and paper cups to drink out of. I was eager to see what the game would be like.

I didn't have to wait long. Once we had been around a

number of wretched little drinking joints, to "make contact," as Jojo put it, everyone knew that there would be a
game of craps in our place at eight that evening. The last
joint we went to was a shed with a couple of tables
outside, four benches and a carbide lamp hanging from a
covering of branches. The boss, a huge, ageless redhead,
served the punch without a word. As we were leaving he
came over to me and, speaking French, he said, "I don't
know who you are and I don't want to know. But I'll just
give you this tip. The day you feel like sleeping here,
come along. I'll look after you."

He spoke an odd sort of French, but from his accent I
realized he was a Corsican. "You a Corsican?"

"Yes. And you know a Corsican never betrays. Not
like some guys from the north," he added, with a knowing
smile.

"Thanks. It's good to know."

Toward seven o'clock, Jojo lit the carbide lamp. The
two blankets were laid out on the ground. No chairs. The
gamblers would either stand or squat. We decided I
shouldn't play that night. Just watch, that's all.

They started to arrive. Extraordinary mugs. There were
few short men: most were huge, bearded, moustachio'd
types. Their hands and faces were clean, and they didn't
smell, but their clothes were all stained and very nearly
worn out. Every single one of the shirts, though, was
spotlessly clean.

In the middle of the cloth, eight pairs of dice were
neatly arranged, each in a little box. Jojo asked me to
give each player a paper cup. There were about twenty of
them. I poured out the rum. Not a single guy there jerked
up the neck of the bottle to say enough. After just one
round, three bottles vanished.

Each man deliberately took a sip, then put his cup
down in front of him and laid an aspirin tube beside it. I
knew there were diamonds in those tubes. A shaky old

Chinese set up a little jeweler's scales in front of him. Nobody said much. These men were exhausted: they'd been laboring under the blazing sun, some of them standing in water up to their middles from six in the morning till the sun went down.

Ha, things were beginning to move! First one, then two, then three players took up a pair of dice and examined them carefully, pressing them tight together and passing them on to their neighbor. Everything must have seemed in order, because the dice were tossed back onto the blanket without anything said. Each time, Jojo picked up the pair and put them back in their box, all except for the last, which stayed there on the blanket.

Some men who had taken off their shirts complained of the mosquitoes. Jojo asked me to burn a few handfuls of damp grass, so the smoke would help to drive them out.

"Who kicks off?" asked a huge copper-colored guy with a thick black curly beard and a lopsided flower tattooed on his right arm.

"You, if you like," Jojo said.

Out of his silver-mounted belt, the gorilla—for he looked very like a gorilla—brought an enormous wad of bolívar notes held in a rubber band.

"What are you kicking off with, Chino?" asked another man.

"Five hundred bolos." *Bolos* is short for "bolívars."

"Okay for five hundred."

And the craps rolled. The eight came up. Jojo tried to shoot the eight.

"A thousand bolos you don't shoot the eight with double fours," said another player.

"I take that," Jojo said.

Chino managed to roll the eight, by five and three. Jojo had lost. For five hours on end the game continued without an exclamation, without the least dispute. These men were uncommon gamblers. That night Jojo lost seven

thousand bolos and a guy with a game leg more than ten
thousand.

It had been decided to stop the game at midnight, but
everyone agreed to carry on for another hour. At one
o'clock Jojo said this was the last crack.

"It was me that kicked off," said Chino, taking the
dice. "I'll close it. I lay all my winnings, nine thousand
bolívars."

He had a mass of notes and diamonds in front of him.
He covered a whole lot of other stakes and rolled the
seven first go.

At this terrific stroke of luck, a murmur went around
for the first time. The men stood up. "Let's get some
sleep."

"Well, you saw that, man?" Jojo said when we were
alone.

"Yes, and what I noticed most were those tough mugs.
They all carry a gun and a knife. There were even some
who sat on their machetes, so sharp they could take your
head off in one swipe."

"That's a fact, but you've seen others like them."

"Still and all . . . I ran the table on the islands, but I
tell you I never had such a feeling of danger as
tonight."

"It's all a matter of habit, mac. Tomorrow you'll play
and we'll win; it's in the bag. As you see it," he added,
"which are the guys to watch closest?"

"The Brazilians."

"Well done! That's how you can tell a man—the way
he spots the ones who may turn lethal from one second to
another."

When we had locked the door (three huge bolts) we
threw ourselves into our hammocks, and I dropped off
right away, before Jojo could start his snoring.

The next day, a splendid sun arose fit to roast you—
not a cloud or the least hint of a breeze. I wandered

about this curious village. Everyone was welcoming. Disturbing facts on the men, sure enough, but they had a way of saying things (in whatever language they spoke) so there was a warm human contact right away. I found the enormous Corsican redhead again. His name was Miguel. He spoke fluent Venezuelan with English or Brazilian words dropping into it every now and then, as if they'd come down by parachute. It was only when he spoke French, which he did with difficulty, that his Corsican accent came out. We drank coffee that a young brown girl had strained through a sock. As we were talking he asked, "Where do you come from, brother?"

"After what you said yesterday, I can't lie to you. I come from the penal colony."

"Ah? You escaped? I'm glad you told me."

"And what about you?"

He drew himself up, six feet and more, and his redhead's face took on an extremely noble expression. "I escaped, too, but not from Guiana. I left Corsica before they could arrest me. I'm a bandit of honor—an *honorable* bandit."

His face, all lit up with the pride of being an honest man, impressed me. He was really magnificent to see, this honorable bandit. He went on, "Corsica is the paradise of the world, the only country where men will give their lives for honor. You don't believe it?"

"I don't know whether it's the only country, but I do believe you'll find more men who are fugitives on account of their honor than because they're just plain bandits."

"I don't care for town bandits," he said thoughtfully.

In a couple of words I told him how things were with me; and I said I meant to go back to Paris to present my bill.

"You're right; but revenge is a dish you want to eat cold. Go about it as carefully as you can; it would be terrible if they picked you up before you had had your satisfaction. You're with old Jojo?"

"Yes."

"He's straight. Some people say he's too clever with the dice, but I don't believe he's a wrong 'un. You've known him long?"

"Not very; but that doesn't matter."

"Why, Papi, the more you gamble the more you know about other men—that's nature; but there's one thing that worries me for you."

"What's that?"

"Two or three times his partner's been murdered. That's why I said what I did yesterday evening. Take care, and when you don't feel safe, you come here. You can trust me."

"Thanks, Miguel."

Yes, a curious village all right, a curious mixture of men lost in the bush, living a rough life in the middle of an explosive landscape. Each one had his story. It was wonderful to see them, wonderful to listen to them. Their shacks were sometimes no more than a roof of palm fronds or bits of corrugated iron, and God knows how they got there. The walls were strips of cardboard or wood or sometimes even cloth. No beds; only hammocks. They slept, ate, washed and made love almost in the street. And yet nobody would lift a corner of the canvas or peer between the planks to see what was going on inside. Everybody had the utmost respect for others' privacy. If you wanted to go and see anyone, you never went nearer than a couple of yards before calling out, by way of ringing the bell, "Is anyone home?" If someone was, and he didn't know you, you said, *"Gente de paz,"* the same as saying, I'm a friend. Then someone would appear and say politely, *"Adelante. Esta casa es suya."* Come in; this house is yours.

A table in front of a solid hut made of well-fitting logs.

On the table, necklaces of real pearls from Margarita Island, some nuggets of virgin gold, a few watches, leather or expanding metal watch straps, and a good many alarm clocks. Mustafa's jewelry shop.

Behind the table was an old Arab with a pleasant face. We talked awhile; he was a Moroccan and he'd seen I was French. It was five in the afternoon, and he said to me, "Have you eaten?"

"Not yet."

"Nor have I. I was just going to. If you'd like to share my meal . . . ?"

"That would be fine."

Mustafa was a kind, cheerful guy. I spent a very pleasant hour with him. He was not inquisitive, and he didn't ask me where I came from.

"It's odd," he said, "in my own country I hated the French, and here I like them. Have you known any Arabs?"

"Plenty. Some were very good and others were very bad."

"It's the same with all nations. I class myself among the good ones. I'm sixty, and I might be your father. I had a son of thirty who was killed two years ago—shot. He was good-looking; he was kind." He eyes brimmed with tears.

I put my hand on his shoulder; this unhappy father so moved by the memory of his son reminded me of my own—he, too, retired in his little house in the Ardèche, must have his eyes fill with tears when he thought of me. Poor old Dad. Who could tell where he was, or what he was doing? I was sure he was still alive—I could feel it. Let's hope the war had not knocked him about too much.

Mustafa told me to come to his place whenever I felt like it—for a meal or if I ever needed anything: I'd be doing a kindness if I asked him a favor.

Evening was coming on: I said thank you for everything and set off for our shack. The game would be
beginning soon.

I was not at all on edge about my first game. "Nothing
ventured, nothing gained," Jojo had said, and he was
quite right. If I wanted to deliver my trunk filled with
dynamite at 36, quai des Orfèvres and to deal with the
others, I needed dough, plenty of dough. I'd be getting my
hands on it precious soon; that was a certainty.

As it was a Saturday, and as the miners religiously took
their Sundays off, the game was not to begin before nine,
because it would last until sunrise. The men came crowding to the shack, too many of them to get inside. It was
impossible to find room for them all, so Jojo sorted out the
ones who could play high. There were twenty-four of
them: the rest would play outside. I went to Mustafa's,
and he very kindly lent me a big carpet and a carbide
lamp. As the big-time gamblers dropped out, they could
be replaced from outside.

Banco, and banco again! On and on: every time Jojo
rolled the dice, so I kept covering the stakes. "Two to one
he won't shoot six with double threes . . . ten with double
fives. . . ." The men's eyes were ablaze. Every time one of
them lifted his cup an eleven-year-old boy filled it with
rum. I'd asked Jojo to let Miguel supply the rum and the
cigars.

Very soon the game heated up to boiling point. Without asking his permission, I changed Jojo's tactics. I laid
odds not only on him but also on the others, and that
made him look sour. Lighting a cigar, he muttered angri-
ly, "Quit it, man. Don't squander the jack." By about four
in the morning I had a pile of bolívars, cruzeiros, American and West Indian dollars, diamonds and even some
little gold nuggets in front of me.

Jojo took the dice. He staked five hundred bolívars. I
went in with a thousand.

And he threw the seven!

I left the lot, making two thousand bolívars. Jojo took out the five he had won. And threw the seven again! Once more he pulled out his stake. And seven again!

"What are you going to do, Enrique?" Chino asked.

"I leave the four thousand."

"Banco alone!" I looked at the guy who had just spoken. A little thickset man, as black as boot polish, his eyes bloodshot with drink. A Brazilian for sure.

"Put down your four thousand bolos."

"This stone's worth more." And he dropped a diamond on the blanket, just in front of him. He squatted there in his pink shorts, bare to the waist. The Chinese picked up the diamond, put it on his scales and said, "It's only worth three and a half."

"Okay for three and a half," said the Brazilian.

"Shoot, Jojo."

Jojo shot the dice, but the Brazilian grabbed them as they rolled. I wondered what was going to happen; he scarcely looked at the dice but spat on them and tossed them back to Jojo. "Shoot them like that, all wet," he said.

"Okay, Enrique?" asked Jojo, looking at me.

"If that's the way you want it, *hombre*."

Jojo hitched the fold in the blanket deeper with his left hand, and without wiping the dice he shot them—a long, long roll. And up came the seven again.

As if he was jerked by a spring, the Brazilian leapt to his feet, his hand on his gun. Then quietly he said, "It's not my night yet." And he went out.

The moment he shot up like a jack-in-the-box my hand darted to my gun—it had a round in the breech. Jojo never stirred or made a move to defend himself. And yet it was him the black man was aiming at. I saw I still had a lot to learn before I knew exactly when to draw and fire.

At sunrise we stopped. What with the smoke of the damp grass and the cigars and cigarettes, my eyes stung so much they ran. My legs were completely numb from having squatted like a tailor more than nine hours on end. But there was one thing that pleased me: I hadn't had to get up and piss, not once, and that meant I was entirely in control of my nerves and of my life.

We slept until two in the afternoon. When I woke up, Jojo wasn't there. I put on my trousers—nothing in the pockets! Shit! Jojo must have swiped the lot. But we hadn't settled our accounts yet: he shouldn't have done that. He was taking too much upon himself—assuming that as the boss he was beyond all question. I wasn't, and never had been, a boss; but I couldn't bear people who thought themselves superior—who thought they could get away with anything. I went out and found Jojo at Miguel's, eating a dish of macaroni. "Okay, buddy?" he said to me.

"Yes and no."

"How come, no?"

"Because you never ought to have emptied my pockets when I wasn't there."

"Don't talk bullshit, boy. I know how to behave and the reason why I did that is on account of everything depends on mutual trust. Don't you see, during a game you might very well stuff the diamonds or the liquid someplace else besides your pockets, for example? Then again, you don't know what I won either. So whether we empty our pockets together or not, it's all one. A matter of confidence."

He was right; let's say no more. Jojo had paid Miguel for the rum and the tobacco of the night before. I asked whether the guys wouldn't think it odd that he paid for them to drink and smoke.

"But I'm not the one who pays! Each man who wins a

bundle leaves something on the table. Everyone knows
that."

And night after night this life went on. We'd been here
two weeks, two weeks in which every night we played
high and wild, gambling with the dice and gambling with
our lives too.

One night an appalling rain came hurtling down. Black
as ink. A gambler got up after winning a fair pile. He
went out at the same time as a huge guy who'd been just
sitting there for some time, not playing anymore for want
of the wherewithal. Twenty minutes later the big guy who
had been so unlucky came back and started gambling like
crazy. I thought the winner must have lent him the
dough, but still it seemed queer he should have lent him
so much. When daylight came they found the winner
dead, stabbed less than fifty yards from our place. I
talked to Jojo about it, telling him what I thought.

"It's nothing to do with us," he said. "Next time, he'll
watch out."

"You're crazy, Jojo. There'll be no next time for him,
on account of he's dead."

"True enough: but what can we do about it?"

I was following José's advice, of course. Every day I
sold my foreign notes, the diamonds and the gold to a
Lebanese buyer, the owner of a jeweler's shop in Ciudad
Bolívar. Over the front of his hut there was a notice,
"Gold and diamonds bought here: highest prices given."
And underneath it, "Honesty is my greatest treasure."

Carefully I packed the credit notes payable on sight to
my order in a balataed envelope—an envelope dipped in
raw latex. They couldn't be cashed by anyone else or
endorsed in any other name. Every jailbird in the village
knew what I was doing, and if any buster made me feel
too uneasy or didn't speak French or Spanish, I showed
him. So the only time I was in danger was during the

game or when it ended. Sometimes that good guy Miguel came and fetched me when we stopped for the night.

For two days I'd had the feeling the atmosphere was getting tenser, more mistrustful. I'd learned the smell in the clink: when trouble was brewing in our barrack on the islands, you realized it without being able to tell how. When you're always on the alert, do you pick up vibes from the guys getting ready for the rough stuff? I don't know. But I've never been wrong about things like that.

For example, one time four Brazilians spent the whole night propped up in the corners of the room, in the darkness. Very occasionally one of them would come out of the shadows into the hard light that shone on the blanket and lay a few ridiculous little bets. They never took the dice or asked for them. Something else: *not one of them had a weapon that could be seen*. No machete, no knife, no gun. And that just didn't go with their killers' faces. It was on purpose, no doubt of it.

They came back the next evening. They wore their shirts outside their pants, so they must have their guns up against their bellies. They settled into the shadows, of course, but still I could make them out. Their eyes never left the players' movements. I had to watch them without their noticing it; and that meant I must not stare straight at them. I managed by coughing and leaning back, covering my mouth with my hand. Unfortunately there were only two in front of me. The others were behind, and I could only get quick glances of them by turning round to blow my nose.

Jojo's coolness was something extraordinary. He remained perfectly unmoved. Still, from time to time he did bet on other men's throws, which meant the risk of winning or losing by mere unaided chance. I knew that this kind of gambling set him all on edge, because it forced him to win the same money two or three times before keeping it for good. The disadvantage was when the game grew red-hot he became too eager to win and passed me over great wads of dough too fast.

As I knew these guys were watching me, I left my pile there in front of me for everyone to see. I didn't want to behave like a living safe deposit.

Two or three times I told Jojo, in quick crook's slang, that he was making me win too often. He looked as if he didn't understand. I had worked the outhouse trick on them the day before and I had not come back; so it was no good doing it now—if these four guys meant to move in tonight, they were not going to wait for me to return: they'd get me between the shack and the shit house.

I felt the tension mount: the four images in each corner were more on edge than ever. Particularly one who kept smoking cigarette after cigarette, lighting each from the butt of the last.

So now I started making bancos right and left, in spite of Jojo's ugly looks. To crown it all I won instead of losing and, far from shrinking, my pile kept on piling up. It was all there in front of me, mostly in five-hundred-bolívar notes. I was so keyed up that as I took the dice I put my cigarette down on them, and it burned two holes in a folded five hundred. I played and lost this note together with three others in a two-thousand-bolo banco. The winner got up, said, "See you tomorrow," and went out.

In the heat of the game I took no notice of how the time passed, and then all at once, to my amazement, I saw the note there on the blanket again. I knew perfectly well who'd won it, a very thin, bearded white man of about forty, with a pale mark on the lobe of his left ear, standing out against the sunburn. But he was not here anymore. In a couple of seconds I had put the scene together again: he'd gone out alone, I was certain of that. Yet not one of those four guys had stirred. So they must have one or two accomplices outside. They must have a system of signaling from where they were that a guy was coming out loaded with cash and diamonds.

There were a good many gamblers standing up, so I couldn't make out who had come in since the thin guy left. As for the ones sitting down, they had been the same for hours, and the place of the thin guy with the burned note had been filled the moment he left.

But who had played the note? I felt like picking it up and asking. But that would be very risky.

I was in danger: no doubt about that. There before my eyes was proof that the thin guy had got himself killed. My nerves were tense but they were under control; I had to think very fast. It was four in the morning; there'd be no daylight before six-fifteen, because in the tropics the sun comes up all at once, some time after six. If something was going to happen, it would happen between four and five. Outside it was as dark as hell: I knew, because I had just got up, saying I wanted a breath of fresh air in the doorway. I'd left my pile there where I sat, neatly stacked. I saw nothing unusual outside.

I came back and sat down calmly, but all my senses were on the alert. The back of my neck told me there were two pairs of eyes drilling into it.

Jojo rolled the dice, and I let other people cover his stakes. And now he began to have a fair-sized pile in front of him—something he hated.

The temperature was rising, rising; I felt that for sure, and in a very natural voice, not as if I were taking precautions, I said to Jojo in French, "I'm dead certain there's trouble in the air, man; I can smell it. Get up at the same time as me and let's cover the lot with our guns."

Jojo smiled as though I were saying something pleasant: he no more bothered about me than about someone else understanding French, and he said, "My good friend, what's the sense of this damn-fool attitude? And just who's to be covered in particular?"

True enough. Cover who? And what reason could you give? But the situation was explosive, that was certain. The guy with the everlasting cigarette had two full cups of rum and he tossed them straight off one after the other.

It would be no good going out alone in the inky darkness, even holding a gun. The men outside would see me and I wouldn't see them. Go into the next-door room? Worse still. Nine chances out of ten there was already a guy there: someone could easily have got in by lifting one of the planks in the wall.

There was only one thing to do, and that was to openly put all my winnings into my canvas bag, leave the bag there where I was sitting and go out and have a piss. They wouldn't signal, because I wouldn't have the dough on me. There were more than five thousand bolos in my pile. Better lose them than my life.

Anyhow, there was no choice. It was the only way to get out of this trap, which might snap shut any minute.

I'd worked all this out very quickly, of course: it was now seven minutes to five. I gathered everything together, notes, diamonds, the aspirin tubes and all: everyone saw me. I deliberately stuffed this little fortune into the canvas bag. As naturally as could be I pulled the strings tight, put the bag down about a foot from me, and so that everybody should understand I said in Spanish, "Keep an eye on the bag, Jojo. I don't feel so good. I'm going to take a breath of air."

Jojo had been watching all my movements; he held out his hand and said, "Give it to me. It'll be better off here than anywhere else."

Unwillingly I held it out, because I knew he was putting himself in danger, immediate danger. But what could I do? Refuse? Impossible: it would sound very strange.

I walked out, my hand on my gun. I could see no one

in the darkness, but I didn't have to see them to know they were there. Quickly, almost running, I made for Miguel's place. There was just a chance that if I came back with him and a big carbide lamp we might avoid the crunch. Unfortunately Miguel's was more than two hundred yards from our shack. I began to run.

"Miguel! Miguel!"

"What's the matter?"

"Get up quick! Bring your gun and your lamp. There's trouble."

Bang! Bang! Two shots in the pitch-black night.

I ran. First I got the wrong shack—insults from inside and at the same time they asked me what the shooting was about. I ran on. This was our shack—all lights out. I flicked my lighter. People came running with lamps. There was nobody left in the room. Jojo was lying on the ground, blood pouring from the back of his neck. He was not dead, but in a coma. A flashlight they'd left behind showed just what had happened. First they'd shot out the carbide lamp, at the same time knocking Jojo out. Using the flashlight, they'd swept up the pile lying in front of Jojo—my bag and his winnings. His shirt had been torn off, and the canvas belt he wore next to his skin had been ripped open with a knife or a machete.

All the gamblers had escaped, of course. The second shot had been fired to make them move faster. Anyhow, there had not been many of us left when I'd got up. Eight men sitting down, two standing, the four guys in the corners and the kid who poured out the rum.

Everybody offered to help. Jojo was carried to Miguel's hut, where there was a bed made of branches. He lay there in a coma all the morning. The blood had clotted; it no longer ran out, and according to an English miner that was a good sign but also a bad one, because if the skull was fractured, the bleeding would go on inside. I decided not to move him. A miner from El Callao, an old friend of Jojo's, set off for another mine to fetch a so-called doctor.

I was all in. I explained everything to Mustafa and Miguel, and they comforted me by saying that since the whole business had been, as you might say, signaled hours ahead, and since I had given Jojo a clear warning, he ought to have followed my lead.

About three in the afternoon, Jojo opened his eyes. We made him drink a few drops of rum, and then, the words coming hard, he whispered, "It's all up with me, buddy: I know it. Don't let me be moved. It wasn't your fault, Papi; it was mine." He paused for a while and then went on, "Miguel, there's a can buried behind your pigsty. Let the one-eyed guy take it to Lola, my wife." His mind was clear for a few minutes after that, and then he relapsed into coma. He died at sunset.

Doña Carmencita, the fat woman from the first joint, came to see him. She brought a few diamonds and three or four notes she had found on the floor at our place during the morning. God knows hundreds of people had been there, yet not one of them had touched either the money or the diamonds.

Almost the whole of the little community came to the funeral. The four Brazilians were there, still wearing their shirts outside their trousers. One of them came up to me and held out his hand; I pretended not to see it and gave him a friendly shove in the belly. Yes: I had been right. The gun was there, just where I had thought it would be.

I wondered whether I ought to deal with them. Do it now? Later? Do what? Nothing: it was too late.

I wanted to be alone, but after a burial it was the custom to go and have a drink at every joint whose owner had turned up at the graveyard. They always came, all of them.

When I was at Doña Carmencita's she came and sat by

me, with her glass of anisette in her hand. When I put mine to my lips, she raised hers, too, but only to hide the fact that she was talking to me. "It was better him than you," she said. "Now you can go wherever you want in peace."

"What do you mean, in peace?"

"Because everybody knows you always sold your winnings to the Lebanese."

"Yes, but suppose the Lebanese is killed?"

"That's true. One more problem."

I told Doña Carmencita the drinks were on me and walked off by myself leaving my friends sitting there. Without really knowing why, I took the path that led to what they called the graveyard, a piece of cleared ground of about fifty square yards.

Eight graves there in the cemetery: Jojo's was the latest. And there in front of it stood Mustafa. I went over to him. "What are you doing, Mustafa?"

"I've come to pray for an old friend—I was fond of him—and to bring him a cross. You forgot to make one."

Hell, so I had! I'd never thought of it. I shook the good old Arab's hand and thanked him.

"You're not a Christian?" he asked. "I didn't see you pray when they threw the earth on him."

"Well, I mean . . . there's certainly a God, Mustafa," I said, to please him. "And what's more, I thank Him for having looked after me instead of sending me away forever, along with Jojo And I do more than say prayers for this old man; I forgive him: he was a poor little kid from the Belleville slums and he was able to learn just one profession—shooting craps."

"What are you talking about, brother? I don't understand."

"It doesn't matter. But remember this: I'm really sorry he's dead. I did try to save him. But no one should ever think he's brighter than the rest, because one day he'll find a man who moves faster than him. Jojo is fine here. He'll sleep forever with what he loved, adventure and the wild landscape; and he'll sleep with God's forgiveness."

"Yes, God will forgive him for sure, because he was a good man."

"That's a fact."

I walked slowly back to the village. It was true that I did not feel resentful toward Jojo, although he had very nearly been the death of me. His enthusiasm, his prodigious energy, and, in spite of his sixty years, his youth, and his underworld good breeding—"Behave properly, God almighty, behave properly!" And then I'd been warned. I'd willingly send up a little prayer to thank José for his advice. Without him I shouldn't be here.

Swinging gently in my hammock and smoking fat cigar after fat cigar, as much to soak myself in nicotine as to chase the mosquitoes away, I took stock of my accounts.

Right. I had ten thousand dollars after only a few months of freedom. And both here and at El Callao I had met men and women of all races and backgrounds, every one of them full of human warmth. Because of them and this life in the wild, in this atmosphere so unlike that of the city, I'd come to know how wonderful freedom was, the freedom I'd fought for so hard.

Then again the war had come to an end, thanks to Charlie de Gaulle and the Yankees, and in all this churning about of millions of people, a convict didn't amount to much. So much the better for me: with all these problems to settle, they would have other things to do besides worrying about what I had been.

I was thirty-nine: fourteen years of penal settlement, fifty-three months of solitary confinement, counting the Santé, the Conciergerie and Beaulieu as well as the prison on the island, the Réclusion. It was hard to put a label on me. I wasn't a poor bastard only capable of working with a pick or a shovel or an ax; nor did I have a real trade that would let me earn a decent living anywhere in the world, as a mechanic or an electrician, say. On the other hand, I couldn't take on important responsibilities; I hadn't enough education for that. While you're in school you should always learn a good manual trade; then if school goes wrong you can always look after yourself in life. It wasn't that you felt better than a street sweeper if you had a certain amount of education—I had never despised any man except screws and pigs—but that, without it, you couldn't do justice to your true self. You were stymied—you felt you might have been happy, but that you wouldn't be, after all. I had both too much education and not enough. Hell, that was hardly the brightest outlook in the world.

And it was true that I had to take my revenge, too: it was true I could not possibly forgive the people who had done me and my family so much harm. Calm down, Papi, calm down. You've got plenty of time. You must gradually learn to trust in the future. You've sworn to go straight in this country, but here you are, already hustling, forgetting your promise.

I couldn't help going to the doorway and gazing for a long while at the stars and the moon, and listening to the countless noises coming from the mysterious bush that surrounded the village with a wall as dark as the moon was brilliant.

And then I slept, rocking gently in my hammock, happy to the core in the knowledge that I was free, free, free, and *master of my fate*.

4

Farewell to El Callao

At about ten the next morning I went to see the Lebanese. "So I go to El Callao or Ciudad Bolívar, to the addresses you've given me, and they pay me your bills of exchange?"

"That's right: you can go off with an easy mind."

"But what if they kill you too?"

"It doesn't matter, as far as you're concerned. You will be paid whatever happens. You're going to El Callao?"

"Yes."

"What part of France are you from?"

"Around Avignon, not far from Marseille."

"Why, I've got a friend from Marseille, but he lives a great way off. Alexandre Guigue is his name."

"Well, what do you know! He's a close friend of mine."

"Of mine, too. I'm glad you know him."

"Where does he live, and how can I get there?"

"He's at Boa Vista. A very long and complicated journey."

"What does he do there?"

"He's a barber. Easy to find him—you just ask for the French barber-dentist."

"So he's a dentist too?"

I couldn't help laughing, because I knew Alexandre Guigue very well: an extraordinary guy. He was sent out the same time as me, in 1933; we made the crossing together, and he had all the time in the world to tell me every last detail of his job.

One Saturday night in 1929 or 1930, Alexandre and a friend climbed quietly down from the ceiling of Lisbon's biggest jewelry shop. They had broken into a dentist's office on the next floor up. To memorize the layout of the building, to be sure the dentist went away every weekend with his family and make impressions of the lock of the front door and the surgery, they had had to go there several times and have their teeth filled.

"Very good work he did, too," Alexandre told me, "seeing the fillings are still there. In two nights we had all the time we needed to shift the jewels and open two safes and a little steel cabinet. doing it neatly and without any noise. The dentist must have been fantastic at describing people, because as we were on the platform leaving Lisbon the pigs jumped on us without any hesitation at all. The Portuguese court sent us down for ten and twelve years. So there we were. a little while later, at their prison in Angola, down under the Belgian and French Congo. No problem about escaping: our friends came to get us in a taxi. Like an idiot I went to Brazzaville: my buddy, he chose Leopoldville. A few months later I was picked up by the French police. The French wouldn't give me back to the Portuguese: they sent me back to France and there I copped a twenty-year stretch instead of the ten they'd given me in Portugal."

He made a break from Guiana. I'd heard that he had passed through Georgetown. and that he'd gone to Brazil through the bush, riding on an ox.

What if I went to see him? Yes: I'd go to Boa Vista. That was a brilliant idea!

I set off with two men. They said they knew how to get to Brazil, and they were to help me carry the food and bedding. For ten days and more we wandered about the bush without even managing to reach Santa Helena, the last mining village before the Brazilian frontier, and after a fortnight we found ourselves at Aminos, a gold mine almost on the edge of British Guiana. With the help of some Indians we reached the Cuyuni River, and that led us to a little Venezuelan village called Castillejo. There I bought machetes and files as a present for the Indians, and I left my so-called guides. I had to control myself so as not to smash their faces in, because in fact they no more knew those parts than I did.

In the end I found a man in the village who really did know the country and who agreed to guide me. Four or five days later I reached El Callao. Exhausted, worn out, thin as a lath, I knocked on Maria's door at nightfall.

"He's here! He's here!" shrieked Esmeralda at the top of her voice.

"Who?" asked Maria from another room. "And why do you shout so?"

All stirred up by finding this sweetness again after the weeks I had just been through, I caught hold of Esmeralda and put my hand over her mouth to keep her from answering.

"Why all this noise about a visitor?" asked Maria, coming in. Then with a cry of joy, of love, of hope fulfilled, she threw herself into my arms.

When I had embraced Picolino and kissed Maria's other sister—José was away—I lay there a long, long while beside Maria. She kept asking me the same questions; she couldn't believe I had come straight to her house without stopping at Big Charlot's or at any of the village cafés.

"You're going to stay a little while in El Callao, aren't you?"

"Yes. I'll fix things so I stay for some time."

"You must take care of yourself and put on weight; I'll cook such dishes for you, sweetheart. When you go, even if it wounds my heart forever—not that I blame you in any way, since you warned me—when you go, I want you to be strong, so that you can avoid the snares of Caracas as well as you can."

El Callao, Uasipata. Upata, Tumeremo: little villages with names strange for a European, tiny points on the map of a country three times the size of France, lost at the back of beyond. where the word *progress* has no meaning and where men and women, young and old, live as people lived in Europe at the beginning of the century, overflowing with genuine passions, generosity, joy in life and kindness. Almost all the men who were more than forty had had to bear the most terrible of all dictatorships, the rule of Gomez They were hunted down and beaten to death for nothing· any man in authority could flog them with a bull's pizzle When they were between fifteen and twenty in the years 1925 to 1935, all of them had been hunted like animals by the army's recruiting agents and dragged off to the barracks Those were the days when a pretty girl might be picked out and kidnaped by an important official and thrown into the street when he was tired of her; and if her family raised a finger to help her they were wiped out.

Now and then. to be sure, there were uprisings, suicidal revolts by men who were determined to have their revenge even if. they died for it. But the army was always there at once. and those who escaped with their lives were so tortured they were crippled for the rest of their days.

And yet in spite of all that. the almost illiterate people of these little backward villages still retained their love for other men and their trust in them. For me it was a continual lesson, and one that touched me to the bottom of my heart.

I thought of all this as I lay beside Maria. I had suffered, that was true; I had been condemned unjustly, that was true again; the French wardens had been as savage as the tyrant's police and soldiers, and maybe even more devilish; but here I was, all in one piece, having just gone through a terrific adventure—a dangerous adventure, certainly, but how utterly fascinating! I'd walked, paddled my canoe, ridden through the bush; but as I lived it each day was a year, so full it was; that life of a man with no laws, free from all restraints, from all moral limits, all obedience to orders from outside.

So I wondered whether I was doing the right thing, going to Caracas and leaving this corner of paradise behind me. Again and again I asked myself that question.

The next day, bad news. The correspondent of the Lebanese, a little jeweler who specialized in gold orchids with Margarita pearls and in all kinds of other truly original ornaments, told me he couldn't pay anything on my notes of credit because the Lebanese owed him a huge sum of money. Okay, so I'd go and get my money at the other address in Ciudad Bolívar.

"Do you know this man?" I asked.

"Only too well. He's a crook. He's run off, taking everything, even some choice pieces I'd left with him on trust."

If what this goddamn fool said was true, then I was even more broke than before I went off with Jojo. Fine, fine! Fate—what a mysterious business. These things only happened to me. And done by a Lebanese, into the bargain!

Bowed down and dragging my feet, I came back to the house. To win those wretched ten thousand dollars I'd risked my life ten and twenty times over; and now not the smell of a cent was left to me. Well, well; that Lebanese did not have to load the dice to win at craps. Better still, he did not even bother to move—he sat there at home, waiting for the cash to be brought to him.

But my zest for life was so strong that I bawled myself out. You're free, man, and here you are whining about fate! You can't be serious. So maybe you did lose your banco; what a marvelous caper it was! Lay your bets!

I was in control again now, and I could see the position clearly enough. I'd have to hurry back to the mine, before the Lebanese sneaked off. And since time is money, don't let's lose any. I'd go and find a mule, some stores and be on my way! I still had my gun and my knife. The only question was, would I find the way? I hired a horse—Maria thought it far better than a mule. The only thing that worried me was the idea of taking the wrong *pique*, because there were places where others came in from all directions.

"I know the paths: would you like me to go with you?" Maria asked. "Oh how I should love that! I'd only go as far as the *posada*, where you leave the horses before taking to the canoe."

"It's too dangerous for you, Maria. Above all, too dangerous coming back alone."

"I'll wait for somebody who's returning to El Callao. That way I'll be safe. Please say yes, *mi amor!*"

I talked it over with José, and he agreed she should go. "I'll lend her my revolver. Maria knows how to use it," he said.

And that's how we came to be sitting there alone on the edge of the *pique*, Maria and I, after a five hours' ride—I had hired another horse for her. She was wearing breeches, a present from a friend, a *llanera*. The Venezuelan *llana* is a huge plain, and the women who live there are brave and untamable; they fire a rifle or a revolver like a man, wield the machete like a fencer and ride like an Amazon—yet in spite of that they are capable of dying for love.

Maria was exactly the opposite. She was gentle and sensual and so close to nature you felt she was part of it. Not that that prevented her from knowing how to look after herself, with a weapon or without: she was courageous.

Never, never shall I forget those days of traveling before we reached the *posada*. Unforgettable days and nights when it was our hearts that sang after we were too tired to speak our happiness.

I'll never be able to describe the delight of those dreamlike halts when we played in the coolness of the crystal-clear water and then, still wet and mother-naked, made love on the grassy bank with butterflies and hummingbirds and dragonflies all around us.

We would go on, tottering with love and sometimes so filled with ecstasy that I felt myself to make sure I was still all in one piece.

The nearer we came to the *posada* the more closely I listened to Maria's pure natural voice singing love songs. And the more the distance shortened, the more often I pulled in my horse and found excuses for another rest.

"Maria, I think we ought to let the horse cool a while."

"At this pace, he's not going to be the one who's tired when we get there, Papi; we're the ones who'll be worn out," she said, breaking into a laugh that showed her pearly teeth.

We managed to spend six days on the road before we came in sight of the *posada*. The instant I saw it, I was overcome with a longing to spend the night there and then go back to El Callao. The idea of having the purity of those six days of passion all over again suddenly seemed to me a thousand times more important than my ten thousand dollars. The desire was so strong it made me tremble. But even stronger, there was a voice that said, "Don't be a fool, Papi. Ten thousand dollars is a fortune, the first big chunk of the amount you need to carry out your plan. You must not give it up."

"There's the *posada*," said Maria.

And against myself, against everything I thought and felt, I said the opposite of what I wanted to say. "Yes, there's the *posada*. Our journey's over; tomorrow I leave you."

Four good men at the paddles, and in spite of the current the canoe raced over the water. Every stroke took me farther from Maria, and standing on the bank she watched me disappear.

Where was peace, where was love, where perhaps was the woman with whom I was fated to build a home and a family? I forced myself not to look back, for fear I should call out to the paddlers, "Let's turn around!" I had to go on to the mine and get my money and then head for other adventures as soon as possible, to make enough for the great journey to Paris and back. If there was to be any return.

Only one promise: I'd not hurt the Lebanese, I'd just take what belonged to me, neither more nor less. He'd never know he owed this forgiveness to my six days of traveling through paradise with the most wonderful girl in the world, Maria, the nymph of El Callao.

"The Lebanese? But I'm pretty sure he's gone," said Miguel, having crushed me in his embrace.

I had found the shack closed, true enough, but the wonderful sign was still there: "Honesty is my greatest treasure."

"You think he's gone? Oh, the worthless shit!"

"Calm down, Papi. We'll soon find out."

My doubt did not last long, nor my hope; Mustafa confirmed that the Lebanese had gone. But where had he gone? It was only after two days of inquiry that a miner told me he had lit out for Brazil with three bodyguards. "All the miners say he's an honest man for sure." Then I told the story of El Callao and all I'd learned about the disappearing Lebanese in Ciudad Bolívar. Four or five guys, including an Italian, said that if I was right, they were broke. There was only one old character from Guiana who would not see it our way. According to him, the real thief was the Ciudad Bolívar Greek. We looked the situation over from every angle for quite a while, but in my heart of hearts I felt I'd lost the whole works for good and all. What was I going to do?

Go to see Alexandre Guigue at Boa Vista? It was a long way off, Brazil. You had to reckon about three hundred miles through the bush to reach Boa Vista. My last experience had been too risky—just a little farther, and it would have been my last journey. No, I'd fix things so I was in contact with the mine, and as soon as I heard the Lebanese had surfaced again I'd pay him a visit. Once that was settled, I'd be on my way for Caracas, picking up Picolino as I went by. That was the most sensible answer. The next day I'd set off for El Callao.

A week later I was back with José and Maria. I told them everything. Gently, kindly, Maria found the right words to restore my spirits. Her father urged me to stay with them. "We'll raid the Caratal mine, if you like." I smiled, and patted him on the shoulder.

No, really that did not appeal to me; I mustn't stay there. It was only my love for Maria and hers for me that could keep me in El Callao. I was more hooked than I had believed and more than I wanted. It was a strong, genuine love; but still it wasn't powerful enough to overcome my desire for revenge.

Everything was settled: I had made arrangements with a truck driver and we were to leave at five the next morning.

While I was shaving, Maria slipped out and hid in her sisters' room. That mysterious sense women possess had told her that this was the real parting. Picolino was sitting at the table in the big room, washed and tidy, with Esmeralda standing next to him, her hand on his shoulder. I took a step toward the room where Maria was. Esmeralda stopped me. "No, Enrique." Then she too darted to the door and disappeared.

José went with us as far as the truck. We did not say a word.

5

Caracas

It was a tough journey, particularly for Picolino. Six hundred miles and more; twenty hours of driving, not counting the stops. We spent a few hours in Ciudad Bolívar, and then having crossed the splendid Orinoco on a ferry, we tore along, the truck racing like crazy, driven by a man with nerves of steel; which was just as well.

The next afternoon at four o'clock we reached Caracas. And there I was in the big city. The movement, the crowds, the coming and going of thousands and thousands of people, sucked me right in.

1931, Paris. 1946, Caracas. Fifteen years had passed since I had seen a genuine big city. A lovely city, Caracas, beautiful with its one-story colonial houses; and it stretched right down the valley with the Avila mountains rising all round it. A city three thousand feet up, with an everlasting spring, neither too hot nor too cold.

"I trust you, Papillon," said Dr. Bougrat's voice in my ear, just as if he were there, watching us drive into this huge, swarming city.

Crowds of people everywhere, of all colors from the darkest to the lightest, without any complexes about race. All these people, black, brick-red or purest white, were alive with a happiness that went to my head in the first moments.

With Picolino leaning on my arm, I walked toward the middle of the city. Big Charlot had given me the address of an ex-con who kept a boardinghouse, the Pension Maracaibo.

Yes, fifteen years had gone by and a war had shattered the lives of hundreds of thousands of men of my age in a great many lands, including my own country, France. Between 1939 and 1945 they, too, had been prisoners, or had been killed or maimed. But I was thirty-nine. I was young and strong.

How beautiful it is, a great city! And it was only four o'clock now. What must it be like at night, with its millions of electric stars? Yet we were still only in a working-class district, and a pretty tough one, at that. I'd spend a little money for once. "Hey there, taxi!"

Sitting beside me, Picolino laughed and dribbled like a kid. I wiped his poor mouth; he thanked me with shining eyes, trembling, he was so moved. For him, being in a town, a great capital like Caracas, meant above all the hope of finding hospitals and doctors who could turn the wreck he had become into a normal man once more. The miracle of hope. He held my hand, while outside the streets went by and then still more streets with people and still more people, so many of them they entirely hid the pavement. And the cars, and the horns, and the siren of an ambulance, the clang of a fire engine, the bawling of the hawkers and the newsboys selling the evening papers, the shriek of a truck's brakes, the ting-a-ling of the trolleys, the bicycle bells—all these shouts and the deafening noise around made us feel almost drunk. The din destroys some people's nerves, but it had the opposite effect on us; it woke us up and made us thoroughly understand that we were right back in the crazy rhythm of modern mechanical life—and instead of being tensed up we felt wonderfully happy.

It wasn't surprising that the noise struck us most. For I'd known silence for fifteen years, the silence of the prisons, the silence of the penal settlement, the more than silence of solitary confinement, the silence of the bush and of the sea, the silence of the little remote villages where happy people live.

I said to Picolino, "We are coming into a foretaste of Paris—Caracas, a real city. Here they'll make you well, and as for me, I'll find my right path and work out my fate; you can be sure of that."

His hand squeezed mine; a tear ran from his eye. His hand was so brotherly and affectionate that I held on to it so as not to lose that marvelous contact; and since his other arm was dead, it was I that wiped away my friend's tear.

At last we reached the place run by Emile S., the ex-con, and settled in. He wasn't there, but as soon as his wife, a Venezuelan, heard we were from El Callao, she grasped what we were and gave us a room with two beds right away, and some coffee.

Having helped Picolino take a shower, I put him to bed. He was tired and overexcited. When I left he made violent signs; and I knew he meant to say, "You'll come back, won't you? You won't leave me in the lurch, all by myself?"

"No, Pico! I'll just spend a few hours in the town: I'll be back soon."

And here I was in Caracas. It was seven o'clock when I walked down the street toward the Plaza Simón Bolívar, the biggest in the city. An explosion of light everywhere, a magnificent pouring out of electricity, neon signs of every color. What enchanted me most were the advertisements in colored lights, flaming dragons that came and went like

will-o'-the-wisps, flashing on and off like a ballet run by a
magician.

It was a splendid square, with a huge bronze statue of
Simón Bolívar on an enormous horse in the middle of it.
He looked terrific, and the statue showed how noble he
must have been. I walked right around him, the man who
set Latin America free, and I could not help greeting him
in my bad Spanish, speaking low so no one would hear,
"Hombre! What a miracle it is for me to be here at your
feet—at the feet of the Man of Freedom. A poor bastard
like me, who has been fighting all the time for that
freedom you personify."

The *pension* was a quarter of a mile from the square,
and I went back twice before I found Emile S. He said
Charlot had written to tell him we were coming; we went
out to have a drink so we could talk quietly.

"It's ten years now I've been here," Emile said. "I'm
married, with a daughter, and my wife owns the *pension*.
That's why I can't put you up for nothing; but you'll only
pay half price." The wonderful solidarity of ex-cons when
one of them is in a jam! He went on, "Is he an old friend,
that poor guy with you?"

"You've seen him?"

"No, but my wife's been telling me about him. She says
he's an absolute wreck. Is he senile?"

"Far from it, and that's what's so terrible. His mind is
as clear as a bell, but his tongue and his mouth and his
right side down to the waist are paralyzed. That's the way
he was when I first knew him in El Dorado. Nobody
knows who he is or whether he's a con or a detainee."

"I can't see why you want to drag this stranger around
with you. You don't even know if he's a regular fellow or
not. And then on top of that, he's a burden to you."

"I've realized that, these eight months I've been looking
after him. In El Callao I found some women who took
charge. Even so, it's not easy."

"What are you going to do with him?"

"Get him into a hospital if I can. Or find a room—rough, if need be, but with a shower and a toilet—to look after him until I can find a place for him somewhere."

"You got dough?"

"A little, but I've got to be careful; because although I understand all they say, I speak Spanish badly and it's not going to be so simple to make things work out."

"You're dead right, it's not easy here—more people wanting work than there are jobs. But anyhow, Papi, don't you worry; you can stay in my place the few days you'll need to find something."

I got the message. Emile was generous, but he was unhappy about the whole thing. His wife must have drawn a pretty picture of Picolino with his tongue lolling out and his animal grunts. She must have thought of the impression he would make on the boarders.

Tomorrow I'd carry his meals up to our room. Poor Picolino, sleeping there next to me in your little iron bed. Although I pay for your room and board, they don't want you. People who are well don't like to see the sick. But don't you worry, pal. Even if I'm not as gentle as the El Callao girls, you'll always have me by you; something better than a friend—a crook who's adopted you and who'll do everything he can to keep you from dying like a dog.

Emile gave me several addresses, but there was no job for me anywhere. And twice I went to the hospital to try to get Picolino in. Nothing doing. According to them there were no empty beds; and his papers, saying he'd been let out of El Dorado, were no help at all. Yesterday they asked me how he came to be under my care and why, and what was his nationality and so on. When I told the little cunt of a clerk that the chief of El Dorado had put him in my charge and that I had undertaken to look after him, this is what the bastard answered: "Well then, since he's been let out because you agreed to take care of him, all you have to do is keep him where you live and have him treated there. If you can't do that, you ought to have left him at El Dorado."

When he asked for my address I gave him a false one. I didn't trust the jackass, a perfect example of the petty official who wants to throw his weight about.

I moved Picolino; I moved him quick. I was desperate, both for him and for me. I felt I couldn't stay at Emile's any longer; his wife was moaning about having to change Picolino's sheets every day. I did wash the dirty places every morning as well as I could in the washbasin, but they took a long time to dry and it was soon noticed. So I brought an iron and dried the places I had washed with it.

What was to be done? I couldn't be sure. One thing was certain—I had to find an answer quick. Now for the third time I'd tried to get him into a hospital with no result. It was eleven o'clock when we came out. Since that was the way things were, we'd have to set about it properly; I decided to devote the whole of that fine afternoon to my friend. I led him to the Calvario, a wonderful garden filled with tropical plants and flowers on a little hill plumb in the middle of Caracas.

Sitting there on a bench and admiring the splendid view, we ate *arepas* with meat in them and drank a bottle of beer. Then I lit two cigarettes, one for Pico, one for me. It was hard for Picolino to smoke; he drooled on his cigarette. He felt this was an important moment and that I meant to tell him something that might hurt him badly. His eyes were full of anxiety and they seemed to say, "Speak, speak right away. I can feel you've taken a big decision. Tell me; I beg you to tell me." Yes, I could read all that in his eyes as plain as if it was written. It made me wretched, and I hesitated. At last I brought it out. "Pico, it's three days now I've been trying to get you into a hospital. There's nothing to be done; they don't want you. You understand?"

"Yes," said his eyes.

"On the other hand, we can't go to the French consulate without the risk of them asking the Venezuelans for an extradition order." He shrugged his good shoulder. "Listen: you've got to get well, and to get well you've got to be treated. That's the main thing. But you know I haven't got enough money to have you looked after. So this is what we'll do: we'll spend the evening together, and I'll take you to the cinema. Then tomorrow morning I'll take you to the Plaza Bolívar without any papers on you. There you lie at the foot of the statue and you don't stir. If they want you to stand or to sit up, you refuse. It's dead certain that after a minute they'll call a cop and he'll call an ambulance. I'll follow in a cab to see what hospital they take you to. Then I'll wait two days before coming to see you, and I'll come in visiting hours so as to mix with the crowd. The first time maybe I won't talk to you, but as I go past your bed I'll leave you some cigarettes and a little money. Okay? You agree?"

He put his good arm on my shoulder and looked straight into my face. His expression was an extraordinary mixture of sadness and gratitude. His throat contracted; he made a superhuman effort to force his twisted mouth to bring out a hoarse sound very like "Yes, thank you."

Next day, everything happened just as I had foretold. Less than a quarter of an hour after Picolino lay down at the foot of the Bolívar statue, three or four old men sitting under the shade of the trees told a cop. Twenty minutes later an ambulance came for him. I followed in a cab.

Two days later—no difficulty about mingling with the visitors—I found him in the third ward I went through. A piece of luck: he was between two very sick patients and I could talk to him a while without any risk. He was flushed with joy at seeing me, and maybe he jerked about a little too much.

"They look after you all right?"

He nodded yes.

I looked at the chart at the foot of his bed. "Paraplegia or malaria with secondary complications. To be checked every two hours." I left him six packs of cigarettes, matches and twenty bolívars in change.

"Bye, Pico!" Seeing his desperate and imploring eyes I added, "Don't worry, pal; I'll come back and visit you." I mustn't forget that I'd grown absolutely necessary to him. I was his one link with the world.

I'd been in Caracas for two weeks, and the hundred-bolívar notes were disappearing fast. Fortunately I had decent clothes when I got to Caracas. I found a little room, cheap, though still too dear for me. There were no women anywhere on the horizon, but the girls of Caracas were lovely to look at, intelligent and full of life. The difficulty was getting to know them. This was 1946, and it wasn't the custom for women to sit in a café alone.

A big city has its secrets. To be able to take care of yourself, you have to know them; and to learn them, you have to know the teachers. And just who are these teachers of the streets? A whole mysterious tribe with their own language, laws, customs and vices, their own ways of managing to make enough to live on for twenty-four hours every day. Earning a living, as honestly as possible: that was the problem, and it wasn't easy.

Like all the others, I had my own little ways, often good for a hearty laugh and far from wicked. For example, one day I met a Colombian I'd known in El Dorado.

"What are you doing?"

He told me just then he was earning his living by running a lottery for a magnificent Cadillac.

"Hell, so you've made your fortune already? You must have, to own a Cadillac."

He choked with laughter, then he explained the job. "The Cadillac belongs to the director of a big bank. He drives himself, gets there at nine on the dot and parks like a good citizen a hundred or a hundred and fifty yards from the bank. There are two of us. One—not always the same, so we don't get spotted—follows him to the door of the bank where he sits on his ass all morning. If there's a hitch, a whistle you can't mistake for anything else; it's only happened once. So between the time he gets there and the time he goes, which is around one, we put an elegant white streamer on the Cadillac, with red letters saying, 'On sale here: tickets that may win you this Cadillac. Winning numbers the same as the Caracas lottery. Draw next month.' "

"Man, that's a better-than-average racket. So you sell tickets for a Cadillac that isn't yours? Christ, what a nerve! What about the pigs?"

"They're never the same; and seeing as there's no vice in them, it never comes into their heads that maybe the deal's a swindle. If they get a little too interested we give them a ticket or two and off they go, dreaming perhaps they'll win a Cadillac. If you want to make a little money with us, come along and I'll introduce you to my partner."

"You don't think it stinks a little, duping the poor?"

"Never on your sweet life. The tickets cost ten bolívars, so it's only well-off folk that can afford them. So there's no harm done."

Once the partner had checked me out, there I was, all involved with this knavery. It's not very elegant, but you have to eat, sleep and be, if not well dressed, at least clean. And I had to hold on to my reserve as long as possible—the few diamonds I'd brought from El Dorado and two five-hundred-bolívar notes that I hoarded like a

miser in my *plan*— a short aluminum tube that I shoved
up my ass for safekeeping—just as if I were still in the
clink. I'd never left off carrying my *plan* inside me, for
two reasons: my hotel was in a pretty rough part of the
town, where I might be robbed; and if I carried money in
my pocket, I might lose it. In any case, I'd been storing
this tube up my ass for fourteen years now, so a year
more or less didn't make much difference, and that way I
was easy in my mind.

The selling of the lottery tickets lasted more than a
fortnight, and it would be going on still but for the fact
that one day a very eager customer bought two tickets
and examined every detail of this marvelous car he
dreamed of winning. All at once he straightened up and
cried, "But doesn't this car belong to Dr. Fulano, the bank
director?"

Without batting an eyelid, the Colombian replied cool-
ly, "Just so. He put it into our hands to dispose of like
this. He reckons a lottery will bring him in a better price
than a straight sale."

"Odd . . . ," said the customer.

"But above all, don't mention it to him," the Colombian
went on, still very calm. "He made us promise to say
nothing, because he'd find it awkward if it was known."

"I can't understand it; it's really most unusual for a
man of his kind."

As soon as he'd got far enough away, moving in the
direction of the bank, we whipped off the streamer and
folded it up. The Colombian vanished, carrying it, and I
went to the door of the bank to tell our partner we were
breaking camp. Inside myself I was laughing like a hyena
and I couldn't help hanging around near the door so I
could catch what I expected would be the sequel. It came
off, all right. Three minutes later, there was the director
together with the suspicious customer. He was waving his

arms wildly and walking so fast I knew he was in a real fury.

They saw there was nobody left around the Cadillac, and surprised, no doubt, they came back slower, stopping at a café to have a drink at the bar. As the customer hadn't recognized me, I went in, too, to hear what they would say, for the laugh.

"By God, that was a nerve! Don't you think that was an infernal nerve, Dr. Fulano?"

But the owner of the Cadillac, who, like all good Caraqueños, had a sense of humor, burst out laughing and said, "When I think that if I had walked by they might have offered me a ticket for my own car! And that sometimes I'm so absentminded that I might actually have bought it. You must admit it makes you laugh."

Naturally enough, that was the end of our lottery. The Colombians vanished. For my part, I'd made close to fifteen hundred bolívars, enough to live on for over a month; which was important.

The days went by, and it was not at all easy to find anything worthwhile to do. This was the period when Pétain's supporters and the men who had collaborated with the Germans started reaching Venezuela from France, on the run from the justice of their own country. Since I didn't know enough about the possible distinction between collaborators and Pétainists, I lumped them all together under the label of ex-Nazis. So I did not associate with them.

A month went by and nothing much happened. At El Callao I had never thought it would be so hard to get myself going. I was reduced to selling coffee pots from door to door; they were supposed to be specially designed for offices.

You look rather foolish walking about the streets with a coffee pot in your hand; and I was doing just that when I bumped into Paulo the Boxer, an old Montmartre acquaintance.

"Why, what do you know? You must be Paulo the . . ."

"And you're Papillon?"

He grabbed my arm and towed me into a café.

"Well, talk of coincidence—this is a coincidence, all right."

"What are you up to, walking around the street with that coffee pot?"

"I'm selling them: it's a goddamn disaster. What with getting it out and shoving it back again, the box tore just now." I told him how things were with me and then I said, "How about you?"

"Let's drink our coffee. I'll tell you somewhere else."

We paid and stood up; I reached for my coffee pot.

"Leave that where it is. You won't want it anymore, I give you my oath."

"You don't think so?"

"I know it, man."

I left the vile pot on the table and we went out.

An hour later, in my room, after we had tossed memories of Montmartre to and fro, Paulo came to the point. He had a big job in a country not far from Venezuela. He knew he could rely on me. If I agreed, he'd take me on as one of his team.

"It's as easy as falling off a log—it's in the bag, man! I tell you very seriously, there are going to be so many dollars you'll need an iron to flatten them so they don't take up too much room."

"And where is it, this prodigious job?"

"You'll know when you get there. I can't say anything before."

"How many of us will there be?"

"Four. One's already on the spot. I came here to fetch the other. You know him, by the way. He's a friend of yours: Gaston."

"Right. But I've lost touch with him."

"Not me," said Paulo, laughing.

"You really can't tell me any more about the job?"

"Impossible, Papi. I've got my reasons."

I thought quickly. Placed as I was, there wasn't much choice. Either I went on dragging about with a coffee pot or some other goddamn nonsense in my hand or I took up the adventurous life again, with the possibility of making a bundle and making it quick. I'd always known that Paulo was a sober, reflecting type, and if in his opinion there had to be four of us, then that meant this job was serious, too. Technically, it would be a fancy piece of work. And that, I must admit, tempted me, too. So what about it, Papi—banco?

"Banco!"

The next day we set off.

6

The Tunnel under the Bank

More than seventy-two hours of driving. We relieved one another at the wheel. Paulo took endless precautions; every time we stopped for gas, the man who was driving put the others down three hundred yards from the pump and picked them up afterward.

Gaston and I had been waiting half an hour in the driving rain, waiting for Paulo to come back. I was furious. "You really think all this act is necessary, Paulo? Just look at us. We'll catch our goddamn deaths."

"What a fucking bore you are, Papi. I had air put in

the tires, changed a back wheel and filled up with oil and water. You can't do that in five minutes."

"I never said you could. But I tell you I don't see the point of all these precautions."

"Well, I do, and I'm the boss. You may have had a fourteen-year stretch, but I copped ten of solitary in our loving homeland; so I don't think you can ever do enough in the way of precautions. Suppose there's a tip about a car, a Chevrolet with one man in it, say—well, it's not the same as a car with three men in it."

He was right. Ten hours later we reached the town we were aiming for. Paulo dropped us at the end of a road with villas on either side.

"Take the pavement on the right. The villa's called Mi Amor; it's along there. Walk in like you owned it, and inside you'll find Auguste."

There was a yard bordered with flowers, and a neat path leading to the door of a pretty little house. The door was shut; we knocked.

"Hi there, brothers, come right in," said Auguste, opening the door. He was in shirtsleeves; he was covered with sweat, and his hairy arms had earth on them. We told him Paulo had gone to park the car at the other end of the town. It made sense not to have a Venezuelan license plate seen too often in the road.

"Did you have a good trip?"

"Yes."

No more than that. We sat down in the dining room. I felt the decisive moment was coming, and I was rather tense. Gaston had no more idea than I what the job was all about. "It's a matter of trust," Paulo had said in Caracas. "Either you come along or you don't. Take it or leave it. Just one thing: it means more liquid cash than you've ever dreamed of." Okay, but now it was all going to have to be clear, open and exact.

Auguste gave us coffee. Aside from a few questions

about our journey and how we were, there wasn't a word that shed any light at all. They were prudent, tight-mouthed, in this family.

I heard a car door slam in front of the house. It must be Paulo, who'd hired a car with local plates. Just so.

"Here we are," Paulo cried, coming in and taking off his leather jacket. "Everything's going just fine, boys." Calmly he drank his coffee. I said nothing; I was waiting. He asked Auguste to put the cognac bottle on the table. Without any hurry, and still looking thoroughly pleased with life, he poured some for us; and then at last he came to the point. "Well, boys, here you are on the spot; this is where we work. Listen, now: just in front of this little house, on the other side of the street you came by, there's the back of a bank. Its main entrance is on the big avenue that runs parallel with our little road. And the reason why you see Auguste's arms all covered with clay is because he knew you were idle, good-for-nothing bums, and he set to work so there would be less for you to do."

"Do what?" asked Gaston, who was no fool but still wasn't very quick on the uptake.

"Not much," said Paulo, smiling. "Just dig a tunnel. It starts in the room next to this; it'll go under the yard, then under the street and come out just beneath the bank's vault. If my calculations are right. If they're not, then maybe we'll find ourselves nearer the street side. If that happens, we go deeper and try again for under the very middle of the vault." A short silence; and then he said, "What do you say about it?"

"Just a second, man. Give me time to think. It's not quite the kind of job I was expecting."

"Is it a big bank?" Gaston asked; this was not one of his brighter days. If Paulo had set all this going, and on such a scale, it was certainly not just for three packs of licorice.

"You walk by the bank tomorrow, and you'll have

something to say," Paulo said, roaring with laughter. "Get this: there are eight cashiers. That gives you some idea of what they must handle by way of bills in the course of a day."

"Christ!" said Gaston, slapping his thigh. "So it's a real bank! Well, I am pleased. For once I'll be in on a big-time job, in keeping with my title of big-time crook."

Still with his broad grin of happiness, Paulo turned to me. "You got nothing to say, Papillon?"

"I don't need any titles. I'd rather stay just plain mister with enough dough to carry out a job I have in mind. I don't need millions. I'll tell you what I think, Paulo: it's a prodigious job, and if it comes off—*when* it comes off, I should say, because you must always believe in a job— we're set up for the rest of our lives with enough for the rent and the telephone. But . . . there are a good many buts to get around. I can ask questions, boss?"

"As many as you like, Papi. I meant to talk over every part of the job with you anyhow. For although I'm the top man, since it was me who worked it out, each one of us is risking his freedom and maybe his life. So ask all the questions you want."

"Right. The first is this: from the room next door, where the shaft is, how far is it to the pavement on this side of the road?"

"Exactly eighteen yards."

"Second, how far from the edge of the pavement to the bank?"

"Ten yards."

"Third, inside the bank, have you worked out exactly where the door to the vault is?"

"Yes. I've hired a box in the safe-deposit room. It's just next to the bank's own vault and separated from it by an armored door with two combination locks. There's only one way in, and that's from the safe-deposit room. You go from there into the main vault. One day, after I'd been down there a good many times, I was waiting for them to give me the second key to my safe and I saw the armored door open. As it swung around, I caught a glimpse of the vault and big safes lined up all round it."

"Could you get an idea of how thick the wall was between the two rooms?"

"It was hard to tell on account of the steel casing."

"How many steps down to the vault door?"

"Twelve."

"So the floor of the vault is about ten feet below street level. What's your plan?"

"We must try and hit just under the wall between the two rooms. We can guide ourselves by the bolts under the floor of the vault—the ones that hold the safes. That way we get into both rooms at once with just one hole."

"Yes, but since the safes stand right against the wall, you're likely to come out under one of them."

"I hadn't thought of that. If that happens, all you have to do is make the hole larger toward the middle of the room."

"I think two holes would be better: one in each room, and each in the middle, if possible."

"I think so, too, now," said Auguste.

"Okay, Papi. We aren't there yet, you know, but it's just as well to think of these things well ahead. What next?"

"How deep's the tunnel going to be?"

"Three yards."

"How wide?"

"Two feet six. You have to be able to turn around inside."

"Have you reckoned the height?"

"A yard."

"The height and the width are fine; but I don't agree

with the depth. Six feet of earth overhead isn't solid
enough. If a heavy truck goes by, or a steamroller, it
might collapse."

"I dare say, Papi; but there's no reason why trucks or
heavy stuff should come along this street."

"Sure. But it doesn't cost us anything to make the shaft
four yards deep. You do that, and you've got three yards
of earth between the top of the tunnel and the street. Any
objection? The only extra work is digging the shaft a yard
deeper. It doesn't change anything about the tunnel itself.
Then four yards down, you're almost certain of reaching
the bank at the level of its foundations or even lower.
How many stories in the building?"

"Ground floor and one over it."

"The foundations can't be very deep, then."

"You're right, Papi. We'll go down to four yards."

"How are you going to cope with the vault? What
about the alarm system?"

"As I see it, Papi, that's the main snag. Still, looking at
it logically, systems are set up *outside* bank vaults. So long
as you don't touch a door, either of the bank or of the
vault itself, it shouldn't go off. And there can hardly be
one right inside the rooms. Still, I think we'd better not
touch the safes on either side of the door to the safe-
deposit room or the ones by the armored door."

"I agree with you. There is one risk, of course, and that
is when you get to work on the safes the vibration might
set things off. But taking precautions like you said, we've
a pretty good chance."

"Is that the lot, Papi?"

"You've thought of lining the tunnel?"

"Yes. There's a workbench and everything we need in
the garage."

"Fine. What about the earth?"

"First we'll spread it out right over the whole yard, and
then we'll make raised flower beds and lastly a platform

all along the walls a yard wide and as high as it'll go without looking queer."

"Are there any inquisitive bastards around here?"

"On the right everything's fine. A tiny little old couple who apologize every time they see me, because their dog shits just outside our gate. On the left, not so hot. There are two kids of eight and ten who never get off their swing for an instant, and the silly little buggers fly so high they can easily look over the wall and see what's happening in our place."

"But however high they swing they can't see more than part of the yard—they can't possibly see the stretch against their own wall."

"True enough, Papi. Okay. Now, suppose we've made the tunnel and we're under the vault. There we'll have to make a big hollow, a kind of room, so as to store the tools and be able to work properly, perhaps two or three of us together. And then once we've hit the center of the rooms we'll make a space under each, two yards square."

"Right. And what are you going to cut the steel of the safes with?"

"That's something we'll have to talk over."

"You start."

"Well, the job could be done with oxyacetylene: that's something I understand—it's my trade. Or there's the electric welder, and I understand that, too. But there's a snag—you need two hundred and twenty volts and this villa only has one hundred and twenty. So I decided to let another guy in on the job. But I don't want him to work on the tunnel: he'll come a couple of days before we move in."

"What'll he come with?"

"Here comes my big surprise. Thermit is what he'll come with. He's a positive artist in the Thermit line. What do you say to that, everybody?"

"It'll make five shares instead of four," said Gaston.

"There'll be more than you can carry, Gaston! Five or four, it's all one."

"As for me, I'm in favor of the Thermit guy; because if there are a dozen safes to open, it goes quicker with Thermit than with anything else."

"Well then, there's the overall plan. Are you all in agreement?"

Everyone said yes. Paulo said one other thing: neither Gaston nor I should show our noses out of doors during the daytime on any pretext whatsoever. We could go out at night from time to time, but as little as possible and then very carefully dressed, with a tie and all. Never all four of us together.

We went into the room next door; it had once been an office. They had already dug a hole a yard across and three deep, and I was admiring the sides, as straight as a wall, when the thought of ventilation came to me. "And what have you laid on for air down there?"

"We'll pump it down with a little compressor and plastic tubing. If the one working begins to suffocate, someone'll hold the tube to his face while he gets on with the job. I bought a compressor in Caracas—it's almost silent."

"What about an air conditioner?"

"I thought of that, and I've got one in the garage; but it blows the fuses every time you switch it on."

"Listen, Paulo. Nobody can tell what may happen to the Thermit guy. If he doesn't turn up, the oxyacetylene is slow and the electric welder is the only thing for the job. We have to install two hundred and twenty volts. To make it look natural, you say you want a deepfreeze and air conditioning and so forth, and a little circular saw in the garage as well, because you like screwing around with wood. There shouldn't be any difficulty."

"You're right. There's everything to be said for putting in two hundred and twenty volts. Well now, that's enough about the job for the moment. Auguste's the spaghetti king; as soon as it's ready, let's eat."

Dinner was very cheerful. After we'd exchanged a few unpleasant memories, we all agreed that when talking about the past we'd never bring up stories about life inside—only about happy things like women, the sun, the sea, games in bed, etc. We laughed like a pack of kids. Nobody had a second's remorse at the idea of attacking society in the shape of the greatest symbol of its selfish power, *a bank*.

There was no difficulty about installing the 220-volt current, because the transformer was close to the house. No problem at all. To finish the shaft, we gave up the short-handled pick, which was too awkward in such a confined space. Instead we cut out blocks of earth with the circular saw, digging out each block with a handy trowel and putting it into a bucket.

It was a titanic job, but little by little it advanced. In the house you could scarcely hear the sound of the circular saw at the bottom of the shaft, now four yards deep. From the yard you heard absolutely nothing; there was nothing to be feared.

The shaft was finished. We started the tunnel, and it was Paulo, compass in hand, who dug the first yard through the very wet clay earth that stuck to everything. We no longer worked half naked but in dungarees that came down under our feet; so when we quit and took the dungarees off, there we were, as clean as a butterfly coming out of its cocoon. Apart from our hands, of course.

According to our calculations, we still had thirty cubic yards of earth to bring out.

"This is genuine convict's work," said Paulo, when he was feeling rough.

But gradually we pushed on. "Like moles or badgers," Auguste said.

"We'll get there, men! And we'll roll in cash for the rest of our lives. Isn't that right, Papillon?"

"Sure, sure! And I'll have the prosecutor's tongue and I'll get my false witness and I'll spring such fireworks at thirty-six quai des Orfèvres! On with the job, boys—this is no time to talk bullshit or play games. Here, lower me down the hole. I'm going to work another couple of hours."

"Calm down, Papi. We're all of us on edge. Sure, it's not going fast, but we're getting on, and the jackpot's only fifteen yards ahead of us."

I agreed to play a hand of cards to please the others and to relax a little.

No difficulty about carrying the earth out into the yard; it was eighteen yards long and ten wide, and we spread the stuff out over the whole width except for the garage path. But seeing the earth we dug was not the same as the topsoil, we had a truckload of garden loam brought in from time to time. Everything was going fine.

How we dug, and how we heaved up the buckets full of earth! We laid a wooden floor in the tunnel, because the water seeping in turned it to mud; and the buckets slid easily on these planks when you heaved on the rope.

This is how we worked: There was one man at the far end of the tunnel; with the circular saw and a little pick he filled a bucket with the earth and stones. Another stood at the bottom of the shaft and pulled the bucket back along the tunnel. At the top there was a third who hauled it up and emptied it into a rubber-wheeled barrow. We broke through the wall that divided the house from the garage, so the fourth man only had to take the wheelbarrow, push it out through the garage and appear quite naturally in the yard.

We worked for hours on end, spurred on by a furious urge to win. The far end of the tunnel was very uncomfortable in spite of our precautions: the air conditioner and the blast of pure air coming down the pipe we carried rolled around our neck so as to take a suck every now and then. I was covered with little red heat pimples; there were great blotches of them all over my body. It looked like nettle rash, and it itched horribly. The only one who did not have it was Paulo, because he just looked after the wheelbarrow and spread the earth in the garden. When we came out of that hellhole it took over an hour to recover even after a shower; then, breathing normally and covered with Vaseline and cocoa butter, at last we felt more or less all right. "Anyhow, we were the ones who started this labor of Hercules. Nobody makes us do it. So help yourself, bear it, shut your trap and heaven will help you." That's what I said to myself and what I said two or three times a day to Auguste, whenever he began to beef about having got himself mixed up with this kind of a job.

For slimming, there's nothing like digging a tunnel under a bank. It's amazing how supple you get, bending, crawling and turning yourself inside out. In that tunnel, we sweated as much as if we had been in a sauna. If you do exercises in every conceivable position there's no danger of being overweight; and you work up splendid muscles, too. So there was everything to be said for it; and what's more, there at the end of the tunnel a magnificent prize was waiting—other people's money.

Everything was fine, except for the yard. With the level rising and rising, the flowers did not seem to grow but rather to sink; and that did not look altogether natural. If we went on, soon nothing would be seen but their petals. We hit on a remedy: we stuffed the flowers into pots and kept them flush with the earth as we dug it out. With the pots well covered, the plants looked as if they were coming right out of the surface.

This party was beginning to last rather too long. If only we could take turns at having a rest. . . . But there was no

question of that. We all four had to be there to keep
things running smoothly. With only three of us it would
never end, and we'd have to store the earth in the house
for the time being, which would be dangerous.

The trapdoor over the shaft fitted to within a sixteenth
of an inch. When we were resting, we could leave the
room door open—not a thing could be seen. As for the
hole in the garage wall, we covered it on the garage side
with a huge wooden panel with handyman's tools hung on
it, and on the house side with an immense Spanish colonial chest. So when Paulo had to have someone come to
the house, he could do so without worrying at all. Gaston
and I just hid in our first-floor bedroom.

For two days there had been nonstop torrential rain,
and the tunnel was flooded. There was close to a foot of
water, so I suggested that Paulo should go buy a hand
pump and the necessary piping. An hour later it was set
up. Pumping as hard as we could (another form of exer-
cise) we sucked up the water and poured it down the
drain. A long, tough day's work for nothing.

December was coming nearer. If we could be ready by
the end of November with our little room dug out and
shored up, under the bank, that would be perfect. And if
the Thermit specialist appeared, there was no doubt Father Christmas would cram our stockings to the brim. If
the Thermit specialist did not turn up, then we'd decided
to work with the electric welder. We knew where to find a
set complete with all its fittings. General Electric turned
out some terrific models. We'd buy it in another town
much more safely.

The tunnel crept on. On November 24 we reached the
foundations of the bank. Only three yards to go and the
room to make—about twelve cubic yards of earth to bring
out. We celebrated with champagne, genuine *brut* from
France.

"It tastes a little green," Auguste said.

"All the better. That's a good sign—it's the color of dollars!"

Paulo summed up what there was left to do. Six days for bringing out the earth if there's not too much of it. Three days for the casing. Total, nine. "It's November twenty-fourth today, so that brings us to December fourth. That's the big day, and we'll be sitting pretty. The bank shuts at seven in the evening on Friday, so we go into action at eight. We'll have the whole of Friday night, all day Saturday, Saturday night and the whole of Sunday. If all goes well, we ought to be able to leave the hideout at two in the morning on Monday. That makes fifty-two hours of work altogether. Everyone agreed?"

"No, Paulo, I don't agree at all."

"Why not, Papi?"

"The bank opens at seven for the cleaners. At that moment the whole thing may turn sour: at seven in the morning, that is to say not long after we've left. This is what I suggest: we finish the job by six on Sunday evening. By the time we've shared it out, it'll be about eight. If we leave at eight, that will give us at least eleven hours' start if the thing blows up at seven, and thirteen hours if it holds tight till nine."

In the end everybody fell in with my suggestion. We drank our champagne, and as we drank it we put on records Paulo had brought—Maurice Chevalier, Piaf, the Paris of the little dance halls. . . . Sitting there with his glass, each of us dreamed of the great day. It was there, so close you could almost touch it with your finger.

Your bill, Papi, the bill you've got there engraved on your heart, you'll be able to collect on it in Paris pretty soon. If all goes well and if luck's with me, I'll come back from France to El Callao and fetch Maria. My father: that would be for later on. Poor wonderful Dad! Before I go and embrace him I'll have to bury the man I was, the hustler. . . . It won't take long once I've had my revenge and I'm fixed up properly.

It was two days after our champagne celebration that the thing happened, but we didn't know it until the day after that. We'd been to look at a General Electric welding-and-cutting set in a neighboring town. My pal and I, dressed very properly, set out on foot and joined up with Paulo and Auguste in the car about a mile away.

"We've deserved this trip, boys. Breathe it in, breathe it in deep; this is the wonderful air of freedom!"

"You're dead right, Paulo; we've certainly deserved it. Don't drive too fast; let's have time to admire the countryside."

We split up and stayed in two different hotels, spending three days in this charming port stuffed with ships and swarming with cheerful, motley crowds. Every evening we all met. "No nightclubs, no brothels, no girls off the street; this is a business trip, men," Paulo said. He was right.

Paulo and I went to look at the set, taking our time about it. It was terrific but it had to be paid for in cash and we didn't have enough. Paulo wired Buenos Aires and fortunately gave the address of the hotel in the port where he was staying. He decided to take us back to the villa and then return by himself a day or two later to get the dough and the welder. We drove back, thoroughly set up by these three days of holiday.

Paulo dropped Gaston and me at the corner of our little road as usual. The villa was a hundred yards away. We were walking calmly along, pleased with the idea of seeing our masterpiece of a tunnel again, when all at once I grabbed Gaston's arm and stopped him dead. What was going on outside the villa? There were cops, a dozen people milling around, and then I saw two firemen heaving earth out of the middle of the road. I didn't have to be told what had happened. The tunnel had been discovered!

Gaston began to tremble as though he had a fever, and then with his teeth chattering he stammered out, "They've smashed our beautiful tunnel in! Oh, the shits! Such a beautiful tunnel!"

At this very moment this guy with a pig's face you could tell a mile off was watching us. But the whole situation seemed so comic to me I burst out in such cheerful, genuine, open laughter that if the pig had had some slight doubt about us, it passed off right away. Taking Gaston's arm I said out loud in Spanish, "What a fucking great tunnel those robbers have dug!"

And slowly we turned our back on our masterpiece and walked away from the road—no hurry and no hitch. But now we had to get moving quick. I asked Gaston, "How much have you got on you? I've nearly six hundred dollars and fifteen hundred bolívars. What about you?"

"Two thousand dollars in my *plan*," said Gaston.

"Gaston, the best thing to do is for us to part right here in the street."

"What are you going to do, Papi?"

"I'll go back to the port we came from and try to get a boat for no matter where—straight for Venezuela, if possible."

We could not embrace one another there in the open street, but Gaston's eyes were as wet with emotion as mine as we shook hands. There's nothing that makes such a bond between men as the experience of danger and adventure.

"Good luck, Gaston."

"Same to you, Papi."

Paulo and Auguste went home by different roads, the one to Paraguay, the other to Buenos Aires.

I managed to get on a boat for Puerto Rico: from there I took a plane to Colombia and then another boat to Venezuela.

It was only some months later that I learned what had

happened. A water main had burst in the big avenue on the other side of the bank and the traffic was diverted into the streets running parallel. A huge truck loaded with iron girders took our road, passed over our tunnel, and plunged its back wheels into it. Shrieks, amazement, police; they grasped the whole thing in a moment.

7

Carotte: the Pawnshop

In Caracas it was Christmas. Splendid lights in all the big streets, cheerfulness everywhere, carols sung with the Venezuelans' marvelous sense of rhythm. For my part I was rather depressed by our failure, but I wasn't bitter. We'd gambled and we'd lost, but I was still alive and freer than ever. And then after all, as Gaston said, it had been a lovely tunnel!

Gradually the atmosphere of these songs about the Child of Bethlehem seeped into me; and easy in my mind, my heart peaceful again, I sent Maria a telegram: "MARIA, MAY THIS CHRISTMAS FILL THE HOUSE WHERE YOU GAVE ME SO MUCH JOY."

I spent Christmas Day at the hospital with Picolino, sitting on a bench in the little hospital garden. I'd bought two *hallacas,* specialties they make only at Christmas, and they were the most expensive and the best I could find. I also had two little flat bottles of delicious Chianti in my pockets.

It was a Christmas of two men brought back to life, a Christmas ablaze with the light of friendship, a Christmas of total freedom—freedom even to splash money about as

I had done. The snowless Christmas of Caracas, filled
with the flowers of this little hospital garden: a Christmas
of hope for Picolino, whose tongue no longer hung out
now he was being treated, who no longer dribbled. Yes, a
miraculous Christmas for him, since he distinctly—and
happily—pronounced the word "Yes" when I asked him
if the *hallacas* were good.

But Lord above, how hard it was to make a new life! I
went through some very tough weeks, yet I did not lose
heart. I had two things in me: first, an unshakable confidence in the future, and second, love for life. Even when
it would have been more sensible for me to be worrying, a
mere trifle in the street would make me laugh; and if I
met a friend I might spend the evening with him, having
fun like a twenty-year-old.

Dr. Bougrat gave me a little job in his beauty-products
laboratory. I didn't earn much, but enough to be well
dressed, almost elegant. I left him for a Hungarian
woman who had a little yogurt factory in her villa; and it
was there that I met a pilot whose real name I won't
mention because at this moment he's in command of an
Air France jet. I'll call him Carotte.

He was working for the Hungarian woman, too, and we
made enough to be able to have some fun. Every evening
we'd stroll around the Caracas bars, and we often had a
drink or two at the Hotel Majestic, in the Silencio district.
It has vanished now, but at that time it was the only
modern place in the city.

It was then, during one of those periods when you think
nothing fresh can possibly turn up, that a miracle took
place. One day Carotte vanished, a little while later he
came back again, from the United States, with a plane—a
little observation plane with two seats, one behind the
other. A wonderful gadget. I asked no questions about

where it came from; the only question I did ask was what he was going to do with it.

He laughed and said, "I don't know yet. But we might be partners."

"To do what?"

"It doesn't matter what, as long as we have fun and make a little dough."

"Okay. We'll look around."

The sweet Hungarian woman, who couldn't have had many illusions about how long our jobs would last, wished us good luck; and then began an utterly demented and extraordinary month.

Oh, the things we did with that huge great butterfly!

Carotte was an ace. During the war he used to fly French agents out of England, land them by night in fields guarded by the Resistance and fly others back to London. He often came down with no more guidance than torches held by the men who were waiting for him. He was completely reckless, and he dearly loved a laugh. Once, without a word of warning, he banked so hard, right over, that I almost lost my pants, and all this just to frighten a fat woman who was quietly doing her business in the garden, her bottom bare to the winds.

I so loved that machine and our darting about in the air that when we had no money to buy juice, I brought up the brilliant idea of turning myself into a planeborne peddler.

This was the only time in my life that I ever conned anyone. He was called Coriat and he owned a men and women's clothes shop, the Almacen Rio. He was in business with his brother. Coriat was a medium-sized Jew, dark, with an intelligent head; he spoke very good French. His shop was well run and he was making money hand over fist. On the women's side he had all the newest, most fashionable dresses imported from Paris. So I had the choice of a whole range of very salable merchandise. I persuaded him to let me have a quantity of blouses, trousers and dresses, on sale or return; they were worth a good deal of money and the idea was that we would sell them in the remoter parts of the country.

We set off, going wherever we liked and coming back whenever it suited us. But although we sold our stuff pretty well, we didn't make enough to cover our expenses, and Coriat's share vanished in gas for the plane. There was nothing left for him.

Our best customers were the whores, and of course we never failed to go around the brothels. It was a great temptation for them when I spread our things out on the dining-room table—garish blouses, the latest in the way of pants, silk scarves, flowered skirts—and started my spiel. "And listen to what I say, ladies. This is not a useless luxury as far as you are concerned. If I may say so, it is more like a business investment, because the more attractive you are, the more the customers come crowding in. As for those ladies who just think of saving, I can tell them for sure that it's a deeply unwise economy not to buy from me. Why? Because all the really well-dressed girls are going to be dangerous competitors."

There were some pimps who didn't much care for our doing business this way; it made them feel bad to see money going into pockets other than their own. A good many of them sold "professional equipment" to their girls on credit, sometimes—and the bastards wanted to monopolize the profit.

We often went to Puerto La Cruz, because there was a good airfield at Barcelona, a town a short way off. The best-run, classiest brothel there had sixty women in it, but the boss was an ugly great sod of a man, vulgar, pretentious and obstinate. He was a Panamanian. His wife was a Venezuelan, and she was charming; but unfortunately he was the one who gave the orders, and there was no question of even opening our cases for a quick look, far less of spreading things out on a table.

One day he went too far. He fired a girl then and there for having bought a scarf I was wearing around my neck. The argument turned nasty, and the cop on duty told us to get out and never come back.

"Okay, you fat shit," Carotte said. "We won't come back by land but by air. You can't keep us from doing that."

I didn't understand the threat until the next morning, when we were taking off at dawn from Barcelona and he said to me on the intercom, "We'll go and say hello to the Panamanian. Don't be frightened and hold on tight."

"What are you going to do?"

He made no reply, but when we came within sight of the brothel he climbed a little and then he dived straight for it at full throttle, shot under the high-tension cable just outside and roared over the corrugated-iron roof, almost touching it. Several of the sheets of iron were loose, and they flew off, displaying the rooms, with their beds and the people in them. We banked, climbed and flew back a little higher to contemplate the sight. I've never seen anything more utterly comic than those naked women and their naked customers, hopping mad in their lidless boxes, shaking furious fists at the plane, which had cut them short either in their games or in an exhausted sleep. Carotte and I laughed until we were almost sick.

We never went back, because now there'd be not only a furious boss, but a furious pack of women, too. Later I did find one girl who had the good taste to laugh at the whole thing with us. Apparently, in his rage, the fat cunt of a Panamanian had insisted on fixing the corrugated sheets on all the women's rooms himself, with enormous bolts.

Carotte and I were both devoted to nature, and we often flew off just to look for beautiful places. That was how we came to find one of the real wonders of the world—Los Roques, about a hundred and fifty miles out at sea, a scattering of more than three hundred and sixty little islands, close together in an oval and forming a huge lake in the ocean. A calm lake, because the islands made a barrier, and its pale green water was so clear you could see the bottom sixty or seventy feet down. Unfortunately, in those days there was no landing strip, and we flew the whole length and breadth of the cluster ten times before pitching on another island called Las Aves, some twenty miles to the west.

Carotte really was a wonderful pilot. I've seen him land on a steeply sloping beach with one wing touching the sand and the other sweeping the sea. *Isla de Aves* means "island of birds." There were thousands and thousands of them, and they had gray feathers except when they were young; then they were white all over. They were rather slow-witted and perfectly trusting. It was an extraordinary feeling, being there, just the two of us, stark naked on an island as flat as a pancake and being surrounded by birds that landed on you or walked about without the least fear, never having seen a man. We spent hours browning in the sun, lying on the narrow beach that ran all around the island. We played with the birds, taking them in the hollow of our hands; some were deeply interested in our heads, and gently pecked our hair. We swam, sunbathed again, and when we were hungry we could always find crayfish warming themselves on the surface. We'd catch a few with our hands and grill them on the spot. The only difficulty was finding enough dry stuff for the fire, because almost nothing grew on the island.

Sitting there on that untouched beach, eating those succulent crayfish and drinking a full-bodied white wine— we always had a few bottles on board—with the sea, the sky and the birds all around us and nothing else at all, gave us such a feeling of paradise that we didn't have to speak to be wholly in touch with one another.

And when we took off again, before nightfall, our hearts were filled with sun and happiness and zest for life; we did not give a damn for anything, not even for finding the money for the fuel for the trip—a trip whose only reason was to let us live in a beautiful and unexpected world.

At Las Aves we discovered a huge sea cave: at low tide its mouth was above the surface, and light and air came in. I had a passion for this splendid grotto; you could swim into it, and inside the water was clear and shallow—not more than three feet deep. When you stood up in the middle and looked around, the roof and the walls seemed to be covered with cicadas. They weren't cicadas, of course, but thousands of little crayfish clinging to the rock. We sometimes stayed there a long while, never disturbing them. The only time we interfered was when a big octopus, a great lover of baby crayfish, put out an arm to gather a few. We jumped on him right away and turned him inside out. There he could lie and rot, if he had the time, because he was an unusual treat for the crabs.

We often went to Las Aves and spent the night there. Each of us had a big flashlight, and we gathered crayfish, each weighing about two and a half pounds, until we had filled two sacks with them. We dumped all the finery we were meant to be selling at Carlotta, the airfield in the middle of Caracas, and that meant we could bring back close to half a ton of crayfish. It was insane to load the plane like that, but it was all part of the fun. We could just about get off the ground, and as for gaining height, the stars were in no danger! We would labor up the twelve miles of valley from the coast to Caracas, just skimming the housetops; and there we would sell our crayfish at the ridiculous price of two bolívars fifty apiece.

At least it paid for the fuel and kept us going. But when you go after crayfish with your hands you often get hurt, and sometimes we'd come back without any. It didn't matter; we never gave a damn—we were living to the full.

One day as we were on our way to Puerto La Cruz and not very far from it, Carotte said to me over the intercom, "Papi, we're short of juice. I'm going to put her down on the San Tomé oil company's field." We flew over the strip to show we wanted to come down on their private landing place, and the jackasses instantly ran a tanker full of gasoline or water, God knows which, right out into the middle of the strip. Carotte had nerves of steel, and although I told him again and again I couldn't see where he could possibly touch down, he just said, "Hold on, Papi," and sideslipped toward a fairly wide road. He landed without bumping too much, but the speed carried him along toward a turn in the route, and around this corner came a trailer filled with bullocks, tearing along as fast as it could go. The shriek of the brakes must have drowned our shrieks of horror, because if the driver hadn't lost control and run his trailer into the ditch, we should certainly have been done for. We jumped out of the plane and Carotte hushed the swearing driver—he was an Italian. "Help us push the plane and you can beef later." The Italian was still trembling all over and as white as a sheet. We helped him catch his beasts—they had escaped when the trailer came to pieces.

This prodigious landing made such a stir that the government bought Carotte's plane and made him a civilian instructor at the Carlotta camp.

My life as an airman was over. Sad. I'd had a few hours of lessons and I was coming on well. Never mind. The only one who came out of this business a loser was Coriat. The extraordinary thing was he never sued me. Some years later I paid him back every penny; and here I should like to thank him for the generosity of his attitude.

But at that particular moment, not only had I lost the plane, and not only had my job with the Hungarian woman been taken by someone else, but I also had to avoid the central parts of Caracas, because Coriat's shop was there and I had no wish to bump into him. So once more the position was far from brilliant. But I didn't care: those few weeks with Carotte had been too marvelous for me to regret anything at all.

Carotte and I often saw one another after that; we used to meet in a quiet little joint run by an old Frenchman who had retired from the Compagnie Transatlantique. One night when we were playing dominoes in a corner with a Spanish republican and an ex-con who now made a peaceful living by selling perfume on credit, two men wearing sunglasses came in—we didn't know them—and asked if it was true that a Frenchman often came here, a pilot.

Carotte stood up and said, "That's me."

I examined these strangers from head to foot and right away, in spite of his dark glasses, I recognized one of them. I felt a sudden wave of emotion. I went up to him. Before I could speak he knew me. "Papi!"

It was Big Léon, one of my best friends in the penal colony. A tall guy with a thin face; a real man, open-hearted. This was not the moment to seem too friendly and he just introduced me to his sidekick Pedro the Chilean and said no more. We had a drink in a corner, and Léon said he was looking for a light plane with a pilot, and he had been told about this Frenchman.

"The pilot's here," said Carotte, "and I'm him. But the plane is not. It belongs to other people now."

"That's sad," Léon said laconically.

Carotte returned to his game of dominoes; someone

else took my place. Pedro the Chilean went and stood at the bar, so we could talk quietly.

"Well, Papi?"

"Well, Léon?"

"The last time we met was more than ten years ago."

"Yes. You were coming out of solitary just as I was going in. How are you doing, Léon?"

"Not bad, not bad at all. And you, Papi?"

Since it was Léon, I felt I could talk. "I'll tell you plain, Léon: I'm a little pissed off. It's not so easy to climb up the hill. It's all very well coming out of stir filled with the best intentions: life's so tough when you have no trade that all you think of is hustling again. Léon, you're older than me and you aren't the ordinary bum. I can tell *you* what's on my mind. Speaking dead serious and dead straight, as far as I'm concerned I owe this country everything. I came back to life here and I've promised myself to respect this great community—to do the least possible number of things that could be criticized. It's not easy, but I'm perfectly certain that even with my love for pulling things off I could set myself up here, starting from nothing and going straight, if only I hadn't a long bill to present to some people in Paris, *and I can't wait, in case those assholes should die before I get there.*

"When I see the young people of this country, utterly carefree and full of the joy of life, then in spite of myself I look back at the best years of my life. And I see the black holes of the Réclusion, and the three years of waiting before the trial and after it, and that stinking clink where I was treated far worse than a mad dog. And then for hours, sometimes for whole days on end, I walk about the streets of Caracas turning it all over in my mind. I feel I'm back in those places where I was buried alive; I keep seeing them, and I go back to my *one, two, three four, five, turn,* just as I did when I was buried there and walked to and fro like a bear in a cage. It's beyond my control; it's a real obsession. I can't tolerate the idea that those who unjustly put me through that hell should die in peace, without having paid.

"So when I'm walking along the streets like that, I don't look around like an ordinary man. Every jeweler's shop, every place that is sure to hold the money I need—I can't help casing it and working out just how I could get my hands on everything it contains. It's not because I don't feel like it that I haven't yet pulled anything off; there are jobs here so dead easy they almost cry out to be done.

"Up until now I've managed to keep a hold on myself; I've done nothing serious against this country that trusts me. That would be vile, as odious as raping the daughters of a house that had taken you in. But I'm afraid one day I may not be able to resist the temptation of pulling off a big job. Because I'll never, never be able to scrape together the huge sum I need for my revenge, not by working honestly. Between you and me, Léon, I'm at the end of my rope."

Big Léon listened to me in silence, gazing at me attentively. We had a last drink, hardly exchanging another word. He got up and gave me a time to come and have lunch with him and Pedro the Chilean the next day.

We met in a quiet restaurant with an arbor. The sun was shining.

"I've been thinking about what you said to me, Papi. So listen, and I'll tell you why we're in Caracas."

They were only passing through, on their way to another South American country. There they were going to pay serious attention to a pawnshop, where, according to their own inquiries and information supplied by one of the chief employees, there was enough jewelry for each of them to come out with a very elegant fortune, once the jewels were turned into dollars. That was why they were looking for Carotte. They had meant to make him a proposition for his plane and himself; but now there was no point in talking about it.

"You can come in with us, if you like, Papi," Léon concluded.

"I've no passport and nothing much in the way of savings either."

"We'll look after the passport. Isn't that right, Pedro?"

"It's just as if you had it already," said Pedro. "In a phony name: that way you'll officially neither have gone out of Venezuela nor come back."

"What'll it cost, roughly?"

"About a thousand dollars. Have you got that much dough?"

"Yes."

"Well then, considering how you're placed, you shouldn't hesitate."

Two weeks later I was some miles from a South American capital, having hired a car the day after the job, busy burying a cookie tin with my share of the jewels in it.

The carefully programmed operation had been simple. We went in through a tie shop next door to the pawnbroker's. Léon and Pedro had been there to buy ties several times so as to get a good look at the lock and settle on the exact spot where they would make the hole in the wall. There were no safes, only locked cupboards all around. We went in at ten on Saturday evening, and we came out at eleven on Sunday night.

A smooth, well-run job. So there I was, a dozen miles from the town, burying my tin at the foot of a huge tree. I knew I would find the place again without any difficulty, because even without the mark I'd cut with my knife, the tree was easy to spot: the forest began just after a bridge, and the first tree of this forest, right by the road, was mine. Driving back, I threw the pick away some five miles along the road.

That evening we all met in a classy restaurant. We walked in separately and behaved as if we'd met by chance at the bar and then decided to have dinner together. Each of us had hidden his share, Léon with a friend and Pedro in the forest, like me.

"It's much better for each to have his own private hole," Léon said. "That way, no one of us knows what the others have done with theirs. It's a precaution they often take in South America, because if the pigs pull you in, what they put you through is no fun at all. Then if a poor guy starts to talk, why, he can only rat on himself. So that's sewn up: tell me, Papi, are you satisfied with the shares?"

"I think our rough estimate of each piece was dead right. Everything's fine: I don't have any gripes."

So all was satisfactory and everyone was pleased.

"Hands up!"

"Why, what the hell?" cried Léon. "Are you crazy?"

No time for further observations: in a flash we were clubbed, handcuffed and wheeled off to the police headquarters. We hadn't even finished the oysters.

In that country, the pigs do not coddle you at all; the party went on all night. Eight hours at the very least. First questions: "Do you like ties?"

"Go fuck yourself."

And so it went. By five in the morning we were nothing but lumps of bruised flesh. The pigs were furious at not having been able to get anything out of us; they frothed with rage. "Okay. Since you're all in a sweat and your temperature's too high, we'll cool you." We could scarcely stand, but they tossed us into a paddy wagon and a quarter of an hour later we were in front of a huge building. The pigs went in and then we saw workmen coming out; the pigs must have asked them to leave. Then it was our turn to go in, each propped up by two pigs and almost dragged along.

An enormous corridor; steel doors right and left, each with a kind of clock over it: a clock with only one hand. Thermometers. Right away I grasped that we were in the corridor of the deepfreeze of a big slaughterhouse. We stopped at a place where there were several tables standing in the corner. "Well, now," said the chief pig. "I'll give you one last chance to think it over. These are meat lockers. You understand what that means? So for the last time, where have you put the jewels and the other things?"

"We know nothing about any jewels or about any ties," said Léon.

"Okay, lawyer. You can go first."

The cops unbolted a door and opened it wide. A kind of icy fog came out and wafted down the corridor. Having taken off Léon's shoes and socks they shoved him in.

"Shut it quick," said the chief, "or we'll be frozen, too."

"Now, Chilean. Are you going to talk, yes or no?"

"I've nothing to talk about."

They opened another door and pushed the Chilean in.

"You're the youngest, Wop [my passport had an Italian identity]. Take a good look at these thermometers. They show minus forty. That means that if you don't talk and we stuff you in there in a sweat, after the party you've been through, it's ten to one you'll catch pneumonia and die in hospital in less than forty-eight hours. I'm giving you one last chance, you see: did you rob the pawnbroker's by going through the tie shop, yes or no?"

"I've nothing to do with those men. I only knew one of them, long ago, and I just met them by chance in the restaurant. Ask the waiters and barmen. I don't know whether they had anything to do with this job, but I'm dead certain I didn't."

"Well, Macaroni, you can perish, too. I'm sorry to think

of you dying at your age; but it's your own fault. You asked for it."

The door opened. They shot me into the darkness, and hitting my head on an iron-hard side of beef hanging from a hook, I fell flat on the floor: it was covered with ice and hoarfrost. Immediately I felt the appalling cold seize upon my flesh, pierce right through and reach my bones. With a terrible effort I got to my knees, then, clinging to a side of beef, I stood upright. Every movement hurt, after the beating they had given us, but in spite of that I thumped my arms and rubbed my neck, cheek, nose and eyes. I tried warming my hands under my armpits. All I had on were my pants and a torn shirt. They had taken my shoes and socks, too, and the soles of my feet hurt terribly as they stuck to the ice; I felt my toes beginning to freeze.

I said to myself, "This can't go on for more than ten minutes—a quarter of an hour at the most. Otherwise I'll be like one of these sides of beef: a lump of deep-frozen meat. No, no, it's not possible. They can't do that to us! Surely they can't freeze us alive? Stick it out, Papi. A few minutes more and the door will open. That icy corridor will seem as warm as toast." My arms were not working anymore; I could no longer close my hands or move my fingers; my feet were sticking to the ice and I no longer had the strength to pull them away. I felt I was going to faint, and in the space of a few seconds I saw my father's face, then the prosecutor's floating over it, but that was not so clear, because it merged with the faces of the cops. Three faces in one. "How strange," I thought. "They are all alive, and they are laughing because they've won." Then I passed out.

What was happening? Where was I? As I opened my eyes there was a man's face leaning over me, a handsome face. I could not speak, because my mouth was still frozen stiff with cold, but inside my head I asked myself what I was doing here, stretched out on a table.

Big, powerful, efficient hands rubbed me all over with warm grease, and gradually I felt heat and suppleness coming back. The chief cop was watching, two or three yards away. He looked hot and bothered. Several times they opened my mouth to pour a drop of spirits into it. Once they poured too much; I choked and shot it out.

"There we are," said the masseur. "He's saved."

They went on rubbing me for at least half an hour. I felt that I could talk if I wanted to, but I preferred keeping my mouth shut. I realized that over there on the right there was another body lying on a table the same height as mine. He was naked, too, and they were rubbing and massaging him. Who was it? Léon or the Chilean? There had been three of us: but with me on this table and the guy on the other, that only made two. Where was the third? The other tables were empty.

Helped by the masseur I managed to sit up, and I saw who the other one was. Pedro the Chilean. They dressed us and put us into those padded overalls specially made for men who work inside deepfreezes.

The chief pig returned to the attack. "Can you speak, Chilean?"

"Yes."

"Where are the jewels?"

"I don't know anything."

"And what about you, Spaghetti?"

"I wasn't with those men."

"Okay."

I slipped off the table. I could barely stand, but once I was up I felt a healthy burning on the soles of my feet. That pleased me although it hurt, and I felt the blood flowing inside me, racing round my whole body with such strength that it thumped in the farthest veins and arteries.

I thought that for one day I had gone as far in horror as possible, but I had got it wrong, quite wrong.

They put Pedro and me side by side, and the chief, who had now recovered his self-assurance, called out, "Take off their overalls."

They took them off, and there I was, naked to the waist: straight away I started shivering with cold again.

"And now take a good look at this, *hombres.*"

From under a table they dragged a kind of rigid parcel and stood it up on end in front of us. It was a frozen corpse, as stiff as a board. Its eyes were wide open and fixed, like two marbles: it was hideous to see, terrifying. Big Léon. They had frozen him alive!

"Take a good look, *hombres*," said the chief again. "Your accomplice wouldn't talk; so all right, we went all the way with him. Now it's your turn, if you're as stubborn as he was. I've been given orders to be merciless, because this job of yours is much too serious. The pawnshop is run by the state, and there's an ugly rumor in the town—people think it's a racket worked by some of the officials. So either you talk, or in half an hour you'll be like your friend here."

My wits had not yet come back, and the sight so churned me up that for three long seconds I felt like talking. The only thing that prevented me was that I didn't know where the other hiding places were. They'd never believe me and I'd be in worse danger than ever.

To my utter amazement I heard a very collected voice, Pedro's voice, say, "Come on now; you can't frighten us with that stuff. Why, of course it was an accident—you never meant to freeze him; it was an error of judgment, that's all; but you don't want another error with us. One you can get away with; but three, three foreigners turned into blocks of ice, that mounts up. And I can't see you giving airtight explanations to two different embassies. One, okay. Three, it's too much."

I could not help admiring Pedro's steely nerve. Very calmly the pig looked at the Chilean, not speaking. Then, after a little pause, "You're a crook, and that's for sure; but I have to admit that you've also got guts." Turning to the others he said, "Find them each a shirt and take them back to the prison: the judge will look after them. With brutes like this there's no point in going on with the party—it's a waste of time." He turned his back and walked off.

A month later they let me out. The tie merchant admitted I had never been to his shop, which was true: the barmen stated that I had had two whiskies by myself, that I had already booked a table for one before the other two appeared, and that we had seemed very surprised to meet one another in this town. Still, they ordered me to leave the country in five days, because they were afraid that as Léon's so-called countryman (Léon also had an Italian passport) I would go and tell the consulate what had happened.

During the inquiries, we had been brought face to face with a guy I did not know but Pedro did—the pawnshop employee who had put him on to the job. The very evening we divided up the take, this silly cunt presented a girl from an all-night bar with a splendid antique ring. The pigs were tipped off and they had no difficulty in making him talk: that was why Big Léon and Pedro were identified so quickly. Pedro the Chilean stayed there, hooked on this business.

I took the plane with five hundred dollars in my pocket. I never went near my hiding place; it was too risky. I took stock, to see how things stood after the hideous nightmare I had just been through; the papers reckoned the pawnshop job at two hundred thousand dollars; even if they had exaggerated and doubled it, that still left a hundred thousand; so in my hole I had about thirty thousand. Since the value had been reckoned according to the amount lent on the jewels, that is to say half their real value, and if I sold them without going through a fence, then by my calculations I should be the owner of more than sixty thousand dollars! So I had what I needed for my revenge, as long as I did not break into it for living. This money was sacred; it was for a sacred purpose, and I must never use it for anything else *upon any pretext whatsoever*.

In spite of the horrible way it ended for my friend Léon, this job had been a triumph for me. Unless indeed I was forced to help the Chilean; but in a few months he was sure to send a trusted friend to collect his nest egg so he could pay his lawyer and maybe organize a break. Anyhow, that was our agreement—each with his own hiding place so that no one of us should be connected with the fate of the others. I hadn't been in favor of that method, but it was the customary way of working in the South American underworld—once the job was done, then each for himself and God for all.

And God for all . . . if it was really Him that had saved me, then He had been more than noble; He had been magnanimous. And yet God could not possibly have been the artisan of my revenge. He did not want me to take it, and that I knew. I remembered that day in El Dorado, the day before I was to be let out for good. I had wanted to thank the God of the Catholics, and in my emotion I had said to Him, "What can I do to prove that I am sincerely grateful for your kindness?" And it seemed to me that I heard the words, just as though a voice were speaking to me, "Give up your revenge."

And I'd said no; anything else, but not that. So it could not have been God who took care of me in this business. Impossible. I'd had luck, that was all, the luck of the devil. The good Lord above had nothing to do with that kind of shit.

But the result—oh, the result was there all right, buried at the foot of an ancient tree. It was a huge weight off my mind, knowing I possessed what I needed to carry out the plan I had been feeding my heart with these last fourteen years.

How I hoped the war had spared the villains who sent me down! Now all I had to do, while I waited for my D-Day, was to look for a job and live quietly until I could go and dig up my treasure.

The plane was flying at a great height in a brilliant sky, way above a carpet of snow-white clouds. It was purity up here, and I thought of my people, my father, my mother, my family and of my childhood bathed in light. Beneath that white cumulus there were dirty clouds, a grayish, unclean rain—a fine image of the earthly world: that desire for power, that desire to prove to others that you are better than them, that dry, heartless desire you see in the kind of people who do not give a damn if they destroy a human being as long as by doing so they gain something or prove something.

8

The Bomb

Caracas again. It was with real pleasure that I walked the streets of this great living city once more.

I had been free twenty months now, and yet I still hadn't become a member of this community. It was all very well to say, "All you have to do is get a job," but besides not being able to find any suitable work, I had trouble speaking Spanish, and many doors were closed to me because of this. So I bought a textbook, shut myself in my room and determined to spend however many hours it took to learn Spanish. I grew angrier and angrier; I could not manage to hit the pronunciation, and after a few days I flung the book to the other end of the room and went back to the streets and the cafés, looking for someone I knew who could find me something to do.

More and more Frenchmen were coming over from Europe, sickened by its wars and political upheavals. Some were on the run from an arbitrary justice that varied according to the political climate of the moment; others were looking for peace and quiet—a beach where they could breathe without someone coming up every other moment to take their pulse.

These people were not like Frenchmen, though they were French. They had nothing in common with Papa Charrière or any of the people I had known in my childhood. When I was with them, I found they had ideas so different and so twisted in comparison with those of my young days that I was quite at sea. Often I'd say to them, "I believe that maybe you shouldn't forget the past, but that you should stop talking about it. Is it possible that even now, after the war is over, there are supporters of Nazism among you? I'll tell you something: when you talk about the Jews, it's like seeing one race spew out hatred against another race.

"You're living in Venezuela, in the midst of its people, and yet you aren't capable of grasping their wonderful philosophy. Here there's no discrimination, either racial or religious. If anyone should be infected with the virus of revenge against the privileged classes, the poorest class should be because of their wretched conditions of life. Well now, *that virus doesn't even exist in this country*.

"You aren't even capable of settling down to living for the sake of living. Please, don't come here as Europeans filled with notions of the superiority of your race. True, you have had more intellectual training than the majority of the people here, but what of it? What good is it to you, since you're a more stupid bunch of clods than they are? As far as you're concerned education doesn't mean intelligence, generosity, goodness and understanding, but only learning things from books. If your hearts stay dry, selfish, rancorous and fossilized, what you've learned doesn't mean a thing.

"When I look at you and listen to you, it occurs to me that a world run by bastards like you will mean nothing but wars and revolutions. Because although you say you long for peace and quiet, you only long for it if it agrees with your point of view."

Every one of them had his list of people to be shot, proscribed or shoved into jail; and although it upset me, I couldn't help laughing when I heard these people, sitting in a café or the lounge of some third-rate hotel, criticizing everything and coming to the conclusion that they were the only ones who could really run the world.

And I was afraid, yes, I was afraid, because I had a very real feeling of the danger that these newcomers brought with them—the virus of the old world's fossilized ideological passions.

1947. I'd come to know an ex-con by the name of Pierre-René Deloffre. He had only one object of worship, and that was General Medina Angarita, the former president of Venezuela, who had been overthrown by the last military coup d'état, in 1945. Deloffre was a high-powered character. Very active, but open-hearted and enthusiastic. He summoned all his passion to persuade me that the people who had profited by this coup d'état weren't worth Medina Angarita's bootlaces. To tell the truth, he did not convince me; but since I was in a tricky position I was not going to cross him.

He found me a job through a financier, a truly remarkable guy called Armando. He came from a powerful Venezuelan family; he was noble-minded, generous, intel-

ligent, well educated, witty and unusually brave. There
was only one drawback—he was burdened with a stupid
brother, Clemente. (Some of this brother's recent capers
have made it clear to me that he hasn't changed in these
last twenty-five years.) Deloffre introduced me to the
financier with no beating about the bush: "My friend
Papillon, who escaped from the French penal settlement.
Papillon, this is the man I was telling you about."

Armando adopted me right away, and with the di-
rectness of a real nobleman he asked me whether I was in
need of money.

"No, Monsieur Armando; I'm in need of a job."

I wanted to see how the land lay first; it was better to
take one's time. What's more, I was not really short of
cash for the moment.

"Come and see me at nine tomorrow."

The next day he took me to a garage, the Franco-
Venezuelan it was called, and there he introduced me to
his associates, three young men full of life, ready to break
into a furious gallop at the drop of a hat. Two of them
were married. One to Simone, a magnificent Parisienne of
twenty-five; the other to Dédée, a twenty-year-old blue-
eyed girl from Brittany, as delicate as a violet and the
mother of a little boy called Cricri.

They were good-looking, open people, frank and unre-
served. They welcomed me with open arms, as if they'd
known me for ever. Right away they made me a bed in a
corner of the big garage, more or less curtained off and
close to the shower. They were my first real family for
seventeen years. This team of young people liked, cher-
ished and respected me; and it made me all the happier
because although I was a few years older I had just as
much zest for life, just as much joy in living without rules
and without limits.

I asked no questions—I didn't really have to—but I
soon saw that not one of them was a genuine mechanic.

They had a vague, a very vague notion of what a motor was: but even less than a notion as far as the motors of American cars were concerned, and American cars were the main or indeed the only customers. One of them was a lathe operator, and that explained the presence of a lathe in the garage—they said it was for correcting pistons. Pretty soon I found that what the machine was really used for was changing gas bottles so they would take a detonator and a Bickford fuse.

For the swarm of newly arrived Frenchmen, the Franco-Venezuelan garage repaired cars, more or less; but for the Venezuelan financier it prepared bombs for a coup d'état. I didn't altogether care for this.

"Hell," I said. "Who's it in support of and who's it against? Tell me about it." It was evening; we were sitting there under the lamp and I was questioning the three Frenchmen—their wives and the kid had gone to bed.

"That's none of our business. We just fix the tubes Armando gives us. And that's fine by us, mac."

"Fine for you, maybe. But I have to know."

"Why? You earn a fat living and you have fun, don't you?"

"Sure. As far as fun goes, we have fun. But I'm not like you. They've given me asylum in this country: they trust me and they let me walk about as free as air."

Hearing me talk like this in my position struck them as very odd. Because they knew what I had in the back of my mind; they knew all about my obsession—I'd told them. But one thing I hadn't told them was about the pawnshop job. So they said to me, "If this business comes off, you can make the money you need to carry out what you have in mind. And of course we don't intend to spend the rest of our lives in this garage. Certainly we have fun, but it brings in nothing like the solid cash we'd dreamed of when we came to South America."

"And what about your wives and the kid?"

"The women know all about it. A month before D-Day they leave for Bogotá."

"They know all about it, then. Just as I thought; so they aren't too surprised at some of the things that go on."

That same evening I saw Deloffre and Armando, and I had a long talk with them. Armando said to me, "In this country of ours, it's Betancourt and Gallegos who run everything, under the cover of the phony AD [Acción Democrática]. The power was put into their hands by simpleminded soldiers who no longer really know why they overthrew Medina—he was a soldier, too, and he was more liberal and far more humane than the civilians. I see the former Medina officials being persecuted, and there's nothing I can say; and I try to understand how it comes about that men who carried out a revolution with slogans like 'Social justice and respect for all without the least exception' can become worse than their predecessors once they're in power. That's why I want to help bring Medina back."

"Fine, Armando. I quite see that what you want above all is to stop the party now in power from going on with their persecution. And as for you, Deloffre, you've got just one God, and that's Medina, your protector and your friend. But listen to me, now: the people who let me, Papillon, out of El Dorado were this very party now in power. Straight after the revolution, the minute the new chief arrived, he stopped the savage reign of terror in the settlement, stopped it dead. He's still there, I believe— Don Julio Ramos, a lawyer and a distinguished writer, the guy who let me out. And you want me to join in a coup against these people? No: let me go. You know you can count on my keeping my mouth shut."

Armando knew the tough spot I was in, and like a real gentleman he said to me, "Enrique, you don't make the bombs; you don't work at the lathe. All you do is look after the cars and pass the tools when the boss asks for them. So stay a little longer. I ask it as a favor; and if we make a move I promise you'll know a month ahead for sure."

So I stayed there with those three young guys; they are still alive and they would be easily recognizable, so I will put the initials P.I., B.L. and J.G. instead of their names. We made up a splendid team, and we were always together, living it up at such a pitch that the French of Caracas called us the three musketeers—as everybody knows, there were four of them. Those few months were the finest, the happiest and liveliest I ever spent in Caracas.

Life was one long laugh. On Saturdays we kept some elegant car belonging to a customer for our own use, saying it wasn't ready yet, and we drove down to one of the gorgeous beaches lined with flowers and coconut palms to swim and have fun all day long. Sometimes, of course, we would meet the owner, far from pleased at seeing the car he thought was in the garage filled with all these people. Then gently, gently, we would explain that we were doing this for his sake—that we could not bear the idea of giving him back a car not in perfect condition, and so it had to be tried out. It always worked, and no doubt the ravishing smiles of the girls helped a great deal.

On the other hand, we did get into some very awkward situations. The Swiss ambassador's gas tank leaked; he brought the car in for us to solder the joint. I carefully emptied the tank with a rubber pipe, sucking out the very last drop. But apparently that wasn't enough, because as soon as the flame of the blowpipe touched it, the damn tank blew up, setting fire to the car and roasting it to a frazzle. While the other guy and I groped about, covered with black oil and smoke and just beginning to grasp that we had escaped from death, I heard B.L.'s calm voice saying, "Don't you think we ought to tell our partners about this little mishap?"

He phoned the brothers, and the half-wit Clemente answered. "Clemente, can you give me the number of the garage's insurance?"

"..."

"What for? Oh yes, I was forgetting. Because the Swiss ambassador's car caught fire. It's just a heap of cinders now."

I don't have to tell you that five minutes later Clemente appeared at a brisk run, waving his arms about and hopping mad because in fact the garage was not covered in any way at all. It took three stiff whiskies and all the charm of Simone's amply displayed legs to quiet him down. Armando only turned up the following day; he was perfectly calm, and this was his charming way of taking it—"Things happen only to people who work. Anyhow, don't let's talk about it anymore; I've fixed everything with the ambassador."

The ambassador got another car, but for some reason we lost his business.

From time to time, while we were living this zestful life, I thought about my little treasure lying there hidden at the foot of a tree in a republic well known for its frozen meat. And I put money aside for the fare there and back when the time came to go and fetch it. The knowledge that I had almost enough to satisfy my revenge had completely transformed me. Because I no longer worried about making money, I could plunge wholeheartedly into our mus-keteering life—plunge into it so deep that one Sunday afternoon at three o'clock there we were, all of us, bathing in a fountain in one of the Caracas squares, with nothing on but our drawers. This time, at least, Clemente rose to the occasion and had his brother's partners released from the police station where they had been shut up for inde-cent exposure. By now a good many months had gone by, and at last it seemed to me safe to go and pick up my treasure.

So fare you well, buddies, and thanks for all your kindness. Then I was on my way to the airport. I got there at six in the morning; I hired a car, and at nine I reached the spot.

I crossed the bridge. Christ above, what had happened? Had I gone mad, or was it a mirage? I stared around, but my tree was not there. And not only my tree but hundreds of others. The road had been made much wider, and the bridge and the stretch leading up to it had been entirely changed. Working it out from the bridge, I managed to more or less pinpoint the place where my tree and my wealth must have been. I was flabbergasted. Not a trace!

A kind of madness came over me, a stupid fury. I ground my heels into the asphalt, just as though it could feel anything. I was filled with an enormous rage and I looked around for something to destroy: all I could see was the white lines painted on the road—I kicked them, as if knocking off little bits of paint could destroy the road.

I went back to the bridge. The approach road on the other side had not been altered, and judging from that I reckoned they must have shifted the earth to a depth of more than twelve feet. And since my loot had not been buried deeper than a yard, it couldn't have lasted long, poor thing.

I leaned on the parapet and for a while I watched the water flow by. Gradually I calmed down, but still the thoughts whirled about inside my head. Was I always going to lose out like this? Should I give up trying to pull things off? What was I going to do now? My knees sagged. But then I got hold of myself and I said, "How many times did you fail before you brought off your break? Seven or eight times, right? Well, it's the same thing in life. You lose one banco, you go and win another. That's life, when you really love it."

I didn't stay long in this country that felt called upon to change its roads so fast. It made me sick to think that a civilized nation didn't even respect ancient trees. And why, I ask you, why widen a road that was quite broad enough for all the traffic it had to carry?

In the plane taking me back to Caracas, I laughed to think that men can suppose they are the masters of their fate, that they imagine they can build the future and foresee what they'll be doing the next year or the year after. All so much bullshit, Papi! The brightest calculator, the cleverest imaginable organizer of his life is no more than a toy before fate. Only the present is certain: all the rest is something we know nothing about—something that goes by the name of luck, misfortune, destiny or indeed the mysterious and incomprehensible hand of God.

Only one thing really matters in life, and that is never to admit you're beaten and to start up again after every flop. That was what I was going to do.

When I'd left, I'd said good-bye for keeps. Because once I'd dug up the loot I meant to go to other countries, not Venezuela, alter the jewels so they could not be recognized, sell them and move on to Spain. From there it would be easy to go and pay a call on Prosecuting Counsel and Co. So you can imagine the terrific uproar when the musketeers saw me turn up at the garage door. Dinner and a party cake to celebrate my return, and Dédée put four flowers on the table. We drank to the re-formed team, and life started off again at full throttle. But still, I was no longer as carefree as I had been.

I felt sure Armando and Deloffre had designs on me that they were keeping back, probably something to do with the coup d'état, although both knew my position as far as that was concerned. They often asked me to come and have a drink or to eat at Deloffre's place. Wonderful food, and no witnesses. Deloffre did the cooking, and his faithful chauffeur Victor waited table. We talked about a great many things, but in the end the conversation always came round to the same subject—General Medina Angarita. The most liberal of all Venezuelan presidents; not a single political prisoner during his régime; no one persecuted because of his ideas; a policy of coexistence with all the other states, all other régimes, even to the point of setting up diplomatic relations with the Soviet Union; he was good, he was noble, and the people so loved him for his simplicity that one day, during a celebration at El Paraíso, they carried him and his wife in triumph, like toreros.

Constantly telling me about this wonderful Medina, who walked around Caracas with just one aide-de-camp and went to the cinema like an ordinary citizen, Armando and Deloffre almost persuaded me that only a man with his heart in the right place would do anything to bring Medina back to power. They painted a very dark picture of the present government's injustice and its vengeful attitude towards a whole section of the population; and to make me like their marvelous president even more, Deloffre told me Medina lived it up with the very best of them. On top of that, he was a personal friend, although he knew Deloffre had escaped from jail.

At last, almost won over—mistakenly, as I learned afterward—I began to think of taking part in the coup d'état. My hesitation vanished entirely (I have to say this because I want to be honest) when I was promised the money and all the facilities I needed to set my plan of revenge in motion.

So this is how it was that one night Deloffre and I were sitting there at his place, me dressed as a captain and Deloffre as a colonel, ready to go into action.

It began badly. To identify one another, the civilian

conspirators were supposed to wear a green armband, and
the password was *Aragua*. We were supposed to be at
action stations at two in the morning. But about eleven
that night four guys turned up in the one horse-drawn cab
left in Caracas; they were totally plastered, and they were
singing at the top of their voices, to the accompaniment of
a guitar. They stopped just in front of the house, and to
my horror I heard them singing songs full of allusions to
tonight's coup d'état—allusions as obvious as an elephant.
One of them bawled out to Deloffre, "Pierre! Tonight the
nightmare comes to an end at last! Courage and dignity,
amigo! Our Papa Medina must return!"

For goddamned utter foolishness you could not have
asked better. The time between some joker's telling the
pigs and the cops' coming to call on us would be very
short. I was hopping mad, and I had every reason to be:
we had three bombs there in the car, two in the trunk and
one on the back seat, covered with a rug.

"Well, they're a terrific bunch, your friends. If they're
all like this, we needn't bother: we might just as well go
straight to prison."

Deloffre howled with laughter, as calm as if he were
going to a ball; he was delighted with himself in his
colonel's uniform, and he kept admiring his reflection in
the mirror. "Don't you worry, Papillon. Anyhow, we
aren't going to hurt anyone. As you know, these three gas
bottles have got nothing but powder in them. Just to make
a noise, that's all."

"And what's going to be the point of this little noise of
yours?"

"It's merely to give the signal to the conspirators scattered about the town. That's all. There's nothing bloody
or savage about it, you see—we don't want to hurt anybody. We just insist on their going away, that's all."

Okay. Anyhow, whether I liked it or not I was up to

the neck in this. It was not my job to quiver with alarm or be sorry: all I had to do was wait for the given time.

I refused Deloffre's port—it was the only thing he drank: two bottles a day at least. He tossed back a few glasses.

The three musketeers arrived in a command car transformed into a crane. It was going to be used to carry off two safes, one belonging to the airline company and the other to the Model Prison; one of the governors—or maybe the man in command of the garrison—was in the plot. I was to have 50 percent of what was inside and I had insisted on being there when the prison safe was grabbed: they had agreed. It would be a sweet revenge on all the prisons in the world. This was a job very near to my heart.

A dispatch rider brought the final orders: arrest no enemies; let them escape. Carlotta, the civilian airport right in the middle of the city, had already been cleared so that the chief members of the present government and their officials could get away in light planes without a hitch.

It was then that I learned where the first bomb was to be let off. Well, well, well: this Deloffre certainly went about things in style. It was to go off right in front of the presidential palace, Miraflores. The others were to explode one in the east and the other in the west of Caracas, to make it look like things were breaking out everywhere. I smiled to myself at the idea of the alarm and despondency we were going to cause in the palace.

This big wooden gate was not the official entrance to the palace. It was the back of the building; the military trucks used it, and big shots and the president would sometimes come and go this way when they wanted to avoid being noticed.

Our watches were all set to the same time. We were to be at the gate at three minutes to two. Someone inside

was going to open it a crack for just two seconds, long
enough for the driver to make the noise of a toad with a
little child's toy that imitated it very well. That was how
they would know we were there. What was the point?
Nobody told me. Were President Gallegos's guards in the
plot and would they take him prisoner? Or would they be
put out of action right away by other conspirators already
inside? I knew nothing about that.

One thing was certain: at two o'clock precisely I had to
light the fuse leading to the detonator on the gas bottle I
had between my knees and then toss it out of the door,
giving it a good shove so it would roll toward the palace
gate. The fuse lasted exactly one minute thirty seconds. So
I was to light it with my cigar, and the moment it started
to fizz, shift my right leg and open the door, counting
thirty seconds as I did so. At the thirtieth, start it rolling.
We had worked out that the wind would make it burn
faster as it rolled along, and that there would be only
forty seconds before the explosion.

Although the bottle had no bits of iron in it, its own
splinters would be extremely dangerous, so we would
have to shoot straight off in the car to take shelter. That
would be Victor the chauffeur's job.

I'd persuaded Deloffre that if there were any soldiers or
cops nearby, he, in his colonel's uniform, would order
them to run to the corner of the street. He promised me
he'd do just that.

We reached this famous gate at three minutes to two
without any difficulty. We drew up along the opposite
pavement. No sentry, no cop. Fine. Two minutes to
two . . . one minute to two . . . two o'clock.

The gate did not open.

I was all tensed up. I said to Deloffre, "Pierre, it's two
o'clock."

"I know. I've got a watch, too."

"This stinks."

"I don't understand what's going on. Let's wait another five minutes."

"Okay."

Two minutes past two . . . the gate shot open; soldiers came running out and took up their positions, weapons at the ready. It was as clear as gin: we had been betrayed.

"Get going, Pierre. We've been betrayed!"

It took more than that to knock Pierre off his perch; he seemed not to have grasped the situation at all. "Don't talk bullshit. They're on our side."

I brought out a forty-five and rammed it against the back of Victor's neck. "Get going, or I kill you!"

I was certain of feeling the car leap forward as Victor stamped on the accelerator with all his force, but all I heard was this unbelievable remark: *"Hombre,* it's not you who gives orders here: it's the boss. What does the boss say?"

Hell: I'd seen some guys with guts, but never one like this half-caste Indian. Never!

There was nothing I could do because there were soldiers three yards away. They'd seen the colonel's stars on Deloffre's epaulet up against the window, so they came no closer.

"Pierre, if you don't tell Victor to get going, it's not him I'll put the chill on but you."

"Little old Papi, I keep telling you they're on our side. Let's wait a little longer," said Pierre, turning his head toward me. As he did so I saw his nostrils were shining with white powder stuck to them. I got it: the guy was stuffed full with cocaine. An appalling fear came over me, and I was putting my gun to his neck when he said with the utmost calm, "It's six minutes past two, Papi. We'll wait two more. We've certainly been betrayed."

Those hundred and twenty seconds lasted forever. I had my eye on the soldiers; the nearest were watching us, but for the moment they were making no move. At last Deloffre said, *"Vamos,* Victor: let's go. Gently, naturally, not too fast."

And by a positive miracle we came out of that mantrap alive. Phew! Some years later there was a film called *The Longest Day.* Well, you could have made one called *The Longest Eight Minutes* out of that party of ours.

Deloffre told the driver to make for the bridge that runs from El Paraíso to the Avenida San Martin. He wanted to let his bomb off under it. On the way we met two trucks filled with conspirators who didn't know what to do now, having heard no explosion at two o'clock. We told them we had been betrayed; but saying this made Deloffre change his mind and he ordered the chauffeur to drive back to his place, fast. A mistake the size of a house, because, since we had been betrayed, the pigs might very well be there already. Still, we went: and as I was helping Victor put my bomb into the trunk I noticed that it had three letters painted on it: P.R.D. I couldn't help roaring with laughter when Pierre-René Deloffre told me the reason for them; we were taking off our uniforms at the time. "Papi, never forget that whenever the business is dangerous you must always do things in style. Those initials were my calling card for the enemies of my friend."

Victor went and left the car in a parking place, forgetting of course, to leave the keys as well. The three bombs were not found until three months later.

No question of hanging around at Deloffre's. He went his way, I went mine. No contact with Armando. I went straight to the garage, where I helped carry away the lathe and the five or six bottles of gas that were lying about. At six o'clock the telephone rang and a mysterious voice said, "Frenchmen, get out, all of you. Each in a different direction. Only B.L. must stay in the garage. You get it?"

"Who's that?"

He hung up.

Dressed as a woman and driven in a jeep by a former officer of the French Resistance, I made my way out of Caracas with no trouble at all and reached Río Chico, about a hundred and twenty-five miles away on the coast. I was going to stay there for a couple of months with the ex-captain and his wife and a couple of friends from Bordeaux.

B.L. was arrested. No torture: only a stiff, thorough-going but correct interrogation. When I heard that, I decided the Gallegos and Betancourt régime was not as wicked as they said; at least not in this case. Deloffre took refuge that same night in the Nicaraguan embassy.

As for me, I was still full of confidence in life, and a week later the ex-captain and I were driving the Río Chico Public Works Department's truck. Through a friend we'd got ourselves taken on by the municipality. We made twenty-one bolívars a day between us, and on that we lived, all five of us.

This road-construction life lasted two months, long enough for the storm raised by our plot to die down in Caracas and for the police to turn their minds to the reports about a new one that was cooking. Very wisely they concentrated on the present and left the past to itself. I asked nothing better, because I had made up my mind not to let myself be dragged into another job of that kind. For the moment, by far the best thing to do was to live here quietly with my friends, drawing no attention to myself.

In the late afternoon I often went fishing, to add to our daily rations. That evening I had hauled out a huge *róbalo,* a kind of big sea bream, and I was sitting on the beach, scaling it in no particular hurry and admiring the wonderful sunset. A red sky means hope, Papi! And in spite of all the flops I had had since I was let out, I began

to laugh. Yes, hope must make me live and win: and it
was going to do just that. But exactly when was success
going to come along? Let's have a look at things, Papi:
let's add up the results of two years of freedom.

I wasn't broke, but I didn't have much: three thousand
bolívars at the outside, the sum total of two years on the
loose.

What had happened during this time?

One: the heap of gold at El Callao. No point in brooding over that: it was something you gave up voluntarily so
the ex-cons there could go living in peace. You regret it?
No. Okay, then forget the ton of gold.

Two: craps at the diamond mines. You nearly got
yourself killed twenty times for ten thousand dollars you
never cashed in on. Jojo died in your place: you came out
alive. Without a cent, true enough; but what a terrific
adventure! You'll never forget all those nights, keyed up
to the breaking point, the gamblers' faces under the carbide lamp, the unmoved Jojo. Nothing to regret there
either.

Three: the tunnel under the bank. Not the same thing
at all; there really was no luck about that job. Still, for
three months you lived at full blast twenty-four hours a
day. Even if you got no more out of it than that, you
don't have to be sorry for yourself. Do you realize that for
three months on end, even in your dreams, you felt you
were a millionaire with never a doubt about getting your
hands on the dough? Doesn't that mean anything? Of
course, just a trifle more luck might have given you a
fortune; but on the other hand you might have been
much more unlucky. Suppose the tunnel had caved in
while you were at the far end? You'd have died like a rat
or they would have caught you like a fox in its earth.

Four: what about the pawnshop and its refrigerators?
No complaints, except for the Public Works Department
of that damnable country.

Five: the plot. Frankly, you were never really whole-hearted about that business. These political jobs and those bombs that might kill anybody—it's not your line. What it really comes to is that you were taken in first by the sales pitch of two very nice guys and then by the promise of being able to carry out your plan. But your heart wasn't in it, because you never felt it was quite legit to attack the government that had let you out.

Still, on the credit side you had four months of fun with the musketeers, their wives and the kid; and you aren't likely to forget those days full of the joy of life.

Conclusion: You were unjustly imprisoned for fourteen years and almost all your youth was stolen from you. But you've been free the last two years, and in those two years you've had countless experiences and terrific adventures. You've had wonderful love; you've known men of every kind who've given you their friendship—men you've risked your life with; and after all this, do you still keep moaning? You're broke, or nearly broke? What does that matter? Poverty's not a difficult disease to cure. So glory be to God, Papi! You're fit, which is the really important thing.

Let's wipe it all out and begin again, gentlemen. The chips are down! Make your last bets—this is it! Banco lost, banco again: banco again and again and again. Banco right along the line. But let your whole being thrill and quiver, singing a song of hope that one day you'll hear, "Nine on the nose! Rake it in, Monsieur Papillon! You've won!"

The sun was almost touching the horizon. Red in the evening, that meant hope. The breeze had freshened, and with a calmer mind I stood up, happy to be free and alive; my feet sank in the wet sand as I went back toward the house, where they were waiting for what I had caught for the evening meal. As I walked back, I gave myself over to all the colors, the countless touches of light and

shade playing on the crests of the little waves stretching
out forever. They stirred me so deeply, what with my
remembering past dangers overcome, that I couldn't help
thinking of their creator, of God. "Good night, Big Guy,
good night! In spite of all these flops, I still thank You for
having given me such a beautiful day full of sun and
freedom and, to finish it off, this marvelous sunset!"

9

Maracaibo: Among the Indians

One day, when I was making a quick trip to Caracas, a
friend introduced me to a former Paris model who was
looking for someone to help her in a new hotel she had
just opened at Maracaibo. I very willingly accepted the
job of being her man Friday. She was called Laurence; I
think she had come to Caracas to show a collection, and
then decided to settle in Venezuela. Six hundred miles lay
between Caracas and Maracaibo, and that suited me fine;
it was always possible the police might reopen their inquiries into our coup d'état.

A friend gave me a lift, and after fourteen hours'
driving I had my first sight of Lake Maracaibo—they call
it a lake, although in fact it is a huge lagoon nearly a
hundred miles long and sixty wide at the broadest point,
and it is joined to the sea by a channel about eight miles
across. Maracaibo lies to the north, on the west bank of
the channel, which is now linked to the east bank by a
bridge. In those days, though, if you came from Caracas,
you had to cross on a ferry.

This lake was really extraordinary, dotted with thousands of derricks. It looked like a huge forest stretching away out of sight, a forest whose trees, all exactly lined up, allowed you to see as far as the horizon. But these trees were oil wells, and each oil well had an enormous pendulum that went to and fro all day and all night, never stopping, perpetually pumping up the black gold from the bowels of the earth.

A ferry ran nonstop between the end of the Caracas road and Maracaibo, carrying cars, passengers and goods. During the crossing I hurried from one side to the other, absolutely fascinated by the iron pylons rising from the lake; and as I stared at them I thought that twelve hundred miles from here, down at the far end of the country in Venezuelan Guiana, the Good Lord had stuffed the ground with diamonds, gold, iron, nickel, manganese, bauxite, uranium and all the rest, while here He had filled it with oil, the motor of the world—with such enormous quantities of oil that these thousands of pumps could suck away day and night without ever sucking it dry. Venezuela, you've got no call to blame the Lord!

The Hotel Normandy was a splendid villa surrounded by a carefully kept garden full of flowers. The lovely Laurence welcomed me with open arms. "This is my kingdom, Henri," she said, laughing.

She had opened the hotel just two months before. There were only sixteen rooms, but all were luxurious and in the best taste, each with a bathroom fit for the Ritz. She had designed all the interior herself, from the bedrooms to the staff bathrooms, taking in the drawing room, terrace and dining room on her way.

I set to work, and it was no laughing matter being Laurence's right-hand man—she was under forty and she got up at six to see to her guests' breakfast or even make it herself. She was tireless, and all day long she hurried about, seeing to this and that, supervising everything, and yet still finding time to look after a rose bush or weed a

garden path. She had grasped life with both hands; she
had overcome almost impossible difficulties to set this
business going; and she had so much faith in its success
that I was seized with a will to work almost as consuming
as her own. I did everything I could to help her cope with
the hundreds of difficulties that kept cropping up. Money
difficulties, above all. She was in debt up to her neck,
because to turn this villa into something like a luxury
hotel she had borrowed every penny.

One day, by a private deal I carried out without consulting her, I got something marvelous out of an oil company.

"Good evening, Laurence."

"Good evening. It's late, Henri: eight o'clock already.
I'm not blaming you, now; but I haven't seen you this
whole afternoon."

"I've been for a stroll."

"Is this a joke?"

"Yes, I'm laughing at life. It's always good for a laugh,
don't you think?"

"Not always. And at this time I should have liked your
support; I'm in a bad jam."

"Very bad?"

"Yes. I've got to pay for all these fittings and alterations, and although the place is running well, it's not
easy. I owe a great deal."

"Here comes the big surprise, Laurence; hold on. You
don't owe anything anymore."

"Are you making fun of me?"

"No. Listen: you've brought me in as a kind of partner, and in fact I've noticed a good many people think
I'm the boss."

"What of it?"

"Well, one of the people who thought that way is a
Canadian belonging to the Lumus Company, and a few
days back he talked to me about a deal he thought we

might make. I went to see him this afternoon; I've just come back."

"Tell me quickly!" cried Laurence, her eyes wide with interest.

"The result is the Lumus Company takes your hotel, the whole of it, with full board, *for a year!*"

"It's not possible!"

"It is, I promise you." In her emotion, Laurence kissed me on both cheeks and collapsed into a chair. "Of course, there was no question of *me* signing this terrific contract, so tomorrow they'll call you to their office."

This contract meant that Laurence made a small fortune out of the Hotel Normandy. The first quarter's advance alone let her pay off all her debts.

After the signing of the contract, Laurence and I drank champagne with the Lumus bosses. I was happy, very happy, as I lay there in my big bed that night. With the help of the champagne I saw life a fine rosy pink. Papi, you're no more of a fool then Laurence: so isn't it possible to get rich *by working?* Well, Christ above, this was a real discovery, because in France, for the few years I'd been able to take a quick glance at life, it had always seemed to me that a workingman stayed a workingman all his life. And this completely wrong idea was even more wrong here in Venezuela, where the man who really wants to do something has every opportunity open to him.

It was not from love of money that I had gone for crooked jobs: I wasn't a thief out of a deep liking for theft. It was just that I'd never been able to believe it was possible to get to the top in life by starting from scratch— nor, as far as I was concerned, to get hold of a lump of money big enough for me to go and present my bill in Paris. But it *was* possible, and only one thing was necessary to start—a little bit of capital, a few thousand bolívars; and it would be easy to save that once I'd found a good job.

The only snag was that if I went about it this way, I would need a good deal of time before being able to take my revenge: I couldn't scrape the necessary cash together in a day. "Revenge is a dish you want to eat cold," Miguel had said at the diamond diggings. I was going to find out about that.

Maracaibo was seething. There was excitement in the air, and so many businesses and oil refineries were springing up that everything, from beer to cement, was sold on the black market. Everything was snapped up right away— there was never enough to meet the demand. Labor was making money, jobs were well paid and every kind of business was doing well.

When there is an oil boom, a district's economy goes through two completely different phases. First comes the period before the wells begin to yield, the period of pre-exploitation. The companies turn up and settle in; they need offices, camps, roads, high-tension lines; they have to drill the wells, put up the derricks and pumps, etc. This is the golden age, golden for all the skilled workers and golden for every level of the community.

The people, the genuine horny-handed people, have dough in their pockets; they begin to discover the meaning of money and of security. Families start to get themselves organized, homes grow bigger or better, and the children go to school in good clothes, often taken by companies' buses.

Then comes the second phase, the one that corresponds to my first view of Lake Maracaibo, with all I could see of it turned into a forest of derricks. This is the period of exploitation. Thousands of pumps, working away there by themselves, tirelessly suck out millions of tons of black gold every day.

But this unbelievable mass of dough does not pass
through the people's hands: it goes straight into the coffers
of the state banks or the companies. Things begin to grow
sticky, staff is cut down to the strict minimum, there's no
more money just floating around, all the active business is
over. The coming generations will only know about it
when they hear their grandfathers say, "Once upon a
time, when Maracaibo was wealthy, there was . . ."

But I was lucky. I came in for Maracaibo's second
boom. It had nothing to do with the pumps on the lake,
but several oil companies had just got new concessions
running from the Perijá Mountains down to the lake and
the sea, and they were wild with excitement. The moment
might have been made for me.

I was going to dig in here. And I swore the hole I made
would be a sizable cavern. I'd work at anything I could
lay my hands on to gather in every possible crumb of this
gigantic cake.

Good French cook, 41, seeks position with oil company.
Minimum salary $800.

I'd learned the rudiments of cooking with Laurence
and her chef, and I decided to try my luck. The advertise-
ment came out in the local paper, and a week later I was
cooking for the Richmond Exploration Company. I was
sorry to leave Laurence, but she could not possibly pay
me wages like that, not by a long shot.

Now, having been through that school, I know a good
deal about cooking; but when I first started my job I
quaked for fear that the other guys in the kitchen would
soon see that the French cook knew precious little about
saucepans. To my surprise I soon saw that they, too, were
all atremble in case the French cook should find out that
they were only dishwashers, every last one of them! I
breathed again; and all the deeper because I had a great

advantage over them—*I owned a cookbook in French*—a present from a retired whore.

The personnel manager was a Canadian, Monsieur Blanchet. Two days later he put me in charge of cooking for the camp executives, a dozen of them—the big chiefs!

The first morning I showed him a menu like something out of the Ritz. But I pointed out that before I could prepare the food the kitchen would have to be better stocked. It was decided that I should have a separate budget, and that I should run it myself. I don't have to tell you I greased my own palm pretty handsomely when I did my buying; but still the executives stuffed themselves heartily, no doubt about that. This way, everybody was happy.

Every evening I stuck up the next day's menu in the hall: written in French, of course. These grand-sounding names out of the cookbook made a terrific impression. What's more, in the town I'd discovered a shop that specialized in French things, so what with canned goods and my recipes I managed so well that the executive guys often brought their womenfolk. Twenty would turn up instead of twelve. From one point of view it was a damn nuisance, but from another, it meant they took less notice of what I spent; because by the rules I was supposed to feed only the people on the list.

I saw they were so pleased that I asked for a raise—twelve hundred dollars a month, an increase of four hundred. They said no, but they gave me a thousand; and although I kept telling them it was wretched pay for a big-time chef like me, I let myself be persuaded.

Some months went by like this, but in time these set hours began to irk me like a shirt collar that's too tight. I'd had about enough of this job and I asked the chief of the geologists to take me with him when he went out on a prospecting expedition into the most interesting regions, even if they were dangerous.

The point of these expeditions was to make a geological survey of the Sierra de Parijá, the mountain chain to the west of Lake Maracaibo that divides Venezuela from Colombia. It is the country of a very fierce, warlike tribe of Indians, the Motilón: so much so that the Sierra de Perijá is often called the Sierra de los Motilónes. Even now nobody knows just where this tribe came from; their language and their customs are quite unlike those of the neighboring tribes, and they are so dangerous that "civilization" is barely beginning to make its way among them. They live in communal huts that house from fifty to a hundred people, men, women and children all mixed up together. Their only domestic animal is the dog. They are so wild that you hear of many cases where Motilón Indians captured by "civilized" people absolutely refuse to eat or drink; and although they may be well treated, they end up by killing themselves, biting the veins in their wrists with their front teeth, which are specially filed for tearing meat. Since the days I am talking about, the Franciscans have bravely settled on the banks of the Rio Santa Rosa, only a few miles from the nearest communal house. The Father Superior uses the most modern methods, dropping food, clothing, blankets and photographs of Franciscans over the huts from a plane. Even better, he parachutes straw figures dressed in Franciscan robes, the pockets filled with different kinds of food and even cans of milk. No fool, the good father: the day he turns up on foot, they'll believe he's dropped from heaven.

But when I asked to take part in these expeditions it was back in 1948, a long time before those attempts at "civilized" penetration.

As far as I was concerned, these expeditions had three positive advantages. In the first place, they meant a completely different life from the one I was leading in the kitchen of the Richmond Company's camp; and I had seen just about all I ever wanted to see of that. It would be an adventure again, but honest-to-god adventure this time. There was real danger, of course, as there is in any adventure—quite often an expedition would come back short one or two members, because the Motilón Indians were highly skilled at archery. (Where a Motilón sets his eyes, there he sets his arrow, as they say in those parts.) But if you were killed, at least you were not eaten, because they were not cannibals. There was always that to be thankful for.

Second advantage: these three-week tours in the deep, unexplored, dangerous bush were very well paid. I'd make more than twice what I earned at my kitchen stove.

Third: I liked being with the geologists. They knew a great deal. Although I was well aware it was too late for me to learn enough to make me a different man, I had the feeling that I would not be wasting my time, going about with these scientists.

So, as a member of their expedition, I set off full of confidence and enthusiasm. No need for any cookbooks; I just had to know how to open cans and make bread and pancakes.

My new friend, the geologist in charge of the expedition, was named Crichet. He had been lent to the Richmond by the California Exploration Company. He knew absolutely everything about the oil side of geology, but he wasn't quite sure whether Alexander the Great came before Napoleon or after. In any case, he didn't give a damn one way or the other; he didn't need to know history to be very fit, to have a splendid wife, to give her babies, and to provide his company with the geological information they needed. Still, I dare say he did know more than he let on—in time I learned to watch out for his sort of half-

English humor, quite unlike what we were used to in my native Ardèche. We got along very well.

An expedition of this kind lasted between twenty and twenty-five days, with a week's leave when you got back. It was made up of a geologist in charge, two other geologists, and from twelve to eighteen porters and helpers—strength and discipline were all that was asked of them. They had their own tents and their own cook. I only looked after the three geologists. The men were not fools in any way, and among them there was a militant member of the left-wing Acción Democrática who saw the union laws were obeyed. His name was Carlos. There was a good overall understanding, and I was the one who kept count of the overtime, which they always put down with absolute precision.

This first expedition fascinated me. Getting hold of geological intelligence about oil fields is a very interesting business. The idea is to follow the rivers up into the mountains as far as possible, keeping to the passage they have cut through the rock. You go as far as you can in trucks, and then take to jeeps; when there is no path anymore, you paddle up the river in canoes; and when the river is too shallow you get out and shove, still going up as far as you can toward the source. The equipment is carried by the porters, about a hundred pounds a man, but the three geologists and the cooks don't carry anything.

Why go so far into the mountains? Because you see all the successive geological formations, just like in a school book, along the course the river has dug out. You cut samples from the walls, sort them, label them and pack them away in little bags. The geologists note the direction of the different layers sloping toward the plain. And so, with these hundreds of geological samples taken from different places, they draw up a map of the strata that should be found in the plain at a depth of, say, between three thousand and six thousand feet. And by working it out very carefully from all this information, one day they hit oil perhaps fifty miles away, in some place where nobody has ever been because they know in advance that the oil will be there at a given depth. Talk about the wonders of science—I was filled with admiration.

All this would have been fine if it hadn't been for the Motilón Indians. Often members of the expeditions were killed or wounded by their arrows. This hazard did not make recruiting any easier, and it cost the companies a great deal of money.

I went on several expeditions, and I had some marvelous experiences. One of the geologists was a Dutchman named Lapp. One day he was gathering alligator's eggs— they are very good, once they are dried in the sun. You can easily find them by following the track the alligator leaves as it crawls on its belly from the river to the dry place where it lays its eggs: it sits on them for hours and hours. Taking advantage of the alligator's absence, Lapp dug up the eggs and calmly carried them back to the camp. He had scarcely reached our clearing before the alligator appeared, tearing along like a racing car and coming straight for him. It had followed the robber's trail and was going to punish him. About ten feet long, it gasped hoarsely as it came, as if it had laryngitis. Lapp started to run, darting around and around a big tree; and I howled with laughter at the sight of this big guy in shorts bounding about and bawling for help. Crichet and his men came running; two explosive bullets stopped the alligator dead. As for Lapp, he fell on his ass, as pale as death. Everybody was shocked by my behavior. I told them there was nothing I could have done in any case, because I never carried a rifle—it got in the way.

That evening, while we ate my canned dinner in the tent, Crichet said to me, in his sort of French, "You not so young; at least thirty-four, eh?"

"Rather more. Why?"

"You living, you behaving like a man of twenty."

"Well, you know, I'm not much more. I'm twenty-seven."

"Not true."

"Yes, it is, and I'll tell you why. For fourteen years I was stuffed into a cupboard. So I didn't live those fourteen years then. I have to live them now. And since fourteen from forty-one makes twenty-seven, I'm twenty-seven years old."

"Don't follow."

"It doesn't matter."

Yet it was true enough: my heart was that of a boy of twenty. I had to live those fourteen years that had been stolen from me; I needed them and I had to get them back. I had to burn them up, not giving a damn for anything at all, the way you do when you are twenty and your heart is filled with a crazy love for life.

One day, just before dawn, a scream jerked us all awake. As he was hanging up the hurricane lamp he had lit before making the coffee, the men's cook had been struck by two arrows—one in his side, the other in his buttock. He had to be taken straight back to Maracaibo. Four men carried him as far as the canoe on a kind of litter; the canoe took him down to the jeep, the jeep to the truck, and the truck to Maracaibo.

The day went by in a heavy, brooding atmosphere. We could sense the Indians all around us in the bush, though we never heard or saw them. The farther we went, the more we had the feeling we were right in their hunting grounds. There was a fair amount of game, and as all the men had a rifle, every now and then they shot a bird or a kind of hare. Everyone was serious, nobody sang; and after they had fired a shot they stupidly talked very low, as though they were afraid someone might hear them.

Gradually a general fear came over the men. They

wanted to cut the expedition short and go back to Maracaibo. Our leader, Crichet, kept on up the river. The union man, Carlos, was a brave guy, but he, too, felt uneasy. He took me aside.

"Enrique, what do you say to turning back?"

"What for, Carlos?"

"The Indians."

"True enough, there are Indians; but they might just as easily attack us on the way back as if we go on."

"I'm not so sure about that, Enrique. Maybe we're close to their village. Look at that stone there: they've been crushing grain."

"There's something in what you say, Carlos. Let's see Crichet."

The American had been through the Normandy landings; it took a lot to shake him, and he was completely in love with his job. When all the men were gathered together, he said we were in one of the richest districts for geological information. He lost his temper, and in his anger he said the one thing he never should have said— "If you're afraid, all right, go back. I'm staying."

They all went off, except for Carlos, Lapp and me. But I stayed only on the condition that when we left we'd bury the equipment, because I did not want to carry anything heavy. Ever since I had broken both my feet during one of my unsuccessful breaks from Barranquilla, walking with a load made me tire very quickly. Carlos would see to the samples.

Crichet, Lapp, Carlos and I went on for five days without anyone else at all. Nothing happened, but I've never had a more thrilling and stirring time than those five days, when we knew we were being watched twenty-four hours a day by God knows how many pairs of unseen eyes. We gave up when Crichet, who had gone down to the edge of the river to relieve himself, saw the reeds move and then two hands gently parting them. That

wrecked his urge; but with his usual calmness he turned
his back on the reeds as though nothing had occurred and
came back to the camp.

He said to Lapp, "I believe the moment has come for
us to return to Maracaibo. We've got enough samples of
rocks, and I'm not sure it's scientifically necessary to leave
the Indians four interesting samples of the white race."

We reached Burra, a hamlet of some fifteen houses,
without trouble. We were having a drink, waiting for the
truck to come pick us up, when a drunken half-caste
Indian of those parts took me aside and said, "You're
French, aren't you? Well, it's not worth being French if
you're as ignorant as all that."

"Ah? How come?"

"I'll tell you. You make your way into Motilón country, and what do you do? You blaze away right and left at
everything that flies or runs or swims. All the men carry
guns. It's not a scientific exploration; it's an enormous
great hunting party."

"What are you getting at?"

"If you carry on that way, you'll destroy what the
Indians look upon as their food reserve. They haven't got
much. They just kill what they need for a day or two. Not
more. Then again, their arrows kill with no noise—they
don't make the other animals run away. Whereas you kill
everything and you frighten away all the game with your
shooting."

It was not so foolish, what this guy said. I was interested. "What'll you drink? It's on me."

"A double rum, Frenchman. Thanks." And he went
on, "It's because of this that the Motilón Indians shoot
arrows at you. They say that because of you it's going to
be hard for them to eat."

"So we are robbing their larder?"

"You're dead right, Frenchman. Then again, when you
go up a stream, have you ever noticed that, where it's

narrow or where there's so little water you have to get out
of the canoe and shove, you destroy a kind of dam made
of branches and bamboos?"

"Yes, I have. Often."

"Well, the thing you destroy like that, never thinking
twice, are fish traps built by the Motilón Indians; so there
again you do them harm. Because there's a great deal of
work in these traps. They are a kind of maze, and the fish
that are running up the stream pass through zigzag until
they reach a big trap at the end, and then they can't
escape. There's a wall of bamboos in front, and they can't
find the entrance again, because it's made of little creepers that the fish pushed aside to get in. The current pushes
them back against the gate once the fish has passed. I've
seen traps more than fifty yards long from one end to the
other. Beautiful work."

"You're right, absolutely right. You have to be vandals
like us to smash work of that kind."

As we traveled back, I thought about what the rum-
soaked half-breed had told me, and I made up my mind
to try something. As soon as we reached Maracaibo, even
before I went home for my week's leave, I left a letter for
Monsieur Blanchet, the personnel manager, asking him to
see me next day.

He called me in, and there with him I saw the top
geologist. I told them there would be no more killed or
wounded in the expeditions if they would leave the man-
agement to me. Crichet would still be the official boss, of
course, but I would be the one who saw to the discipline.
They decided to have a try; Crichet had put in a report
saying that if they could get higher up than the last
expedition, that is to say into an even more dangerous
region, they would find a real treasure-house of information. As to the pay for my new job, which would be in
addition to being cook (I was still to be the geologists'
chef), that would be settled when I came back. Of course

I said nothing about the reasons that I could guarantee the expedition's safety, and since the Yankees are practical people, they asked me no questions either—it was the result that mattered.

Crichet was the only one who knew about the arrangement. It suited him, so he fell in with the scheme and relied on me. He was sure I had found some certain way of avoiding trouble; and the fact that I had been one of the three who stayed when all the others left had made a good impression.

I went to see the governor of the province and explained my business. He was friendly and understanding, and thanks to his letter of recommendation, I got the National Guard to give orders that the last post before Motilón territory should take all the weapons carried by the men on my list before letting the expedition through. They would think up some likely, comforting excuse. Because if the men knew back in Maracaibo that they were going into Motilón country unarmed, they wouldn't even start. I'd have to catch them short and con them on the spot.

It all passed off perfectly. At Burra, the last post, their weapons were taken away from all the men except two, and I told these two never to fire except in immediate danger—never for hunting or for fun. I had a revolver, and that was all.

From that day on, there was no trouble whatsoever in any of our expeditions. The Americans got the message, and being for efficiency above all, they never asked me the reason.

I got along with the men, and they obeyed me. My job fascinated me. Now, instead of smashing the fish traps with our canoes, we worked around them, destroying nothing. Another thing: since I knew the Motilón Indians' chief problem was hunger, I left old cans filled with salt or sugar every time we struck camp; and according to what we could spare, we'd also leave a machete or a knife or a little ax. When we came back through these camping places we never found a thing. Everything had vanished, even the old cans themselves. So my tactics worked, and since nobody in Maracaibo knew what it was all about, there was a rumor that I was a *brujo*, a wizard, or that I had a secret understanding with the Motilón Indians.

It was during one of these expeditions that I had an extraordinary lesson in how to fish—in how to catch a fish without bait, hook or line, just quietly picking it up on the surface. My teacher was a *danta*, a tapir, an animal bigger than a large pig, sometimes more than six feet long. One afternoon, when I was near the stream, I saw a *danta* for the first time. It came out of the water, and I watched, keeping perfectly still so as not to frighten it. Its skin was rather like that of a rhinoceros; its front legs were shorter than its back ones; and over its mouth it had a short but distinct trunk. It went over to a creeper and ate a good deal of it—so it was a herbivore. Then I saw it go down to the stream again, walk in toward a stretch of slack water. There it stopped, and began to sort of belch, like a cow—so it was a ruminant. Then it brought up a green liquid through its trunk. Very cleverly it mixed this stuff with the water, stirring with its big head. I was still wondering about the reason for all this when a few minutes later, to my astonishment, I saw fish come to the surface, belly uppermost, moving slowly as though they had been drugged or put to sleep. And then there was my *danta* taking the fish one by one, not hurrying at all; and calmly he ate them up. I was absolutely amazed.

After that, I had a try. I carefully marked down the creeper I had seen the *danta* eating, gathered an armful and crushed it between two stones, collecting the juice in a gourd. Then I poured the juice into a part of the river where there was no current. Victory! A few minutes later I saw the fish come to the top, knocked out, just as they

had done for the *danta*. There's only one precaution you
have to take: if the fish are edible, you must gut them
right away, otherwise they go bad in two hours. After this
experiment, the geologists' table often had splendid fish
dishes. I told the men that they should never, under any
circumstances, kill such a charming fisherman, particularly since tapirs are perfectly harmless.

Sometimes, in these expeditions, I took a family of
alligator hunters along as guides, the Fuenmayors, a father and his two sons. This suited everybody, because the
Fuenmayors knew the region very well; but if they were
alone they would be easy prey for the Motilón Indians.
Going along with the expedition, they guided us by day in
exchange for their keep, and at night they hunted alligators.

They were people from Maracaibo, Maracuchos, very
sociable souls. They spoke in a musical way, and they had
a very high notion of friendship. There was a great deal
of Indian blood in their veins and they had the Indian
qualities of wisdom and intelligence. I had some wonderful, indestructible friendships with the Maracuchos, and I
have them still. The women are beautiful, and they know
how to love and how to make themselves loved.

Hunting alligators, creatures seven to ten feet long, is a
very dangerous business. One night I went along with
Fuenmayor and his elder son. The father sat at the back of
this very narrow, very light canoe, steering, with me in the
middle and his son in front. It was pitch dark; all you
could hear was the noises of the bush, and, very faintly,
the lapping of the water against the canoe. We didn't
smoke; we didn't make the slightest sound. The paddle
that moved the canoe and at the same time steered it was
never allowed to scrape against the side.

Every now and then we sent the beam of a huge
flashlight sweeping the surface, and pairs of red dots appeared. Two red points: one alligator. In front of these

eyes there would be the nostrils, because the eyes and the nose are the only two parts of an alligator that show when it is resting on the surface. The victim was chosen according to the shortest distance between the hunters and the red dots. Once it was selected, we felt our way toward it with the light out. Old Fuenmayor was wonderfully skillful at fixing the alligator's exact position, by just one flash of the light lasting no more than a second. We paddled quickly toward it and aimed the beam, and almost always the brute just lay there, dazzled. The beam stayed on the alligator until we were two or three yards away. In the front of the canoe young Fuenmayor kept his flashlight aimed with his left hand and with all the strength of his right arm he threw a harpoon weighted with twenty pounds of lead—the only thing that could pierce a hide that tough and go through to the flesh.

Now we had to get moving, because the second the alligator was harpooned it dived; we took our three paddles and rapidly made for the shore. You really have to hop to it, because if you give the alligator time it comes to the surface again, rushes for you and with one sweep of its tail capsizes the canoe, turning the hunters into a quarry for the other alligators, who've been warned by the turmoil. You have scarcely reached the bank before you jump out, rush for a tree and loop the rope around it. He comes along you feel him coming along to see what's holding him. He can't tell what's happening to him, apart from the pain in his back. So he comes to find out. Gently, without pulling, you take in the slack and pass it round the tree. He's going to come out—he's almost at the edge. Just as he emerges, young Fuenmayor, holding a thin, razor-sharp American ax, gives his head a tremendous crack. Sometimes it takes three to finish the alligator off. At each blow the animal gives a sweep with his tail that would send the axman to heaven if it touched him. Occasionally the ax does not kill the alligator, and then you have to give slack right away so the brute can go off into deep water, because he is so strong he would wrench out even a deeply planted harpoon. You wait a minute and then start heaving again.

That was a wonderful night: we killed several alligators, leaving them on the bank. At daybreak, the Fuenmayors returned and skinned the belly and the underside of the tail. The skin of the back is too hard to be of any use. Then they buried each huge creature—if the carcasses were thrown back they would poison the river. Alligators don't eat other alligators, not even dead ones.

I made several of these expeditions, earning a good living and managing to save a fair amount. And then there occurred the most extraordinary event in my life.

10

Rita—the Vera Cruz

When I was in the solitary-confinement cells at Saint-Joseph I used to take off for the stars and invent wonderful castles in Spain, trying to people the loneliness and the terrible silence. Often I would imagine myself free, a man who had conquered "the road down the drain" and who'd begun a new life in some big city. Yes, it was a genuine resurrection; I pushed back the tombstone that crushed me down in the darkness and I came back into the daylight, into real life; and among the pictures my mind thought up, there would appear a girl as good as she was beautiful.

Yes, there in the stifling damp heat that deprived the unhappy prisoners of the Réclusion of the least waft of

living air, when, half smothered, I breathed in that unbearable steam that hurt my lungs—gasping in the hope
of finding some hint of freshness—and when in spite of
my weakness, my unquenchable thirst and the anxiety
that wrung my heart, I took off for the stars where the air
was cool and the trees had fresh green leaves, and where
the cares of everyday life did not exist because I had
grown rich, there, in every vision, appeared the one I
called my *belle princesse*. She was always the same, down
to the very last detail. Nothing ever varied, and I knew
her so well that every time she stepped into these different
scenes it seemed to me quite natural—wasn't it she who
was to be my wife and my good angel?

Coming back from one of these geological trips, I decided to give up my room in the Richmond Company's
camp and live right in Maracaibo. So one day a company
truck set me down with a small suitcase in my hand, in a
shady little square somewhere in the city center. I knew
there were several hotels or *pensions* thereabouts and I
took the Calle Venezuela, a street in a very good position,
running between the two main squares of Maracaibo, the
Bolívar and the Baralt. It was one of those narrow colonial streets lined with low houses—one story or at the
most two. The heat was shattering, and I walked in their
shade.

Hotel Vera Cruz. A pretty colonial house dating from
the conquest, painted a pale blue. I liked its clean, welcoming look and I walked into a cool passage that gave
onto a patio. And there, in the airy, shaded courtyard I
saw a woman; and this woman was *she*.

I could not be wrong—I had seen her thousands of
times in my dreams when I was a wretched prisoner. Now
my *belle princesse* was before me, sitting in a rocking
chair. I was certain that if I went closer I should see her
hazel-colored eyes and even the minute beauty spot on
her lovely oval face. And these surroundings—I had seen

them, too, thousands of times. So it was impossible that I could be wrong: the princess of my dreams was there before me; she was waiting for me.

"*Buenas dias, Señora.* Have you a room to let?" I put my bag down. I was certain she was going to say yes. I did not just look at her; I ate her up with my eyes. She stood up, rather surprised at being stared at so hard by someone she did not know, and came toward me.

"Yes, Monsieur, I have a room for you," said my princess, in French.

"How did you know I was French?"

"From your way of speaking Spanish. Come with me, please."

I picked up my bag, and following her, I walked into a clean, cool, well-furnished room that opened onto the patio.

I cooled myself down with a shower, washed, shaved and smoked a cigarette; and it was only after that, as I sat on the edge of the bed in this hotel room, that I really came to believe I was not dreaming. "She's here, man, here, just a few yards away! But don't go and lose your head. Don't let this stab in the heart make you do or say anything foolish." My heart was beating violently and I tried to calm myself. "Above all, Papillon, don't tell anyone this crazy story, not even her. Who would believe you? Unless you want to get yourself laughed at, how can you possibly tell anyone that you knew this woman, touched her, kissed her, had her, years ago, when you were rotting in the cells of an abominable prison? Keep your trap shut tight. The princess is here; that's what matters. Now you've found her, she won't escape you. But you must go about it gently, step by step. Just from looking at her, you can see she must be the boss of this little hotel."

It was in the patio, a garden in miniature, that one splendid tropical night I said my first words of love. She

was so completely the angel I had dreamed of that it was
as though she had been waiting for me for years. Rita, my
princess was called; she came from Tangiers, and she had
no ties at all to hamper me. I was frank: I told her I had
been married in France, that I did not know just how
things were at present and that there were serious reasons
why I could not find out. And that was true: I couldn't
write to the *mairie* of my village for a statement of my
position—there was no telling how the law might react to
a request like that: maybe by a demand for extradition.
But I said nothing about my past as a crook and a
convict. I devoted all my strength and all the resources of
my mind to persuading her. I felt this was the greatest
chance in my life, and I could not let it go by.

"You are beautiful, Rita, wonderfully beautiful. Let
yourself be loved by a man who has nobody in his life
either, but who needs to love and be loved. I haven't much
money, it's true, and with your little hotel you are almost
rich; but believe me, I want our two hearts to be just one,
forever, until death. Say yes, Rita. Rita as lovely as the
orchids, I can't tell you when or how, but I've known you
and loved you for years and years." But Rita was not an
easy girl; it was only after three days that she agreed to
be mine. She was very shy, and she asked me to hide
when I came to her room. Then one fine morning, without
making any sort of announcement, we quite naturally
made our love obvious and official; and quite naturally I
stepped into the role of the hotel's boss.

Our happiness was whole and entire, and a new life
opened before me, a family life. Now that I, the pariah,
the fugitive from the French penal settlement, had succeeded in overcoming that road down the drain, *I had a
home,* and a girl as lovely in her body as she was in her
soul. There was only one little cloud in our happiness—
the fact that, having a wife in France, I could not marry
her.

Loving, being loved, having a home of my own—God, how great You are to have given me all this!

Wanderers on the roads, wanderers on the seas, men on the loose who need adventure as ordinary people need water and bread, men who fly through life as migrating birds fly through the sky, wanderers of the cities who search the streets of the slums night and day, ransack the parks and hang around the wealthy districts, their angry hearts watching for a job to pull off, wandering anarchists, liberated prisoners, servicemen on leave—all, all without exception suffer from not having had a home at one moment or another; and when Providence gives them one, they step into it as I stepped into mine, with a new heart, full of love to give and burning to receive it.

So I, too, like ordinary people, like my father, like my mother, like my sisters, like all my family, I too had *my home* at last, with a girl who loved me inside it.

For this meeting with Rita to change my whole way of living and make me feel this was the turning point of my life, she had to be someone quite exceptional.

In the first place, like me, she had first come to Venezuela after making a break. Not a break from a penal settlement, of course, nor from prison, but still a break.

She had arrived from Tangiers some six months before with her husband; he had left her about three months later to go try some kind of adventure two hundred miles from Maracaibo—she didn't want to go with him. He left her with the hotel. She had a brother in Maracaibo, a commercial traveler who moved around a great deal.

She told me about her life, and I listened intently: my princess had been born in a poor part of Tangiers; her widowed mother had bravely raised six children, three boys and three girls. Rita was the youngest. When she was a little girl, the street was her field of action. She did not spend her days in the two rooms where the seven members of the family had their being. Her real home was the

town with its parks and its *souks,* among the dense crowds
of people who filled them, eating, singing, drinking, talking in every conceivable language. She went barefoot. To
the kids of her age and to the people of her quarter she
was Riquita. She and her friends, a lively flock of spar-
rows, spent more time on the beach than at school; but
she knew how to look after herself and keep her place in
the long line at the pump when she went to fetch a bucket
of water for her mother. It wasn't till she was ten that she
consented to put on a pair of shoes.

Everything interested her. She spent hours sitting in the
circle around an Arab teller of tales. So much so that one
storyteller, tired of seeing this child who never gave him
anything always there in the front row, butted her with his
head. Ever afterward, she sat in the second row.

She didn't know much, but that didn't keep her from
dreaming vividly about the great mysterious world where
all those huge ships with strange names came from. To
travel far away—that was her great ambition, and one
that never left her. But little Riquita's idea of the world
was rather special. North America was top America and
South America bottom America; top America meant New
York, which covered it completely. All the people there
were rich and film actors. In bottom America lived the
Indians, who gave you flowers and played the flute; there
was no need to work there, because the blacks did everything that had to be done.

But aside from the *souks,* the camel drivers, the mysterious veiled women and the swarming life of the port,
what she liked most was the circus. She went twice—once
by slipping under the edge of the tent, and once thanks to
an old clown who was touched at the sight of the pretty
barefoot kid; he let her in and gave her a good seat. She
longed to go off with the circus; one day she would be the
one who danced on the tightrope, making pirouettes and
receiving all the applause. When the circus left for bottom

America, she yearned with all her heart to go with it—to go far off and come back rich, bringing money for her family.

Yet it was not the circus she went off with, but her family. Oh, not very far, but still it was a voyage. They went and settled at Casablanca, where the port was bigger and the liners longer. Now she was sixteen and always dressed in pretty little dresses she made herself, because she worked in a shop, Aux Tissus de France, and the boss often gave her short lengths of cloth. Her dream of traveling could not fail to grow stronger, because the shop, in the Rue de l'Horloge, was very close to the offices of the Latécoère airline. The pilots often dropped in. And what pilots! Mermoz, Saint-Exupéry, Mimile the writer, Delaunay, Didier. They were handsome, and what's more they were the greatest and the bravest travelers in the world. She knew them all, and they all made passes at her; now and then she would accept a kiss, but that was all, because she was a good girl. What voyages through the sky she made with them, listening to the stories of their adventures as she ate ice cream in the little pastry shop next door. They liked her; they thought of her as their little protégée; they gave her small but highly valued presents; and they wrote her poems, some of which were published in the local paper.

When she was nineteen she married a man who exported fruit to Europe. They worked hard, they had a little daughter, and they were happy. They had two cars, they lived very comfortably, and Rita could easily help her mother and her relations.

Then in quick succession two ships loaded with oranges reached port with damaged cargoes. Two whole cargoes completely lost, that meant ruin. Her husband was deeply in debt, and if he set about working to pay his creditors, it would take him years and years. So he decided to slip off to South America. It wasn't hard for him to persuade Rita to go with him, to make this wonderful voyage to a land of milk and honey where you could just shovel up the diamonds, gold and oil. They entrusted their little girl to Rita's mother, and Rita, full of adventurous dreams, waited impatiently to board the big ship her husband had told her about.

The "big ship" was a fishing boat thirty-six feet long and sixteen wide. The captain, a somewhat piratical Estonian, had agreed to ship them to Venezuela without papers, along with a dozen other irregulars. Price: five hundred pounds. And it was in the crew's quarters of this old fishing boat that Rita made the voyage, packed in with ten Spanish republicans escaping from Franco, one Portuguese escaping from Salazar, and two women, one a twenty-five-year-old German, the captain's mistress, and the other a fat Spanish woman, the wife of Antonio the cook.

A hundred and twelve days to reach Venezuela! With a long stop at the Cape Verde islands, because the boat leaked and during one spell of rough weather very nearly sank.

While it was being repaired in dry dock, the passengers slept ashore. Rita's husband no longer trusted the boat. He said it was madness to launch out into the Atlantic in a rotten tub like that. Rita put courage into him: the captain was a Viking, she said, and the Vikings were the best seamen in the world; they could have total confidence in him.

Then an incredible piece of news. The Spaniards told Rita that the captain was a double crosser, that he had made a deal with another group of passengers and that he was going to take advantage of their being ashore to set off for Dakar by night, leaving them there. Instant turmoil! They warned the authorities and went to the ship in a body. The captain was surrounded and threatened; the Spaniards had knives. Calm returned when the captain

promised they would go to Venezuela. In view of what
had happened, he agreed to remain under the constant
supervision of one of the passengers. The next day they
left Cape Verde and faced the Atlantic.

Twenty-five days later they came in sight of Los Testi-
gos Islands, the most outlying point of Venezuela. They
forgot everything, the storms, the sharks' fins, the backs of
the playful dolphins rushing at the boat, the weevils in the
flour and the business at Cape Verde. Rita was so happy
she forgot the captain had meant to betray them and she
hugged him, kissing him on both cheeks. And once again
they heard the song the Spaniards had made up during
the crossing; because whenever there are Spaniards there
is always a guitar and a singer:

> *A Venezuela nos vamos*
> *Aunque no hay carretera.*
> *A Venezuela nos vamos*
> *En un barquito de vela.*

(We're going to Venezuela, although there is no road.
We're going to Venezuela, in a little boat with a sail.)

On April 16, 1948, after a voyage of 4,900 miles, they
reached La Guaira, the port of Caracas, fifteen miles
from the city.

To call aboard the health authorities, the captain used
a flag made out of a petticoat belonging to Zenda, the
German girl; and when the passengers saw the Venezuelan patrol boat, all their sun-cooked faces beamed
with joy. This was Venezuela: they had won!

Rita had held out splendidly, although she had lost
twenty pounds. Never a complaint nor a sign of fear,
though from time to time there had been plenty to worry
about in that cockleshell right out in the full Atlantic! She
had only faltered once, and even then no one had known

about it. When she left Tangiers she had packed the one book she should have left behind—Jules Verne's *Twenty Thousand Leagues under the Sea*. One day, in really tough weather, she had been unable to bear it anymore and had tossed the book overboard: night after night she had been dreaming that a giant octopus was dragging their boat, like the *Nautilus,* down to the bottom.

A few hours after their arrival, the Venezuelan authorities agreed to allow them into the country, although not one of them had any papers. "We'll give you identity cards later on." They sent two who were ill to the hospital, and they clothed, housed and fed the others for several weeks. Then each found himself a job.

That was Rita's story.

Wasn't it strange that I should have met the woman who had filled my horrible solitude in the Réclusion for two years, and then that this woman should have come here just as I had done, making a break—although indeed a very different kind of break? Without papers, too, and, like me, generously treated by this nation?

Nothing happened to disturb our happiness for more than three months. Then one fine day, unknown hands opened the safe of the Richmond Company, for which I was still organizing and running the geological expeditions. How the local pigs found out about my past I never could discover. But what is certain is that I was pulled in as suspect number one and shut up in the Maracaibo prison.

Naturally enough, Rita was questioned about me, and she suddenly learned everything I had hidden from her— learned it from the pigs. Interpol had given them all the information. But still she did not leave me in the lurch, and while I was in prison she helped me as much as she possibly could. She paid for a lawyer, who got me out within two weeks—charge dismissed. My complete innocence was established; but the damage had been done.

When she came to fetch me from the prison, Rita was deeply moved, but she was very sad, too. She did not look at me the same way as before. I sensed that she was really frightened—that she was hesitating about taking up with me again. I had the feeling that everything was lost. And I wasn't wrong, because right away she asked, "Why did you lie to me?"

No, I must not, must not lose her. I'd never have another chance like this. Once again I had to fight with all my strength. "Rita, you've just got to believe me. When I met you, I liked you so much, I loved you so much right away, that I was afraid you wouldn't want to see me anymore if I told you the truth about my past."

"You lied to me . . . you lied to me," she kept repeating, over and over again. "And I who thought you were a decent man."

She was crazy with fear, as if she were living in a nightmare. Yes, she's afraid, man, *she's afraid of you.*

"And who's to say I can't be a decent guy? I believe that like everybody else I deserve a chance of becoming good, honest and happy. Don't forget, Rita, that for fourteen years I had to fight against the most horrible prison system in the world. I love you with all my heart, Rita; and I love you not with my past but with my present. You must believe me: the reason I didn't tell you the story of my life was just that I was afraid of losing you. I said to myself that although I'd lived crooked before, my future with you would be the complete opposite. I saw the whole of the road we were to travel together, hand in hand, and I saw it all clean and straightforward, all in lovely colors. I swear it's true, Rita, I swear by the head of my father, whom I've made to suffer so much." Then I cracked, and I began to weep.

"Is it true, Henri? Is that really how you saw things?"

I got a hold on myself; my voice was hoarse and

broken as I replied, "It has to be like that, because now in our hearts that's the way it is. You and me—we have no past. All that matters is the present and the future."

Rita took me in her arms. "Henri, don't cry anymore. Listen to the breeze—it's our future that is beginning. But swear to me that you'll never do another dishonest thing. Promise you'll never hide anything from me anymore and that there'll be nothing dirty in our lives to be kept hidden."

We held one another tight, and I made my oath. I felt my life's greatest chance was at stake. I saw that I should never have hidden from this brave, honest woman that I was a man with a life sentence, a fugitive from the penal settlement.

So I told her everything. It was all on the move inside me, even the idea that had been obsessing me since 1931—my revenge. I decided to lay it at her feet—to give it up as a proof of my sincerity. "To prove how much I love you, Rita, I offer you the greatest sacrifice I can make. From this moment on, I give up my revenge. The prosecutor, the pigs, the false witness, all those people fully deserve a woman like you, I must—not forgive, who made me suffer so—let them die in their beds. To because that's impossible—but put out of my mind this desire to punish mercilessly the men who tossed me into the prison cells. Here before you is a completely new man; the old one is dead."

Rita must have thought over this conversation all day, because that evening, after work, she said to me, "And what about your father? Since you're now worthy of him, write to him as soon as you can."

"Since 1933 neither he nor I have heard from one another. Since October, 1933, to be exact. I used to see the convicts being given their letters, those wretched letters, opened by the screws, in which you could say nothing. I used to see the despair on the faces of the poor guys who had no mail at all, and I could make out the disappointment of the ones who read a longed-for letter and didn't find what they had hoped for in it. I've seen them tear letters to pieces and stamp on them; and I've seen tears fall on the ink and blur the writing. And I could imagine just what those damned letters from the penal settlement might mean when they got to the families outside—the Guiana stamp would make the postman and the neighbors and the people in the village café say, 'The jailbird has written. There's a letter, so he's still alive.' I could guess the shame of taking it from the postman, and the pain when the postman asked, 'Is your son getting along all right?' So I wrote to my sister Yvonne just one letter, the only letter I wrote from prison, saying, 'Never expect to hear from me, and never write. Like Alfred de Vigny's wolf, I shall know how to die without howling.' "

"All that belongs to the past, Henri. You'll write to your father?"

"Yes. Tomorrow."

"No. Now—at once."

A long letter set off for France, just telling my father what could be told without wounding him. I described no part of my sufferings; only my resurrection and my life at present. The letter came back: "Moved without leaving an address."

Dear Lord above, who could tell where my father had gone to hide his shame because of me? People were so evil they might have made life impossible for him.

Rita's reaction came at once. "I'll go to France and look for your father." I stared at her. She went on, "Give up your exploring job; it's too dangerous in any case. While I'm away, you'll run the hotel."

Not only was she ready to plunge unhesitatingly into the dangers of this long journey all by herself, but she had so much trust in me—in me, the ex-convict—that she would leave everything in my hands. She knew she could rely on me.

Rita had only rented the hotel, with an option to purchase. So to keep it from slipping out of our hands, the first thing to do was buy it. Now I really learned what it meant, struggling to make one's place in life by honest means.

I got the Richmond Company to let me go, and with the six thousand bolívars I received, and Rita's savings, we gave the owner 50 percent of the price. And then began a positive battle day after day, and night after night, to make money and meet our installments. Both she and I worked like crazy eighteen hours and sometimes nineteen hours a day. We were united by a wonderful will to win at all costs and in the shortest possible time. Neither she nor I ever mentioned our weariness. I did the buying and helped with the cooking and received the guests. We were everywhere at once, always smiling. We died on our feet, and then we began again the next morning.

To make a little more money, I filled a two-wheeled cart with jackets and trousers to sell in the Plaza Baralt market. These clothes were manufacturers' rejects, which meant I could buy them very cheaply at the factory. Under the blazing sun I reeled off my spiel, bawling like a jackass and putting so much energy into it that one day, tweaking a jacket to show how strong it was, I split it from top to bottom. It was all very well explaining that I was the strongest man in Maracaibo, but I sold precious few that morning. I was in the market from eight until noon. At half past twelve I hurried to the hotel to help at waiting in the restaurant.

The Plaza Baralt was the commercial heart of Maracaibo, one of the liveliest places in the town. At the far end stood the church, at the other, one of the most picturesque markets in the world, a market where you would find anything you could possibly think of in the way of meat, game, seafood and shellfish, not forgetting big green iguanas—a lovely dish—with their claws tied so they could not escape; and there were alligator, tortoise, and turtle eggs, armadillos and *morocoys,* a kind of land tortoise, all sorts of fruit and fresh hearts of palm. The market of this ebullient town swarmed with people in the scorching sun—skins of every color, eyes of every shape, from the Chinese slit to the Negro round.

Rita and I loved Maracaibo, although it was one of the hottest places in Venezuela. This colonial town had a lovable, warm-hearted population that lived happily. They had a musical way of speaking; they were fine, generous people with a little Spanish blood and all the best qualities of the Indians. The men were fiery creatures; they had a very strong sense of friendship, and to those they liked they could be real brothers. The Maracucho—the inhabitant of Maracaibo—did not much care for anything that came from Caracas. He complained that they provided the whole of Venezuela with gold by means of their oil, and that the people of the capital always overlooked him: the Maracucho felt like a wealthy man who was being treated as a poor relation by the very people he had enriched. The women were pretty and rather small: faithful, good daughters and good mothers. The whole town seethed with life and the noise of living, and everywhere there was brilliant color—the clothes, the houses, the fruit, everything. Everywhere, too, there was movement, business, activity. The Plaza Baralt was full of street traders and small-time smugglers who scarcely bothered to hide the liqueurs, spirits or cigarettes they were selling. It was all more or less among friends: the policeman was only a few yards away, but he would turn his back just long enough for the bottles of whisky, the French cognac or the American cigarettes to pass from one basket to another.

Running a hotel was no trifle. When Rita first came, she made a decision completely opposed to the customs of the country. The Venezuelan customers were used to eating a substantial breakfast—corn muffins (*arepas*), ham and eggs, bacon, cream cheese. And as the guests were paying full room and board, the day's menu was written up on a slate. The first day Rita wiped the whole list out and in her pointed hand wrote, "Breakfast: black coffee or café au lait, bread and butter." Well, what do you think of that? the guests must have said; by the end of the week half of them had changed their quarters.

Then I turned up. Rita had made some alterations, but my arrival brought a downright revolution.

First decree: double the prices.

Second decree: French cooking.

Third decree: air conditioning throughout.

People were astonished to find air conditioning in all the rooms and in the restaurant of a colonial house turned into a hotel. The clientele changed. First came commercial travelers; then a Basque settled in: he sold "Swiss" Omega watches manufactured entirely in Peru, and he ran his business from his room, selling only to retailers, who hawked them from door to door and all through the oil fields. Although the hotel was safe, he was so suspicious that he had three big locks put on his door at his own expense. And in spite of the locks he noticed that from time to time a watch disappeared. He thought his room was haunted until the day he found that, in fact, there was a female thief, our bitch Bouclette. She was a poodle, and so cunning she would creep in without a sound, and right under his nose would rip off a strap for pure fun, whether it had a watch attached or not. So here he was, shrieking and bawling, saying I had trained Bouclette to steal his things. I laughed till I could laugh no more, and after two or three rums managed to convince him that I'd had nothing to do with his lousy watches and

that I would really be ashamed of selling such phony
stuff. Comforted and easy in his mind, he shut himself up
in his room again.

Among our guests there were people of every possible
kind. Maracaibo was full to overflowing, and it was almost impossible to find a room. A flock of Neapolitans
went from house to house, swindling the citizens by selling
lengths of cloth folded so there seemed to be enough for
four suits when in fact you could only make two. They
were dressed as sailors and carried big bags on their
shoulders; they combed the town and the country round,
above all the oil fields. I don't know how these sharp-
witted creatures discovered our hotel. As all the rooms
were full, there was only one solution—for them to sleep
in the patio. Every evening they came back about seven
and had a shower. They had dinner at the hotel, so we
learned to make spaghetti *à la napolitaine*. They spent
their money freely, and they were good customers.

At night, we brought out iron bedsteads, and the two
little maids helped Rita make them up in the patio. As I
made the Neapolitans pay in advance, there was the same
argument every night—paying the price of a room for
sleeping in the open was too much. And every night I told
them that on the contrary it was perfectly logical and
completely fair. To bring out the beds, put on the sheets,
the blankets and the pillows and then take them all in
again in the morning was a huge amount of work—
beyond price. "And don't you go on beefing too much, or
I'll put up your rent. Because here I am, literally slaying
myself shifting things in and out—all I make you pay is
the cost of moving."

They would pay up and we would all have a laugh. But
although they were making a lot of money, the next
evening the whole thing would start all over again. They
beefed even more one night when it rained and they had

to run in with all their clothes and their mattresses and sleep in the restaurant.

A woman who kept a brothel came to see me. She had a very big house two or three miles from Maracaibo, at the place called La Cabeza de Toro: the brothel was the Tibiri-Tabara. Eléonore was her name, and she was an enormous mass of flesh: intelligent; very fine eyes. More than a hundred and twenty women worked at her place—only at night.

"There are some French girls who want to get out," she told me. "They don't like spending twenty-four hours a day in the brothel. Working from nine in the evening until four the next morning, that's fine. But they want to be able to eat well and sleep in peace in comfortable rooms away from the noise."

I made a deal with Eléonore: the French and Italian girls could come to our hotel. We could raise the price by ten bolívars a day without worrying: they would be only too happy to be able to stay at the Vera Cruz with French people. We were supposed to take six, but after a month, I don't quite know how, we had twice as many.

Rita laid down iron-hard rules. They were all young and all lovely, and Rita absolutely forbade them to receive any male at the hotel, even in the courtyard or the dining room. But there was no trouble at all; in the hotel these girls were like real ladies. In everyday life they were proper, respectable women who knew how to behave. In the evening, taxis came for them, and they were transformed—gorgeously dressed and made up. Discreet, without any noise, they went off to the "factory," as they called it. Now and then a pimp would come from Paris or Caracas, drawing as little attention to himself as possible. His girl could see him at the hotel, of course. Once he had made his haul, collected his money and made his girl happy, he would go off again as quietly as he had come.

There were often little things that were good for a laugh. A visiting pimp took me aside one day and asked to have his room changed. His woman had already found another girl who was willing to switch. Reason: his neighbor was a full-blooded, well-equipped Italian, and every night, when his girl came back, this Italian made love to her at least once and sometimes twice. My pimp was not yet forty, and the Italian must have been fifty-five.

"Man, I just can't keep up with Rital, if you follow me. There's no getting anywhere near that kind of a performance. My broad and me being next door, we hear the lot—groans, shrieks, the whole works. And as I can barely make it with my chick once a week, I ask you to imagine what I look like. She doesn't believe in the headache excuse anymore; and of course she makes comparisons. So if it doesn't put you out, do this for me."

I kept my laughter inside me, and moved by such an unanswerable argument, I switched his room.

Another time, at two o'clock in the morning, Eléonore called me up. The cop on duty had found a Frenchman who could not speak a word of Spanish perched in a tree opposite the brothel. The cop asked him how he came to be in that curious position—was he there to steal or what?—and all the fellow answered was "Enrique of the Vera Cruz." I jumped into my car and darted out to the Tibiri-Tabara.

I recognized the fellow right away. He was from Lyons and he had already been to the hotel. He was sitting there, and the madam, too; standing in front of them were two grim-faced cops. I translated what he told me—he put it very briefly. "No, the gentleman wasn't in the tree with the idea of doing anything wrong. It's just that he is in love with one of the women, but he won't say which. He climbed up to admire her in secret, because she won't have anything to do with him. It's nothing serious, as you see. Anyhow, I know him, and he's a good citizen."

We drank a bottle of champagne; he paid, and I told him to leave the change on the table—someone would surely pick it up. Then I drove him back in my car. "But what the hell were you doing perched up in that tree? Have you gone crazy, or are you jealous of your girl?"

"It's not that. The trouble is the take has dropped off without any reason for it. She's one of the prettiest there and she earns more than the others. So I thought I'd come and watch how often she went to work without her knowing. That way, it seemed to me, I'd soon find out if she was holding out on me and keeping back my money."

Although I was sore at having been pulled out of bed in the middle of the night on account of a pimp, I roared with laughter at his explanation. This "tree-perched pimp," as I called him from that time on, left for Caracas the next day. It was no longer worth his while keeping a check. The whole business had made a lot of noise in the brothel; like everybody else, his woman knew all about it, but she was the only one who knew why her fancy man had chosen just that tree—it was dead opposite her room.

We worked hard, but the hotel was a cheerful place, and we had fun all the time. There were some evenings, after the girls had gone off to their factory, when we made the dead speak. We all sat at a round table with our hands flat on the top, and each one called up the spirit he wanted to question. It was a good-looking woman of about thirty, a painter, who started these seances—she was a Hungarian, I think. She called up her husband every evening, and of course, with my foot under the table, I helped her spirit reply; otherwise we'd be there yet.

She said her husband was tormenting her. Why? She couldn't tell. At last, one night the spirit came through by means of the table, and after that he never left it quiet. He accused her of having round heels. We all exclaimed that that was very serious, and that this jealous spirit might take a horrible revenge; all the more so as she was perfectly willing to admit that in fact her heels were quite round. What was to be done about it? We discussed it very gravely and we told her there was only one thing to do: at full moon she was to provide herself with a brand-new machete, stand stark naked in the middle of the patio with her hair down and no makeup on, having washed all over with yellow soap, but with no trace of scent and no jewels, clean from head to foot. Nothing but the machete in her hand. When the moon was right over the patio, casting no shadow except directly beneath her, she was to slash the air exactly twenty-one times.

It worked perfectly, and the night after the exorcism (we had laughed fit to burst, hidden behind the shutters) Rita said the joke had lasted long enough; so the table replied that from now on her late husband would leave her in peace and her heels could be as round as she liked, always provided she never slashed the air with a sword at full moon anymore, because it hurt him too much.

We had another poodle called Minou, quite a big poodle, which had been given to us by a French guest who was passing through Maracaibo. Minou was always perfectly clipped and brushed, and the stiff, thick hair on the top of his head was cut in the shape of a tall, impressive fez. He had puffed-out thighs, shaved legs, a Chaplin moustache and a little pointed beard. The Venezuelans were astonished at the spectacle, and often one of them would overcome his shyness and ask what kind of animal this strange beast might be.

Minou very nearly brought about a serious clash with the Church. The Vera Cruz stood in the Calla Venezuela; our street led to a church, and processions often went along it. Now Minou loved sitting at the hotel door to watch the people walking about. He never barked, whatever happened in the street. But although he did not bark, he did cause a sensation; and one day the priest and the choirboys belonging to a procession found themselves all alone while, fifty yards behind, the faithful of Maracaibo stood massed in front of the hotel, gazing at this extraordinary object. They had forgotten to follow the procession. Questions ran through the group, and they jostled to see Minou close up; some were of the opinion that the unknown creature might very well be the soul of a repentant sinner, since it had sat there so quietly, watching a priest and his choirboys all dressed in red go by singing heartily. At last the priest realized that things were very silent behind, and turning around he saw there was no one left. He came striding back, crimson with fury and bawling out his parishioners for their lack of respect for the ceremony. Alarmed, they fell back into line and marched off. But I noticed that some who had been most struck by the sight walked backward so as not to lose a minute of Minou. After that we kept an eye on the Maracaibo paper, *Panorama,* for the date and time when a procession should come along our street, so that we could tie him up in the patio.

It seems this was the season for incidents with the clergy. Two French girls left Eléonore's brothel and the hotel; they had made up their minds to be independent and set up a little "house" in the center of the town where they would just work by themselves, the two of them. It was quite a good scheme, because this way the customers would not have to get their cars and drive six miles there and back to see them. To get themselves known, they had cards printed, saying "Julie and Nana: conscientious work" and the address. They handed them out in the town; but instead of giving them directly to the men, they often slipped them under the windshield wipers of parked cars.

They had the bad luck to put two, one under each wiper, on the car belonging to the bishop of Maracaibo.

This set off a hell of an explosion. To show the profane nature of their action, the paper *La Religión* published a picture of the card. But the bishop and the clergy were indulgent: the little brothel was not closed, and the ladies were only begged to be more discreet. Anyhow, there was no point in going on handing out the cards; after the free publicity in *La Religión,* a very considerable number of customers hurried to the given address. Indeed, the crowd was so great that to provide a reasonable excuse for this troop of men at their door, the girls asked a hot-dog seller to wheel his cart quite close, so it would look as if the line was standing there to buy a *perro caliente.*

That was the picturesque side of life at the hotel. But we weren't living on a planet far out in space; we were living it in Venezuela, and we were involved with the country's economic and political ups and downs. In 1948 politics were not so peaceful. Gallegos and Betancourt had been governing the country since 1945, in the first attempt at a democratic régime in the history of Venezuela. On November 13, 1948, scarcely three months after I had set to work with Rita to buy the hotel, there came the first shot directed against the régime. A major called Thomas Mendoza had the nerve to stage an uprising all by himself. He failed.

On the twenty-fourth of the same month the soldiers seized power in a coup d'état run with clockwise precision: there were almost no victims. Gallegos, the president of the republic and a distinguished writer, was forced to resign. Betancourt, a real political lion, took refuge in the Colombian embassy.

In Maracaibo we lived through hours of very tense anxiety. There was one moment when all at once we heard a passionate voice on the radio crying, "Workers, come out into the streets! They want to steal your freedom from you, close down your unions and impose a military dictatorship by force! Everybody occupy the squares, the . . ." Click, and it went dead, the mike snatched from the brave militant's hands. Then a calm, grave voice: "Citizens! The army has withdrawn the power from the men to whom they entrusted it after having dismissed General Medina, because they made an unworthy use of their authority. Do not be afraid: we guarantee the life and property of one and all, without exception. Long live the army! Long live the revolution!"

That was all I saw of a revolution which caused no blood to flow at all; and when we woke up the next day, there was the membership of the military junta in the papers: three colonels—Delgado Chalbaud as president, Pérez Jiménez and Llovera Páez.

At first, we were afraid this new régime would mean the suppression of the rights given by the former one. But nothing of the kind. Life went on just the same, and we scarcely noticed the change of government, except that the key posts were taken over by soldiers.

Then two years later came the assassination of Delgado Chalbaud. A very ugly business with two conflicting explanations. First theory: they meant to murder all three and he was just the first to be killed. Second theory: one or both of the other colonels had had him put out of the way. The truth was never known. The murderer was arrested, and he was shot and killed while he was being transferred to prison—a lucky shot that prevented any embarrassing statement. From that day on Pérez Jiménez was the strong man of the régime, and he officially became dictator in 1952.

So our life went on, and although we never went out for any fun or entertainment or even a drive, this life and our eagerness to work filled us with a wonderful joy. For what we were building up by our labors was our home-to-be, the home where we would live happily, having earned it ourselves, united as two people can be only when they love one another as we did.

And into this home would come Clotilde, Rita's daughter, who would be mine, and my father, who would be theirs. And to this house my friends would come, to catch their breath awhile when they were in need. And in this home filled with happiness we would be so thoroughly contented that never again should I think of taking my revenge upon those who had caused so much suffering to me and my people.

At last the day came—we had won. In December, 1950, a beautiful document was drawn up at the lawyer's, and we became the owners of the hotel for good and all.

11

My Father

Soon thereafter Rita set off on her journey, her heart filled with hope. She was going to find out where my father had hidden himself.

"Rely on me, Henri. I'll bring you back your father."

I was alone in the running of the hotel. I gave up selling my trousers and shirts, although I could make quite a bundle that way in a few hours. Rita had gone to look for my father, so I was going to look after everything not only as well as if she were there, but even better, twice as well.

To look for my father: my father, the schoolmaster of a village in the Ardèche, who twenty years before had been unable to embrace his own son, because of the bars in the visiting room. My father, to whom Rita would be able to say, "I've come as your daughter to tell you that by his own efforts your son has regained his freedom, that he has made himself a life as a good and honest man, and that he and I have built up a home that is waiting for you."

I got up at five o'clock and went shopping with Minou and a twelve-year-old boy called Carlitos, whom I had taken in when he came out of prison. He carried the baskets. In an hour and a half I'd done the buying for the whole day—meat, fish and vegetables. We both came back loaded like mules. There were two women in the kitchen, one twenty-four, the other eighteen. I dumped everything we had brought on the table and they sorted it out.

For me, the best moment in this simple life was at half past six in the morning, when I ate my breakfast in the dining room with the cook's daughter on my knee. She was four; she was coal-black, and she would not eat unless she had her breakfast with me. All these things— her little naked body, still cool from the shower her mother gave her when she got up, her little girl's piping voice, her lovely shining eyes that looked at me so trustingly, the jealous barking of my dogs, cross at being neglected, Rita's parrot pecking at its bread and milk by my coffee cup—yes, all this really made breakfast the top moment of my day.

Rita? No letter. Why? It was more than a month now that she'd been gone. The voyage took sixteen days, true enough; but after all she'd been in France for two weeks now—had she still found nothing, or did she not want to tell me? All I asked for was a cable, a very short cable just to say "Your father is well and he loves you still."

I watched for the postman. I never left the hotel unless I had to in order to keep it running smoothly, and I hurried over the shopping and the other business so I could be on the spot all the time. In Venezuela the people who bring telegrams have no uniform, but they are all young; so the moment any boy walked into the patio I hurried toward him, my eyes fixed on his hands to see if he was carrying a green paper. Not a thing. Most of the time they weren't even telegraph boys, except on two or three occasions when some young fellow did appear with a green slip in his hand: I'd rush out, snatch the telegram and then see with a sinking heart that it was addressed to someone staying at the hotel.

The waiting and lack of news put me on edge. I worked till I dropped; to keep busy, I helped in the kitchen, I worked out extraordinary menus, I checked the rooms twice a day, I talked to the guests about no matter what and listened to whatever they had to say. The only thing that mattered was filling up these hours and days of waiting. There was only one thing I couldn't do—take a hand in the poker game that started up about two o'clock every night.

There was only one really serious hitch. Carlitos got things wrong. Instead of buying paraffin for cleaning the kitchen, he bought gasoline. The cooks swilled the concrete floor with a good deal of it and then, never suspecting a thing, they lit the stove. The whole kitchen blazed up vividly and the two sisters were burned from foot to belly. I barely had time to wrap a tablecloth round Rosa's little black girl and save her—not a second to spare. She was almost unhurt, but the other two were badly burned. I had them looked after in their room in the hotel and engaged a Panamanian cook.

Life in the hotel carried on as usual, but I began to be seriously worried about Rita's silence and her not being there.

Fifty-seven days she had been gone by the time I found myself waiting for her at the airport. Why just that simple telegram—"ARRIVE TUESDAY 15.30 FLIGHT 705. LOVE RITA"? Why nothing more? Had she not found anyone? I couldn't tell what to think anymore, and I didn't want to make any more guesses.

Then there she was, my Rita. She was the fifth coming down the gangway. She saw me right away and we both waved at the same moment. She came toward me, just as usual. From forty yards I searched her face: she was not laughing, just smiling; no, she hadn't waved as a sign of joy and victory but just naturally, to show she'd seen me. At ten yards I saw she'd come back beaten.

"Did you find my father?"

The question hit her point-blank, after no more than a kiss, a single kiss after two months of separation. I couldn't wait any longer.

Yes, she had found him. He was lying in the graveyard of a little village in the Ardèche.

She showed me a photograph. A well-made cement tomb with "J. Charrière" on it. He had died four months before she got there. And all Rita brought me back was this picture of his grave.

My heart, which had seen Rita go off so full of hope, almost stopped at this appalling news. I felt the collapse of all those illusions I had had as a man who still sees himself as a little boy for his father. God, not only have You struck the whole of my youth but You have also refused to let me embrace my father and to hear his voice, which would have said, I am certain of it, "Come to my arms, my little Riri. Fate has been unmerciful to you but I love you still; I am proud that you have had the strength to become what you are." Over and over again Rita told me the little she had been able to find out about my father's life after I was sentenced. I said nothing; something inside me was tied into a furious knot. And then all at once, as though a sluice had burst open, the idea of revenge came over me again. "Pigs, I'll set off that trunk of dynamite at thirty-six, quai des Orfèvres, not just to kill a few but to get as many as possible—a hundred, two hundred, three hundred, a thousand! And you, Goldstein, you perjurer, believe me, you'll get what's coming to you, every last bit of it. As for you, prosecuting counsel, so eager to put me away, it won't take me long to find a way of getting hold of your tongue and tearing it out, to cause as much agony as you can suffer!

"Rita, we must part. Try to understand: they prevented me from embracing my father and having his forgiveness. I must have my revenge; they can't get away with this. I know where to find the money for the journey and to carry out my plan. All I ask is that you let me take five thousand bolívars out of our saving for my first expenses."

An interminable silence settled; I no longer saw Rita; her face disappeared behind the unfolding vision of the plan I had worked out so often.

What did I need to put it into action? Less than two hundred thousand bolívars, in fact. I'd asked too much before. I'd have plenty to spare with these sixty thousand dollars. There were two jobs I'd left alone out of respect for this country. First, El Callao with its heap of gold guarded by ex-cons. Then right in the middle of Caracas, the cashier of a big firm. He was a pushover: he carried large sums of money without an escort. The entrance to the building was perfect; so was the fourth-floor corridor: both were badly lit. I could work alone, unarmed, with chloroform.

As for the getaway, that would have to be through British Guiana. I'd get to Georgetown with just a little gold melted down into nuggets—easy enough with a blow-torch. I'd be certain of finding a buyer for the lot. The fence and I would carry out the deal on the basis of notes cut in two; he'd keep one half and only give it to me when I delivered the goods on the British side of the Caroní, where I would have the stuff hidden. That way, there would be confidence all round.

Transfer the dough to Buenos Aires through a bank; carry a certain amount in notes; take a plane from Trinidad to Rio de Janeiro. At Rio, change passports and get into Argentina.

No problem there. I had friends in Rio, ex-cons; and it must be easy to find former Nazis with their trunks full of papers. Leave for Portugal from Buenos Aires with four sets of passports and identity papers—different nationalities but all in the same name to avoid confusion.

From Lisbon, take the road into Spain and reach Barcelona; still traveling by road, into France on a Paraguayan passport. I spoke Spanish well enough by now for an inquisitive French gendarme to take me for a South American.

In Paris I'd stay at the Georges V. Never go out at night: have dinner at the hotel and send for tea in my suite at ten. The same thing every day of the week. That's the hallmark of a serious man who leads an exactly regulated life. In a hotel such things get noticed right away.

I'd have a moustache, of course, and hair cut *en brosse,* like an officer. Only say what was strictly necessary and use a Spanish sort of French to say it. Have Spanish newspapers put in my pigeonhole at the reception desk every day.

Thousands and thousands of times I'd considered which man or men to begin with, so that the three jobs would never be connected with Papillon.

The first to get their deserts would be the pigs, with the trunk stuffed with explosives at 36, quai des Orfèvres. There would be no reason to think of me if I did it cleverly. To begin with I'd have a look at the premises and check the exact time it took to go up the stairs to the report room and then get back to the entrance. I didn't need anyone to work out the fuse for the detonator; I'd make all the necessary experiments at the Franco-Venezuelan garage.

I'd turn up in a van with MAISON SO-AND-SO: OFFICE EQUIPMENT painted on it. Dressed as a delivery man, with my little crate on my shoulder, I should get away with it easily. But when I first went over the place I'd have to find some inspector's card on a door or else manage to get hold of the name of an important character with his office on that floor. Then I could say the name to the pigs on duty at the door; or indeed I could show them the invoice, as if I didn't remember who the trunk was for. And then all aboard for the fireworks. It would take diabolical bad luck for anyone to connect the explosion—a sort of anarchist's job, after all—with Papillon.

Thus the prosecutor Pradel would remain unsuspecting. To cope with him, and to prepare the trunk, the fuse, the explosives and the bit of old iron, I'd take a villa, using my Paraguayan passport if I hadn't managed to get hold of a French identity card. I was afraid it might be too dangerous to get into contact with the underworld again. Better not risk it: I'd make out with the passport.

The villa would be near Paris, somewhere along the Seine, because I'd have to be able to get there by water and by road. I'd buy a light, fast little boat with a cabin, and it would have moorings right by the villa and on the banks of the Seine in the middle of Paris, too. For the road, I'd have a small, high-powered car. It was only when I got there, when I knew where Pradel lived and worked and where he spent his weekends and whether he took the Métro, the bus, a taxi or his own car, that I'd take the necessary steps to kidnap him and shut him up in the villa.

The main thing was to make dead sure of the times and the places he was alone. Once he was in my cellar, I had him on toast. This prosecutor who, way back in 1931, at the trial, had seemed to say to me, with his vulture look, "You won't escape from me, young cock; I'm going to make use of everything that can look bad for you, all this ugly muck in your file, so the jury will turn you out of society for good and all"—this prosecutor, who had used

all his abilities and all his education to paint the vilest and
most hopeless picture of a boy of twenty-four, and with
such success that the twelve incompetent bastard jurymen
sent me to hard labor for life—this prosecutor I'd have to
torture for at least a week before he died. And at that he
wouldn't have paid too dear.

The last to pay the bill would be Goldstein, the perjurer. I'd take him last, since he was the most dangerous
for me. Because once I'd killed him, they'd look back
over his life, and the pigs were not always half-wits—
they'd soon see the part he had played in my trial. And as
they'd know right away that I was on the run, it wouldn't
take them long to figure out there might be a Papillon
fluttering about in the Paris air. At that point everything—
hotels, streets, stations, ports and airfields—would become
extremely dangerous for me. I'd have to make my getaway quickly.

It would be easy enough to pinpoint and follow him,
because of his father's fur shop. There were several ways
of killing him, but whichever way I chose, I wanted him
to recognize me before he died. If possible, I'd do what I
had so often dreamed of doing—strangle him slowly with
my bare hands, saying, "Sometimes the dead come to life
again. You didn't expect that, brother? You didn't expect
my hands to kill you? Still, you win, because you're going
to die in a few minutes, whereas you sent me down to rot
slowly all my life until I died of it."

I couldn't tell whether I'd manage to get out of France,
because once Goldstein was dead things would be very
dangerous. It was almost certain they would identify me,
but I didn't give a damn. Even if I had to die for it, they
must pay for my father's death. I'd have forgiven them
for my suffering. But the fact that my father should have
died without my being able to tell him his boy was alive
and had gone straight; the fact that maybe he had died of
shame, hiding from all his old friends, and that he should

have lain in his grave without knowing what I was now—that, no, no, no! That I could never forgive!

During the very long silence while I went through every step of the action again to see there was no hitch anywhere, Rita had been sitting at my feet, with her head leaning against my knee. Not a word, not a sound; she almost seemed to be holding her breath.

"Rita, sweetheart, I leave tomorrow."

"You can't go." She stood up, put her hands on my shoulders and looked me straight in the eye. She went on, *"You must not go:* you can't go. There's something new for me, too. I took advantage of my journey to send for my daughter. She'll be here in a few days. You know perfectly well the reason I didn't have her with me was that I needed a settled place for her. Now I've got one, and she'll have a father, too—you. Are you going to spoil everything we've built up with the love and trust between us? Do you think killing the men who were responsible for your sufferings and perhaps for your father's death is really the only thing to do when you compare it with what we have?

"Henri, for my sake and for the sake of this girl who is coming to you, and who I am sure will love you, I ask you to give up your idea of revenge forever. If your father could speak, do you think he would approve of your idea of revenge? No. He'd tell you that neither the cops nor the false witness nor the prosecutor nor what you call the jurymen nor the wardens were worth your sacrificing a wife who loves you and whom you love, and my daughter who hopes to find a father in you, and your good, comfortable home, and your honest life.

"I'll tell you how I see your revenge: it's this—that our family should be a symbol of happiness for everybody; that with your intelligence and my help, we should succeed in life by honest means; and that when the people of this country talk about you not one would say anything

but this—the Frenchman is straight and honest, a good
man whose word is his bond. That's what your revenge
ought to be; the revenge of proving to them all that they
were terribly mistaken about you; of proving that you
managed to come through the horrors of prison unspoiled
and to become a fine character. That is the only revenge
worthy of the love and the trust I have placed in you."

She had won. All night we talked, and I learned to drain
the cup to the dregs. But I could not resist the temptation
of knowing every last detail of Rita's journey. She lay on
a big sofa, exhausted by the failure of this long voyage
and by her struggle with me. Sitting there on the edge of
it, I leaned over her, questioning her again and again and
again, and little by little I dragged out everything she had
meant to hide.

At the very beginning, after she left Maracaibo for the
port of Caracas, where she was to take the boat, she had
a foreboding that she was going to fail: everything seemed
to conspire to prevent her from leaving for France. Just as
she was boarding the *Colombie* she noticed she was missing one of the necessary visas. A race against time to get
it in Caracas, tearing along that dangerous little road I
knew so well. Back to the port with the paper in her bag
and her heart beating for fear the boat should leave
before she got there. Then a terrible storm broke out,
bringing landslides down over the road. It became so
dangerous that the driver lost his head and turned back,
leaving Rita there alone in the storm by the side of the
road, among the landslides. She walked nearly two miles
in the downpour and then by a miracle found a taxi that
was returning to Caracas; but at the sight of the landslides
it turned back for the port. And from the port she could
hear ships' sirens. In her panic she was sure it was the
Colombie leaving.

Then when she reached her cabin at last, weeping with

joy, there was some accident aboard and the ship could not leave for several hours. All this gave her a very uneasy feeling, as if the events were expressions of fate.

Then the ocean: Le Havre, Paris, and without a stop, Marseille, where she stayed with a woman she knew, who introduced her to a municipal councilor, who wrote her a cordial letter to a friend of his called Henri Champel, who lived at Vals-les-Bains in the Ardèche.

Then the train and the bus again, and it was not until she reached these wonderfully kind Champels that Rita could draw breath and begin to organize her search. Even then she was not at the end of her difficulties.

Henri Champel took her to Aubenas in the Ardèche, where Maître Testud, the family lawyer, lived. Ah, that Testud! A heartless bourgeois. In the first place he told her my father was dead—just right out, like that. Then on his own initiative, without consulting anyone, he forbade her to go and see my father's sister and her husband, my uncle and aunt Dumarche, retired teachers who lived in Aubenas. Many years later they welcomed us with open arms, indignant at the thought that because of this wretched Testud they had not been able to put Rita up and so to get in touch with me again. The same thing with my sisters: Testud refused to give their address. Still, Rita did manage to get this stony heart to tell her where my father had died—Saint-Peray.

The journey to Saint-Peray. There Henri Champel and Rita found my father's grave and learned something else as well. After having been a widower for twenty years he had married again—a retired schoolmistress—when I was still in the penal settlement. They found her. The family called her Tante Ju, or sometimes Tata Ju.

A fine woman, said Rita, and with such a noble character that she had kept the memory of my mother alive in this new home. In the dining room Rita had seen big photographs of my mother, whom I worshipped, and of my father. She had been able to touch and fondle objects that had belonged to her. Tante Ju, who now suddenly came into my life—although at the same time I felt I already knew her—had done all she could to let Rita feel the atmosphere she and my father had wanted to keep alive—the memory of my mother and the continual presence of that vanished little boy who was still Riri to my father.

November 16 was my birthday, and every November 16 my father used to weep. Every Christmas there was a chair left empty. When the gendarmes came to tell them their son had escaped again, the Charrières almost kissed them for having brought such wonderful news. Because although Tante Ju did not know me, she had already adopted me in her heart as if I were her own son, and both she and my father shed tears of joy at hearing what was for them news of hope.

So she had received Rita more than kindly. Only one shadow: Tante Ju had not given her the address of my two sisters. Why not? I thought quickly. No doubt about it: she wasn't sure how they would take the news of my reappearance. Since she did not say to Rita, "Hurry over and see them at such-and-such a place; they'll be wild with delight to know their brother's still alive and doing well, and to meet his wife," she must have had her reasons. Maybe Tante Ju knew that neither my sister Yvonne nor my sister Hélène nor my brothers-in-law would care to be visited by the wife of their brother, the escaped jailbird, sentenced to life for murder. No doubt she did not want to take the responsibility for disturbing their peace.

They were married and they had children, and probably these children did not even know of my existence. Take care, she must have said to herself. It seemed to me that although throughout my fourteen years in the clink I had lived with them and through them, they, on the other hand, must have spent those fourteen years doing their best to forget me or at least trying to blot me out of their daily lives. So all my wife brought back was a little earth from my father's grave and a photograph of the tomb where just four months before my father had been laid to rest forever.

Still, through Rita's eyes (for Champel had driven her everywhere) I did see the bridge of Ucel once more, the bridge of my childhood. I listened as she told me every detail about the big primary school where we had lived in the flat over the classrooms. Once again I could see the war memorial opposite our garden, and the garden itself, where a splendid flowering mimosa seemed to have kept itself in full bloom so that Rita, whose eyes drank in the garden, the memorial and the house, should be able to say to me, "Nothing, or almost nothing, has changed; and you've so often described the scenes of your childhood that I did not feel I was seeing something new but rather that I was coming back to a place I knew already."

Often in the evenings I would ask Rita to tell me some part of her journey all over again. At the hotel life went back to what it had been before. But deep inside me something inexplicable had happened. I had not felt this death as a forty-year-old man in the prime of life feels when he hears of the death of a father he has not seen for twenty years, but like a boy of ten—like one who lives with his father, disobeys him, plays truant and then, on coming home, hears of his death.

Rita's daughter Clotilde arrived. She was over fifteen, but she was so frail and slight you would have said she was twelve. She had long, thick, black, curling hair down to her shoulders. Her small jet-black eyes sparkled with intelligence and curiosity. Her little face was not that of a girl but of a child that might still be playing at hopscotch or with a doll. There was immediate sympathy between us.

When she appeared, something new came over me—
the wish that she should be happy and that she should
look upon me, if not as her father, then at least as her
surest support.

Now that Rita was back again, I did the shopping later,
at seven. And now I took Clotilde with me; she led Minou
and Carlitos carried the baskets. Everything was new for
her, and she wanted to see it all at once. When she found
something unexpected she piped up loud and clear to
know what it was. What struck her most were the Indian
women with their long shimmering robes, painted cheeks,
and shoes decorated with huge, many-colored woolen
pompoms.

That in the midst of this hurrying, shouting crowd she
felt completely protected, moved me deeply and filled me
with a hitherto unknown feeling—the feeling of a father's
love. "Yes, Clotilde, go forward into life with a trusting,
easy mind; you can be sure that until the end I shall do
everything I can to keep your path clear of thorns."

And we would go happily back to the hotel, always
with something amusing to tell Rita about what had happened to us or what we had seen.

12

I Become a Venezuelan

I know perfectly well that what the reader expects is my
own personal adventures and not a history of Venezuela.
Forgive me if I feel I should mention certain important
political events that happened during the time I was writ-

ing about; they had a direct influence on my life and on the decisions I took.

For many people Venezuela is just a country in South America (most aren't quite sure just where), a country exploited by the Americans as if it were a kind of oil-producing American colony. This is far from true.

To be sure, the oil companies did once have very great weight; little by little, though, the Venezuelan intellectuals have set the country almost entirely free from the influence of American policy.

At present Venezuela is completely independent politically, as it has proved at the United Nations and elsewhere. One thing all its political parties have in common is a great zeal for Venezuela's freedom of action with respect to all foreign countries. Thus, ever since Rafael Caldera came to power, we have had diplomatic relations with every country in the world, whatever their political régimes.

It is true that economically Venezuela depends on its oil, but it has succeeded in selling the oil at a very high price and in making the oil companies hand over as much as 85 percent of their profits.

Venezuela has other things besides oil, such as iron and other raw materials; and Venezuela has a vast resource of men whose aim is to free their country entirely from all forms of economic pressure. Men who have begun to prove that Venezuela can set up a democracy as good as any other, respected and preserved.

The young people in the universities long for nothing but social justice and the radical transformation of their country. They are full of faith, and confident of succeeding without undermining the foundations of real freedom—confident of bringing happiness to the whole nation without falling into a dictatorship either of the extreme right or of the extreme left. I believe in the young people of this country: they will help make it a nation that can be held up as an example, both for its truly democratic régime and for its economy, because it must not be forgotten that its huge resources of raw materials will soon be completely industrialized. When that happens, Venezuela will have won a great battle—and Venezuela *will* win it.

Venezuela is also an ideal country for the kind of tourism that must develop in the coming years. Everything is in its favor—its beaches of coral sand, shaded by coconut palms; its sunshine, which surpasses all other countries'; its fishing of every kind in a sea that is always warm. Venezuela also offers a lower cost of living than other countries; islands by the hundred: a welcoming, hospitable people without the least trace of a color problem. And within an hour's flying distance from Caracas you can find the Indians, the lake villages of Maracaibo, or the Andes with their everlasting snow.

In short, Venezuela is so rich in resources that the country doesn't really need a politician at the helm so much as a good accountant, who will use the profits from oil to build factories and so increase the labor market for all who need or want work.

1951. . . . Once again, as I remember this date, I have the same feeling I had then—the feeling of having nothing more to tell. You tell about storms and shooting the rapids of a swollen river; but when the water is calm and peaceful, you feel like closing your eyes and resting on the placid current. Then rain comes pouring down again, the streams rise, the quiet water grows rough, the flood carries you away, and even if you longed to live in peace from everything, outside events have such an effect on your life that they force you to follow the current, avoiding the reefs and shooting the rapids in the hope of finding a quiet harbor at last.

After the mysterious killing of Chalbaud at the end of

1950, Pérez Jiménez seized power, although he hid behind Flamerich, the figurehead president of the junta. The
dictatorship began. First sign: the suppression of freedom
of speech. The press and the radio were throttled. The
opposition went underground, and the terrible political
police, the Seguridad Nacional, went into action. The
Communists and the Adecos (the members of the Acción
Democrática, Betancourt's party) were hunted down.

Several times we hid them at the Vera Cruz. We never
closed our doors to anyone at all, never asked for any
man's identification. I was only too glad to pay my tribute
to these followers of Betancourt, whose régime had set me
free and given me asylum. We ran the danger of losing
everything, but Rita saw that there wasn't anything else
we could do.

Then again, the hotel had become something of a refuge for Frenchmen in a jam—the Frenchmen who had
reached Venezuela with little in their pockets and who did
not know where to go. They could eat and sleep at our
place without paying while they were looking for a job.
Our service became so famous that in Maracaibo they
called me the Frenchmen's consul.

In the course of these years something very important
to me happened, something almost as important as my
meeting with Rita—I renewed my ties with my family. As
soon as Rita left, Tante Ju wrote to my two sisters. And
all of them, both my sisters and Tante Ju, wrote to me.
After twenty years the great silence was coming to an
end. I trembled as I opened the first letter. Would they
reject me forever, or would they . . . ?

Victory! These letters were a cry of joy—joy at knowing I was alive, earning an honest living and married to a
woman Tante Ju described with all the kindness she had
felt. Not only had I found my sisters once again, but I had
also found their families, who now became *my* family.

My elder sister had four fine children, three girls and

a boy. Her husband wrote himself to say that his affection had remained unaltered and that he was more than happy to know I was free and doing well. Photos and still more photos, pages and still more pages told the story of their lives and of the war and of what they had had to go through to bring up their children. I read every word, weighing and analyzing so I could understand their story thoroughly and savor all its charm.

After the great black hole of the prison and the penal settlement my own childhood came to the surface: "My dear Riri," wrote my sister. Riri . . . I could hear my mother calling me and see her lovely smile. It seemed that from a photo I had sent them my family decided I was the image of my father. My sister was convinced that if I was like him physically I must be like him in personality. Her husband and she were not afraid of my turning up again. The gendarmes must have heard about Rita's journey in the Ardèche, because they had gone to ask about me, and my brother-in-law had replied, "Yes indeed, we have news of him. He's very happy and he's doing fine, thank you very much."

My other sister was in Paris, married to a Corsican lawyer. They had two sons and a daughter, and he had a good job. The same cry: "You are free, you are loved, you have a home, a good position and you are living like everybody else. Well done, little brother! My children, my husband and I bless God for having helped you to come out a winner from that terrible prison into which they threw you."

My elder sister offered to take our daughter so she could go on with her studies in France. But what warmed our hearts most was that not one of them seemed to be ashamed of having a brother who was an ex-convict who had escaped from the penal settlement.

To round off this influx of wonderful news, I managed to get hold of the address of my friend Dr. Guibert-

Germain, the former doctor of the settlement, who had treated me as one of his family when I was on Royale, inviting me to his house, and protecting me from the screws. It was thanks to Dr. Guibert-Germain that the solitary confinement at Saint-Joseph was done away with; and it was thanks to him that I was able to get myself transferred to Devil's Island and escape. I wrote to him, and one day I had the immense happiness of receiving this letter:

Lyons, 21 February 1952

My dear Papillon,

We are very glad to have news of you at last. For a long while now I have felt sure you were trying to get in touch with me. When I was in Jibuti my mother told me she had received a letter from Venezuela, although she could not say exactly who had sent it. Then, very recently, she sent me the letter you wrote through Mme. Roesberg. So after a fair amount of trial we have managed to find you again. Since September 1945, when I left Royale, a good many things have happened.

. . . And then in October 1951 I was posted to Indo-China; I am to stay there for two years, and I leave very soon, that is to say on 6 March. This time I am going by myself. Perhaps when I am there, and according to where they send me, I may be able to arrange for my wife to come out and join me.

So you see that since the last time we met I have traveled a fair number of miles! I retain some pleasant memories of those days; but alas I have not been able to get in touch with any of the men I used to like asking to the house. For quite a long while I did hear from my cook (Ruche), who settled at Saint-Laurent; but since leaving Jibuti I have had no word. Still, we were very pleased to know that you

*were happy, in good health and comfortably estab-
lished at last. Life is a strange thing; but I remember
you never gave up hope, and indeed you were quite
right.*

*We were delighted with the photograph of you
and your wife—it shows that you have been really
successful. Who knows, perhaps one day we may
come and see you! Events move faster than we do.
We see from the photograph you have excellent
taste: Madame seems charming, and the hotel has a
very agreeable look. My dear Papillon, you must
forgive me for still using this nickname; but it brings
back so many memories for us!*

*. . . So there you have some idea of our doings,
old fellow. We often talk about you, you may be
sure, and we still remember that stirring day when
Mandolini poked his nose into a place he should
have left alone.**

*My dear Papillon, I enclose a photograph of both
of us; it was taken at Marseille, on the Canebière,
about two months ago.*

*And so I leave you, with all kinds of good wishes
and hoping to hear from you now and then.*

*My wife and I send our kind regards to your wife
and our best wishes to you.*

                                A. Guibert-Germain

And following that, a few lines from Madame Guibert-
Germain: "With my best compliments on your success
and kindest wishes to you both for the New Year. Greet-
ings to my protégé."

Madame Guibert-Germain never did join her husband
in Indo-China. He was killed in 1952, so I never saw him

---

* This was Bruet, the warder who found the raft in the grave
in *Papillon.*

again, that self-effacing medico who, together with Major Péan of the Salvation Army and a handful of others, was one of the very few men at the penal settlement who had the courage to stand up for humane ideas in favor of the convicts; and in his case, to succeed in getting some results while he was serving there. There are no words fine enough to express the respect due to people like him and his wife. In opposition to one and all and at the risk of his career, he maintained that a convict was still a man, and that even if he had committed a serious crime he was not lost forever.

The letters from Tante Ju were not the letters of a stepmother who has never known you, but real, motherly letters, saying things that only a mother's heart could think of. Letters in which she told me about my father's life up until the time he died, the life of that law-abiding schoolmaster, full of respect for the legal authorities, who nevertheless cried out, "My boy was innocent, I know it; and these swine have had him found guilty! Where can he be now that he has escaped? Is he dead or alive?" Every time the members of the Resistance in the Ardèche brought off an operation against the Germans, he would say, "If Henri were here, he would be with them." Then the months of silence during which he no longer pronounced his son's name. It was as though he had transferred his affection for me to his grandchildren, whom he spoiled more than most grandfathers.

I devoured all this like a starving man. Over and over again Rita and I read all these precious letters that renewed the links with my family; we kept them like positive relics. Truly I was blessed by the gods—without exception all my people had enough love for me and enough courage not to give a damn for what people might say, and to tell me of their joy that I was alive, free and happy. And indeed courage was necessary, because society does not easily forgive a family for having had a delinquent within it.

In 1953 we sold the hotel. Eventually the shattering heat got us down, and in any case Rita and I had never meant to spend the rest of our days in Maracaibo. All the less so as I'd heard of a tremendous boom in Venezuelan Guiana, where a mountain of almost pure iron had been discovered. It was at the other end of the country, so we were up and away for Caracas, meaning to stop there a while and look into the situation.

One fine morning we set off in my huge green De Soto station wagon, crammed with baggage, and left behind five years of quiet happiness and many friends.

Once again I saw Caracas. But hadn't we hit on the wrong town?

At the end of Flamerich's term Pérez Jiménez had named himself president of the republic; but even before that he had set about turning the colonial town of Caracas into a typical ultra-modern capital. All this during a period of unheard-of cruelty, on the part both of the government and of the underground opposition. Caldera, who has been president since 1970, escaped from a shocking attempt on his life; a powerful bomb was thrown into the room where he was sleeping with his wife and child. By an absolute miracle not one of them was killed; and with wonderful coolness—no shrieks, no panic—he and his wife just went down on their knees to thank God for having saved their lives.

But in spite of all the difficulties he had to deal with during his dictatorship, Pérez Jiménez entirely transformed Caracas, and a good many other things, too. The old road from Caracas to the Maiquetía airfield and the port of La Guaira was still there. But Pérez Jiménez had built a magnificent and technically outstanding thruway that meant you could get from the town to the sea in less than a quarter of an hour, whereas it had taken two hours by the old road. In the Silencio district Pérez Jiménez ran up enormous buildings the size of those in New York. And he built an astonishing six-lane highway right through the city from one end to the other—not to mention the building of working- and middle-class complexes that were models of urbanism, and many other changes. All this meant millions and millions of dollars swirling about; and it meant a great deal of energy burst out in this country that had been dozing for hundreds of years. Foreign capital came flowing in, together with specialists of every kind. Life changed completely; immigration was wide open, and fresh blood came in, giving a positive beat to the country's new rhythm.

I took the opportunity of our stop in Caracas to get in touch with friends and to find out what had happened to Picolino. These last years I had regularly sent people to visit him and take him a little money. I saw a friend who had given him a small sum from me in 1952, a sum Picolino had wanted so he could settle in La Guaira, near the port. I'd often suggested that he should come live with us at Maracaibo, but every time he replied through his friends that Caracas was the only place with doctors. It seemed that he had almost recovered his speech and that his right arm more or less worked. But now nobody knew what had become of him. He had been seen creeping about the port of La Guaira, and then he had completely disappeared. Perhaps he had taken a ship back to France. I never learned; and I have always kicked myself for not having gone to Caracas earlier to persuade him to come to me in Maracaibo.

Everything was clear: if we couldn't find what we wanted in Venezuelan Guiana, where there was this terrific boom and where General Ravard had just dynamited the burgeoning forest and its swollen streams to prove they could be tamed, we would go back and settle in Caracas.

With the De Soto full of luggage, Rita and I drove to the capital of the state, Ciudad Bolívar, on the banks of the Orinoco. After eight years I found myself once more in that charming provincial town with its kindly, welcoming people.

We spent the night at a hotel, and we had scarcely sat down on the terrace for our morning coffee when a man stopped in front of us. A man of about fifty, tall, thin and sun-dried; he had a little straw hat on his head, and he screwed up his small eyes until they almost disappeared.

"Either I'm crazy or you're a Frenchman called Papillon," he said.

"You're not very discreet, buster. Suppose this lady here didn't know?"

"Excuse me. I was so surprised I didn't even notice I was talking like a fool."

"Say no more about it: sit down here, with us."

He was an old friend, Marcel B. We talked. He was quite amazed to see me in such good shape; he felt I had done well for myself. I told him it had mostly been luck, a great deal of luck; he didn't have to tell me, poor soul, that he had not made a go of it—his clothes did the telling. I asked him to lunch.

After a few glasses of Chilean wine he said, "Yes, Madame, although you see me like this, I was a fine upstanding guy when I was young—afraid of nothing. Why, after my first break from jail I reached Canada and joined the Canadian Mounted Police, no less! I might have stayed there all my life, but one day I had a fight, and the other guy fell right onto my knife. It's God's truth, Madame Papillon. This Canadian fell right onto my knife. You don't believe me, do you? Well, I knew the Canadian police wouldn't believe me either, so I made my getaway that very minute, and going by way of the United States, I reached Paris. I must have been sold by some bum or other, because they picked me up and sent me back to the clink. That's where I knew your husband: we were good friends."

"And what are you doing now, Marcel?"

"I grow tomatoes at Los Morichales."

"Do they do well?"

"Not very. Sometimes the clouds don't let the sun come through properly. You can't see it, but it sends down invisible rays that slay your tomatoes for you in a few hours."

"Christ! How come?"

"One of the mysteries of nature, man. I don't know anything about the cause, but the result, I know that all right."

"Are there many ex-cons here?"

"About twenty."

"Happy?"

"More or less."

"Is there anything you need?"

"Papi, I swear if you hadn't said that I wouldn't have asked for a thing. But I can tell you're not doing so badly—so excuse me, Madame, but I'm going to ask for something very important."

The thought flashed through my mind, God, don't let it cost too much, and then I said, "What do you need? Speak up; Marcel."

"A pair of trousers, a pair of shoes, a shirt and a tie."

"Come on: let's get into the car."

"That's yours? Well, by God, you have had luck."

"Yes, plenty of luck."

"When are you leaving?"

"Tonight."

"Pity. Otherwise you could have driven the bridal pair in your bus."

"What bridal pair?"

"Of course! I never told you the clothes were to go to the marriage of an ex-con."

"Do I know him?"

"Don't know. He's called Maturette."

I couldn't get over it! Maturette! The little fairy who had not only made it possible for us to escape from the Saint-Laurent-du-Maroni hospital but had also traveled fifteen hundred miles with us in a boat on the open sea.

No question of leaving now. The next day we went to the wedding, where Maturette and a sweet little black girl were married. We could not do less than pay the bill and buy clothes for the three children they had produced before going to the altar. This was one of the few times I was sorry I had not been christened, because that kept me from being his best man.

Maturette lived in a poor district where the De Soto made a sensation, but still he owned a clean little brick house with a kitchen, a shower, and a dining room. He didn't tell me about his second break and I didn't tell him about mine. Just one reference to the past: "With a little more luck, we'd have been free ten years earlier."

"Yes, but our fates would have been different. I'm happy, Maturette; and you look pretty happy, too."

We parted, our throats tight with emotion, saying "Au revoir," and "See you soon."

As Rita and I drove on toward Ciudad Piar, a town springing up by an iron deposit they were getting ready to mine, I spoke about Maturette and the extraordinary ups and downs in life. He and I had been on the brink of death at sea a score of times; we had been captured and taken back to prison; and like me he had copped two years of solitary. And now as Rita and I were driving in search of some new adventure, I found him on the eve of his marriage. And to both of us at the same moment there came this thought: The past doesn't mean a thing; all that matters is what you have made of yourself.

We found nothing suitable at Ciudad Piar and went back to Caracas to look for some business that was doing well.

Very soon we found one that answered to both our abilities and our purse. It was a restaurant called the Aragon, right next to Carabobo Park, a very beautiful spot, and it was changing hands: it suited us perfectly. The beginning was tough, because the former owners came from the Canaries, and we had to change everything from top to bottom. We adopted half-French, half-Venezuelan menus and our customers increased in number every day. Among them were plenty of professional men, doctors, dentists, chemists and attorneys. Some manufacturers, too. And in this pleasant atmosphere the months went by without incident.

It was on a Monday, on June 6, 1956, to be exact, that the most wonderful news reached us: the Ministry of the Interior informed me that my request for naturalization had been granted.

It was my reward for having spent ten years in Venezuela without giving the authorities anything to criticize in the life I had led as a future citizen. On July 5, 1956, the national holiday, I was to go swear loyalty to the flag of my new country, the country that accepted me, knowing my past. There were three hundred of us there in front of the flag. Rita and Clotilde sat in the audience. It's hard to say what I felt, there were so many ideas milling about in my head and so many emotions in my heart. I remembered what the Venezuelan nation had given me—both material and spiritual help, with never a word about my past. I remembered the legend of the Iano-Mamos, Indians who live on the Brazilian frontier, the legend that says

they are the sons of Peribo, the moon. When the great
warrior Peribo was in danger of being killed by his enemies' arrows, he leapt so high to escape from death that he
rose far into the air, although he had been hit several
times. He kept on rising, and from his wounds there fell
drops of blood that turned into Iano-Mamos when they
touched the ground. Yes, I thought about that legend, and
I wondered whether Simón Bolivar, the liberator of Venezuela, had not also scattered his blood to give rise to a
race of generous, openhearted men, bequeathing to them
the best of himself.

They played the national anthem. Everybody stood up.
I stared hard at the starry flag as it rose, and tears flowed
down my cheeks.

I who had thought I should never sing another national
anthem in my life, I roared out the words of the anthem
of my new country with the others, at the top of my
voice—"*Abajo cadenas. . . .*" Down with the chains.

Yes, that day I really felt them drop off forever, the
chains I had been loaded with. Forever.

"Swear loyalty to this flag, which is now your own."

Solemnly all three hundred of us swore it; but I am
sure the one who did so with most sincerity was myself,
Papillon, the man his mother country had condemned to
worse than death for a crime he had not committed. Yes,
although France was the land that bore me, Venezuela
was my haven.

13

My Childhood

Now events moved very rapidly. As a Venezuelan I could have a passport, and I got one right away. I trembled with emotion when they handed it to me, and trembled again when I got it back from the Spanish embassy with an elegant three months' visa. I trembled when they stamped it as I went aboard the *Napoli,* the splendid liner that was taking Rita and me to Europe, to Barcelona. I trembled when the Guardia Civil gave it back to me in Spain, with the entrance visa. This passport, which had made me the citizen of a country once more, was so precious that Rita sewed a zipper on each side of my inside coat pockets so that I could not lose it, whatever happened.

Everything was beautiful during this voyage, even the sea when it was rough, even the rain when it came driving across the deck, even the ill-tempered guy in charge of the hold, who unwillingly let me go below to make sure the big Lincoln we had just bought was properly stowed. Everything was beautiful because our hearts were on holiday. Whether we were in the dining room, at the bar, or in the saloon, and whether there were people around us or not, our eyes kept meeting so we could speak without anyone's hearing—because we were going to Spain, right up by the French border, and we were going for a reason I hadn't dared to hope for these many years.

The purpose of this hurriedly prepared voyage was to let me see my family once more, on Spanish territory out of reach of the French police. It was twenty-six years since I had seen them. We were going to spend a whole month together, and they were coming as my guests.

Day after day went by, and I often went to the bow, spending a long time there, as if this part of the ship were closer to our destination. We had passed Gibraltar; we had lost sight of land again; we were getting very near.

I settled myself comfortably in a deckchair, and my eyes tried to pierce the horizon where any minute now the land of Europe would appear. The land of Spain, joined to that of France.

1930–1956: twenty-six years I had been twenty-four then; I was fifty now. A whole lifetime. My heart beat violently when at last I made out the coast. The liner ran on fast, carving a huge V in the sea, a V whose far ends spread and spread until gradually they vanished and melted into the ocean.

When I left France aboard *La Martinière,* the accursed ship that was taking us to Guiana—yes, when she steamed away from the coast, I did not see it: I did not see the land, *my land,* drawing gradually away from me forever (as I thought then), because we were in iron cages at the bottom of the hold.

And now here I was with my new passport in the pocket of my yachtsman's blazer, well protected by Rita's zipper—the passport of my new country, my other identity. Venezuelan? You, a Frenchman, born of French parents—of schoolteachers, and from the Ardèche into the bargain?

I was perhaps five when my grandfather Thierry bought me a beautiful mechanical horse. How splendid he was, my lovely stallion! Almost red; and such a mane! It was black, real horsehair, and it always hung down on the right side. I pedaled so hard that on a level surface our maid had to run to keep up with me; then she would push me up the little slope I called the hill; and so, after another level stretch, I reached the nursery school.

Madame Bonnot, the headmistress and a friend of Mama's, welcomed me in front of the school; she stroked the long curly hair that came down to my shoulders like a girl's and said to Louis the caretaker, "Open the door as wide as it will go so that Riri can ride in on his splendid horse."

I pedaled with all my strength and flew into the playground. First I made a great sweep all around it and then I gently dismounted, holding the bridle so it would not roll away. I kissed Thérèse, the maid, who handed Madame Bonnot my sandwiches. And all the other boys and girls, my friends, came to admire and stroke this wonder, the one and only mechanical horse in these two little villages, Pont-d'Ucel and Pont-d'Aubenas.

Every day before I set out, Mama told me to lend it to each one in turn; this I found rather hard, but still I did it. When the bell rang, Louis the caretaker put the horse away under the lean-to, and once we were in line we marched into school, singing, *"Nous n'irons plus au bois."*

I know my way of telling my story will make some people smile; but you have to understand that when I am talking about my childhood it is not a man of sixty-five who is writing but a kid—it is Riri of Pont-d'Ucel who writes, so deeply is that childhood imprinted on his mind, and he writes with the words he used then.

My childhood. . . . A garden with gooseberries that my sisters and I ate before they were ripe, and pears that we were forbidden to pick before Papa said we could. (By crawling like a Red Indian so that no one could see me from a window in the apartment I had my fill from the pear tree, and a bellyache afterward.)

I was eight, but still I would often go to sleep on my father's lap or in my mother's arms. Sometimes, when she tucked me into my little bed, I would half wake up, put my arms around her neck and hold her tight, and we would stay like that for what seemed to me a long, long time, our breath mingling; and at last I would go to sleep without knowing when she left me.

How beautiful Mama was! Tall, slim, always elegant. You ought to have seen how she played the piano, even when I knelt on a chair behind her music stool and closed her eyes with my little hands. Mama was never meant to be a schoolmistress. My grandfather was very rich, and Mama and her sister Léontine had been to the most expensive schools in Avignon. It was not Mama's fault that my grandfather Thierry had liked living high; her father was very kind, but because he had loved giving splendid parties in Avignon and meeting too many pretty farmers' wives, Mama had no dowry, and she was forced to earn her own living.

My grandfather was terrific. He had a little goatee and a snow-white moustache. Hand in hand we went round the farms in the morning, and as he was secretary of the *mairie* ("He has to earn his tobacco money," said Tante Léontine), he always had papers to take to the peasants or to fetch from their homes. I noticed how right my aunt was when she said he always lingered at a certain farm where the woman of the house was good-looking. I was delighted, because it was the only farm where they let me ride the little donkey and where I could meet Mireille, a girl of my age who was much better at playing papa and mama than the girl next door at Pont-d'Ucel.

Eight, and already I was beginning to fool around. Secretly I went to swim in the Ardèche. I had learned by myself in the canal; it was deep, but it was only five yards across. We had no bathing suits, of course, so we swam naked, seven or eight of us, all boys together. Oh, those sunny days in the water of my Ardèche! The trout we

caught with our hands! I never went home until I was
quite dry.

1914. The war, and Papa was called up. We went with
him as far as the train. He was going with the Chasseurs
Alpins, and he would soon be back. He said to us, "Be
good children and always obey your mother. And you
girls must help with the housework, because she is going
to look after both classes, mine and hers, all by herself.
This war won't last long; everybody says so." And standing there on the platform, the four of us watched the train
go, with my father leaning half out of the window to wave
at us a little longer. Those four years of war had no
influence on our happiness at home. We drew a little
closer to one another. I slept in the big bed with Mama; I
took the place of my father, who was fighting at the
front.

Four years in the history of the world is nothing. Four
years for a kid of eight was an eternity.

I was growing fast; we played at soldiers and at battles.
I would come home covered with bruises and with my
clothes torn, but whether I had won or lost I always came
home happy, never crying. Mama bandaged the scrapes
and put raw meat on a black eye. She would scold me a
little, but gently, never shouting. Her reproaches were
more like a whisper. "Be kind, little Riri, your mama is
tired. This class of sixty children is utterly exhausting. I
am completely worn out, you see; it's more than I can
manage. Darling, you must help me by being good and
obedient." It always ended with kisses and a promise to
behave well.

Somebody was stealing our wood, stacked under the
lean-to in the playground; and at night Mama was frightened. I cuddled close, putting my child's arm round her to
make her feel that I was a protection. "Don't be afraid,
Mama; I'm the man of the house and I'm big enough to
defend you." I took down Papa's gun and slipped two

buckshot cartridges into it—he used them for wild boar.

One night Mama woke up, shook me and whispered in my ear, "I heard the thieves. They made a noise, pulling out a log." She was sweating.

"Don't be afraid, Mama."

I got up very quietly, with the gun in my hands. With infinite care I opened the window; it squeaked a little, and I held my breath. Then, pulling the shutter toward me with one hand, I unhooked it with the barrel; holding the butt against my shoulder, ready to fire on the thieves, I pushed the shutter. It opened without a sound. The moon lit up the courtyard as though it were day, and I saw perfectly well that there was nobody at all in the playground. The heap of wood was still neatly arranged. "There's no one, Mama; come and see." And, clinging to one another, we stayed at the window for some time, both comforted by seeing there were no thieves, and Mama happy at finding that her little boy was brave.

In spite of all this happiness, I would sometimes behave badly. A cat tied by the tail to a front-door bell; the water bailiff's bicycle thrown over the bridge into the Ardèche— he had gone down to the river to catch poachers fishing with a net. And other things . . . sometimes we hunted birds with slings; and twice, when I was between ten and eleven, little Riquet Debannes and I went off into the country with Papa's gun to shoot a rabbit Riquet had seen skipping about in a field. Getting the gun in and out of the house without my mother's noticing, and twice at that, was a tremendous feat.

1917. Papa was wounded. He had many little shell splinters in his head, but his life was not in danger. The news came by the Red Cross. Twenty-four hours passed. Mama taught her class as usual—nobody knew a thing. I watched my mother, and I admired her. Normally I was in the front row in class; that day I sat at the back to keep an eye on all the pupils, determined to step in if any of them fooled about during lessons. By half past three Mama was at the end of her rope; I knew it, because we should have had natural science, but she went out, writing an arithmetic problem on the blackboard and saying, "I must go out for a few minutes: do this sum in your arithmetic books."

I went out after her; she was leaning against the mimosa just to the right of the gate. She was crying; my poor dear mama had given in.

I hugged her tight; and of course *I* did not cry. I tried to comfort her, and when she said to me, sobbing, "Your poor papa is wounded," just as if I did not know, my kid's heart found this reply, "So much the better, Mama. This way the war is over for him and we can be sure he'll come back alive." And all at once Mama realized that I was right.

"Why, that's perfectly true! You're quite right, darling; Papa will come back to us alive!"

A kiss on my forehead, a kiss on my cheek, and we went back to the classroom hand in hand.

The Spanish coast was quite visible, and I could make out the specks of white that must be houses. The coast was becoming more distinct, just like those holidays in 1917 that we spent at Saint-Chamas, where Papa had been sent to guard the powderworks. His wounds were not very serious, but the minute splinters could not be removed yet. He was classed as an auxiliary; no more front line for him.

We were all together again, full of happiness.

Mama was radiant: we had got right out of this horrible war; but for other people it was still going on, and she said to us, "Darlings, you must not be selfish and spend all your days running about and picking jujubes; you must set aside three hours a day for thinking of others."

So we went with her to the hospital, where every morning she looked after the patients and cheered them up.
Each of us had to do something useful—push a badly
wounded man in his wheelchair, lead a blind patient
about, make soft bandages, write letters or listen to what
the men confined to bed had to say about their families.

It was when we were going home in the train that
Mama felt so ill at Vogué. We went to my father's sister
at Lanas, about twenty miles from Aubenas—to Tante
Antoinette, who was a schoolmistress, too. We were kept
away from Mama, because the doctor's diagnosis was
some unknown infectious disease, presumably caught
when she was looking after the Indochinese at Saint-
Chamas. My sisters went to the Aubenas high school as
boarders and I to the boys' high school.

It seemed that Mama was getting better. But in spite of
everything I was sad, and one Sunday I refused to go out
for a walk with the others. I was alone, and I threw a
knife at a plane tree; almost every time it stuck there in
the bark.

That was how I was spending my time, in the road
almost opposite the school, low-spirited and depressed.
The road came up from the Aubenas station, some five
hundred yards away. I heard a train whistle as it came in,
and then again as it pulled out. I was not expecting
anyone, so there was no point in looking down the road to
see the people who had got out.

Tirelessly I threw my knife, on and on. My steel watch
showed that it was five o'clock. The sun was low now, and
it was getting in my eyes; so I changed sides. And it was
then that I saw death coming silently toward me.

Death's messengers, their heads bowed, their faces hidden behind black crepe veils almost down to the ground:
I knew them well in spite of their funeral trappings—
Tante Ontine, Tante Antoinette, my father's mother, and
then behind them the men, as though they were using the

women as a screen. My father, bent almost double, and my two grandfathers, all of them in black.

I did not go toward them; my blood was all gone, my heart had stopped, my eyes so longed to weep they could not bring out a single tear. The group stopped more than ten yards from me. They were afraid—or rather they were ashamed: I was certain they would sooner be dead than face me with what I already knew, because without having to utter a sound their black clothes told me, "Your mother has died."

Papa was the first to come forward; he managed to stand almost straight. His poor face was a picture of the most desperate suffering and his tears fell without ceasing; still I did not move. He did not open his arms to me; he knew very well I could not stir. At last he reached me and embraced me without a word. Then at last I burst into tears as I heard the words, "She died saying your name."

The war was over; Papa came home. A man called to see him, and they ate cheese and drank a few glasses of red wine. They enumerated the dead of our region, and then the visitor said a dreadful thing: "As for us, we came out of this war all right, eh, Monsieur Charrière? And your brother-in-law, too. We may have won nothing, but at least we lost nothing either."

I went out before he left. Night had fallen. I waited for the man to go by and then I threw a stone with my sling, hitting him full on the back of the head. He went bellowing into a neighbor's house to have his wound dressed—it was bleeding. He did not understand who could have flung the stone at him, or why. He had no idea that he had been struck for having forgotten the most important victim, the one whose loss could least be mended, in his list of the war dead. My mother.

No, we had not come out of this accursed war all right. Far from it.

Every year when the new term began, I went back as a boarder to the high school at Crest, in the Drôme, where I was preparing for the entrance exam to the Aix-en-Provence *Arts et Méitiers.**

At school I grew very tough and violent. In rugby I tackled hard: I asked no favors and I certainly gave none either.

Six years now I had been a boarder at Crest, six years of being an excellent pupil, particularly in mathematics; but also six years with no marks for good behavior. I was in all the roughest stuff that went on. Once or twice a month, always on Thursdays, I had a fight: Thursday was the day the boys' parents came to see them.

The mothers came to take their sons out to lunch, and then, if it was a fine afternoon, they would stroll about with their boys under the chestnut trees in our playground. Every week I swore I would not watch from the library window; but it was no good. I just had to settle down in a place from where I could see everything. And from my window I discovered that there were two sorts of attitudes, both of which made me furiously angry.

There were some boys whose mothers were plain or badly dressed or looked like peasants. Those fellows had the air of being ashamed of them, the swine, the dirty little creeps! It was perfectly obvious. Instead of going right round the courtyard or walking from one end to the other, they would sit on a bench in the corner and never move. The rascals had already got some idea of what educated, distinguished people were like, and they wanted to forget their origins before they were *Arts et Métiers* engineers.

---

* Roughly equivalent to a college of industrial design and engineering.

It wasn't hard to pick a quarrel with that type. If I saw one send his embarrassing mother away early and come into the library, I would lay into him at once. "Say, Pierrot, why did you make your mother go so soon?"

"She was in a hurry."

"That's not true; your mother takes the train for Gap at seven. I'll tell you why you sent her off: it's because you're ashamed of her. And don't you dare tell me that's not true, you jerk!"

In these fights I nearly always came out on top. I fought so often that I became very good with my fists. Even when I got more than I gave, I didn't give a damn—I almost liked it. But I never went for a weaker boy.

The other kids that sent me into a rage, the kids I fought most savagely, were the ones I called the swaggerers. These were the guys with pretty, well-dressed, distinguished mothers. When you are sixteen or seventeen you are proud of showing off a mother like that, and they would strut about the yard, holding her arm and mincing and simpering until it drove me mad.

Whenever one of them swaggered too much for my liking, or if his mother had a way of walking that reminded me of my own, or if she wore gloves and took them off and held them gracefully in one hand, then I couldn't bear it: I went out of my mind with fury.

The minute the culprit came in I went for him. "You don't have to parade about like that, you big ape; not with a mother dressed in last year's fashions. Mine was better looking, brighter and more distinguished than yours. Her jewels were real, not phony like your mother's. Such trash! Even a guy who knows nothing about it can see that right away."

Naturally, most of the guys didn't even wait for me to finish before hitting me in the face. Sometimes the first swipe would go right to my head. I fought rough: butting, mule-kicking, using my elbows in the infighting; and joy welled up inside me, as though I were smashing all the mothers who dared to be as pretty and fine-looking as my mama.

I really could not control it; ever since my mother's death when I was nearly eleven, I'd had this red-hot fury inside me. You can't understand death when you are eleven: you can't accept it. The very old might die, maybe. But your mother, full of youth and beauty and health, how can she die?

It was because of a fight of this kind that my life changed completely.

The guy was a pretentious asshole, proud of being nineteen, proud of his success in math. Tall, very tall; no good at games because he studied all the time, but very strong. One day, when we were going for a walk, he lifted a massive treetrunk all by himself so that we could get at the hole where a field mouse was hiding.

And this fellow had really let himself go that particular Thursday. A tall, slim mother, in a white dress with blue polka dots. If she had been trying to imitate one of Mama's dresses she couldn't have done better. Big black eyes; a pretty little hat with a white tulle veil.

And this engineer-to-be swaggered about the courtyard the whole of that afternoon, up and down, to and fro, round and round. Often they kissed; they were almost like lovers.

As soon as he was alone I started on him. "Well, you're the wonder of the world, all right. You're as good at putting on a circus act as you are at math. I didn't know you were such a . . ."

"What's wrong with you, Henri?"

"What's wrong with me is that I just have to tell you that you show your mother like they show a bear in a circus, to amaze your buddies. Well, get this: I'm not amazed. Because your mother is just nothing at all compared with mine: she takes after the showy tarts I've seen during the season at Vals-les-Bains."

"Take that back, or I'll spoil your face for you; and you know I hit hard. You know I'm stronger than you."

"Trying to get out of it, eh? Listen: I know you're stronger than me. So to balance things, we'll have a duel. Each with compasses. Go and fetch yours and I'll fetch mine. If you're not a shit and if you can stand up for yourself, I'll be waiting for you behind the john in five minutes."

"I'll be there."

A few minutes later he went down, my compass point buried deep just under his heart.

I was seventeen when my father and I saw the examining magistrate in charge of my case. He told my father that the only way to stop the proceedings was to make me join the navy. At the gendarmerie of Aubenas I signed on for three years.

My father did not really reproach me for the serious thing I had done. "If I understand rightly, Henri," he said—he called me Henri when he meant to be severe—"and I believe what you say, you suggested fighting with a weapon because your opponent was stronger than you?"

"Yes, Papa."

"Well, you did wrong. That is the way ruffians fight. And you are not a ruffian, my boy."

"No."

"Look at the mess you have got yourself into. Think of how you must have hurt your mother."

"I don't think I hurt her."

"Why not, Henri?"

"It was her I was fighting for."

"What do you mean?"

"I mean I can't bear seeing other boys flaunt their mothers at me."

"I will tell you something, Henri: it was not for your mama that this fight and all the others before it came about. It was not out of real love for her. The reason is that you are selfish; because fate took your mother from you, you would like it to be the same for all the other boys.

"If you were really a reflection of your mother's heart, you would be happy at the happiness of others. Now, see, in order to get out of this you have to join the navy: three years at least, and they are not going to be easy ones. I am going to be punished, too, since for three years my son is going to be far away from me." And then he said something that has always remained engraved on my heart: "You know, my dear boy, you can become an orphan at any age. Remember that all your life."

The *Napoli*'s siren made me jump. It wiped out that remote past, those pictures of my eighteenth year, when my father and I walked out of the gendarmerie where I had just enlisted. But immediately afterward there rose up the unhappiest memory of them all, the moment when I saw him for the very last time.

It was in one of those grim visiting rooms at the Santé prison—each of us in a barred box separated by a corridor a yard wide. I was racked by shame and disgust for what my life had been and for what had brought my father here into this wild-beast cage.

He had not come to reproach me for being suspect number one in a dirty underworld job. He had the same ravaged face I had seen the day he told me of my mother's death, and he had come into this prison of his own accord to see his boy for half an hour, not to condemn his bad behavior or to make him understand what this business meant for his family's honor and peace of mind, or to say, "You are a bad son," but to beg my forgiveness for not having succeeded in bringing me up properly. What he said was the last thing I should ever have expected, the one thing that could touch my heart more deeply than all the reproaches in the world: "I believe, Riri, that it is through my fault that you are here. Forgive me for having spoiled you too much."

Nothing could have been more hostile than the iron discipline of the navy in 1923. The ratings were classed in six categories, according to their level of education. I was in the top, the sixth. And this seventeen-year-old boy, just out of the class preparing for the *Arts et Métiers,* could not understand or adapt himself to blind, instant obedience to orders given by quartermasters belonging to the lowest intellectual level.

I was in trouble right away. I could not obey orders that had no rhyme or reason. I refused to go on any specialized course, the normal thing for a man with my education, and I was at once classed among the *estrasses,* the undisciplined, the no-good "unspecialized" types.

We were the ones who had all the nastiest, dullest, stupidest jobs. Potato peeling, head cleaning, brass polishing all day long, coal shoveling, deck swabbing: all for us.

"What the hell are you doing there, hiding behind the smoke-stack?"

"We have finished swabbing the deck, quartermaster."

"Is that right? Well, just you start again, and this time swab it from aft forward. And if it's not cleaner this time, you'll hear from me."

A sailor is a fine sight, with his pompom, his jersey with its wide blue collar, his slightly tilted cap as flat as a pancake and his uniform made to fit properly. But we good-for-nothings were not allowed to have our things recut. The worse we were dressed and the drearier we looked, the better the quartermasters were pleased. In an atmosphere like this a rebel never stops thinking up offenses. Every time we were alongside a quay, for example, we stole ashore and spent the night in the town. Where did we go? To the brothels, of course. With a friend or two I would fix things in no time at all. Right away each of us had our whore; and we not only made love for free but would also get a bill or two for a drink or a meal from our women.

The punishments became more frequent. Fifteen days' detention; then thirty. To get back at a cook who refused us a bit of meat and a crust after the potato-peeling detail, we stole a whole leg of mutton, done to a turn, fishing it out with a hook we slid down a ventilator over the stove when he had his back turned; we ate it in the coal bunker. Result: forty-five days in the naval prison; in the middle of winter I was stark naked in the Toulon prison yard, opposite a washhouse with its huge tub of icy water, into which we had to plunge.

It was a seaman's cap not worth ten francs that brought me up before the disciplinary board. Charge: destruction of naval property.

In the navy, everybody changed the shape of his cap. Not destructively—it was a question of being well turned out. You first wetted it, and then three of you would pull as hard as possible, so that when you put a piece of whalebone around inside, it was as flat as a pancake. "It's terrific, a regular flat cap," said the girls. Particularly a cap with a pretty carrot-colored pompom on it, carefully trimmed with scissors. All the girls in the town knew it brought good luck to touch a pompom, and that you had to pay for touching it with a kiss.

The master-at-arms was a thickheaded brute—I became his pet aversion. He never left me in peace; he kept after me night and day. So much so that three times I went awol. Never more than five days and twenty-three hours, though, because at six days you were put down as a deserter. And a deserter I very nearly was at Nice. I'd spent the night with a terrific girl and woke up late. One more hour and I should have been on the list. I scrambled into my clothes and left at a run, looking for a cop to get myself arrested. I caught sight of one, hurried over to him and asked him to arrest me. He was a fat, kindly old soul. "Come now, boy, don't fly into a panic. Just you go back quietly to your ship and tell them all about it. We've all been young once."

I told him one hour more and I was a deserter; but it was no good, he wouldn't listen. So I picked up a stone, turned to a shop window and said to the cop, "If you don't arrest me, I'll smash this window in one second flat."

"The boy's crazy. Come along, young fellow; the station for you."

But it was for having stretched a cap to make it prettier that they sent me to the disciplinary sections at Calvi, in Corsica. No one can doubt that this was my first step toward the penal settlement.

They called the disciplinary section *la camise,* and you had a special uniform. As soon as you got there you went in front of a reception committee, and they decided whether you were to be rated a genuine *camisard*. You had to prove you were a man by fighting two or three seniors one after another. With my training at the Crest high school, I did pretty well. During the second fight, when my lip was split and my nose a bleeding mess, the seniors stopped the test. I was rated genuine *camisard*.

La camise. I worked in a Corsican senator's vineyards from sunrise to sunset: no break, no little favors; the difficult sort had to be brought to heel. We weren't even sailors anymore: we belonged to the 173 Infantry Regiment at Bastia. I can still see that citadel at Calvi, our three-mile walk, pick or shovel on our shoulder, to Calenzana, where we worked, and our quick march back to the

prison. It was unendurable, we rebelled; and as I was one
of the ringleaders, I was sent, along with a dozen others,
to a still tougher disciplinary camp at Corte.

A citadel right up on top of the mountain: six hundred
steps to go up and down twice a day to work at making a
playing field for the enlisted men near the station.

It was when I was in that hell, with that herd of brutes,
that a civilian from Corte secretly passed me a note:
"Darling, if you want to get out of that horrible place, cut
off your thumb. The law is that the loss of a thumb, with
or without preservation of the metacarpal, automatically
brings about transfer to the auxiliaries; and if this injury is
caused by an accident in the course of duty, it brings
about permanent incapacity for armed services and therefore discharge. Law of 1831, circular of July 23, 1883. I
am waiting for you. Clara. Address, Le Moulin Rouge,
Quartier Réservé, Toulon."

I did not delay. Our work consisted of digging about
two cubic yards of earth out of the mountain every day
and wheeling it off in barrows to a place fifty yards away,
where trucks took away everything that wasn't needed for
leveling the ground. We worked in teams of two. I must
not cut off my thumb with an edged tool, or I should be
accused of self-mutilation, and that would cost me another
five years of *la camise*.

My Corsican mate, Franqui, and I started on the
mountain at the bottom, and we dug a fair-sized cave into
it. One more blow with the pick and everything above
would fall in on me. The supervising NCOs were tough:
Sergeant Albertini was just two or three yards behind us.
This made the job tricky but also afforded one advantage—
if all went well, he would be an impartial witness.

Franqui put a big stone with a fairly sharp edge under
an overhanging piece; I laid my left thumb on it and
stuffed my handkerchief into my mouth so as not to let
out the least sound. There would be five or six seconds for

us to bring the whole mass of earth down on me. Franqui was going to smash my thumb with another stone weighing about twenty pounds: it could not fail. They would be forced to amputate it even if the blow did not take it off entirely.

The sergeant was three yards away from us, scraping earth off his boots. Franqui grasped the stone, lifted it up as high as it would go and brought it down. My thumb was a shattered mess. The sound of the blow mingled with the noise of the pickaxes all round, and the sergeant saw nothing. Two swings with the pick and the earth came down all over me. I let myself be buried. Bellowing, shouts for help: they dug for me and at last I appeared, covered with earth and my thumb destroyed. And I was suffering like a soul in hell. Still, I did manage to say to the sergeant, "They'll say I did it on purpose: you see."

"No, Charrière. I saw the accident: I'm a witness. I'm tough but I'm fair. I'll tell them what I saw, never you fear."

Two months later, discharged with a pension and with my thumb buried at Calvi, I was transferred to the No. 5 Depot at Toulon, and there they let me go.

I went to say thank you to Clara at the Moulin Rouge. She was of the opinion that nobody would even notice the absence of a thumb on my left hand, and that I could make love as well with four fingers as with five. That's what really mattered.

"You've changed in some way, Riri, I can't quite tell how. I hope your three months with those undesirables have not left too many traces."

There I was with my father in my childhood home: I had hurried back after my discharge. Was there some deep change in me? "I can't tell you, Papa: I don't know. I think I'm more violent and less willing to obey the rules of life you taught me when I was a little boy. You must be right: something has changed in me. I feel it, being here in this house, where we were so happy with Mama and my sisters. It doesn't hurt as much as it used to. I must have grown harder."

"What are you going to do?"

"What do you advise?"

"Find a position as soon as possible. You're twenty now, my boy."

Two exams. One at Privas for the post office; the other at Avignon for a civilian job in the military administration. Grandfather Thierry went with me.

Both the written and the oral parts went very well. I was playing the game; I had no objection to following my father's advice—I'd be a civil servant and lead a proper, honorable life. But now I can't help wondering how long the young Charrière would have stayed a civil servant with everything that was boiling up inside him.

When the morning post brought the results of the exam, my delighted papa decided to have a little party in my honor. A huge cake, a bottle of real champagne and a colleague's daughter invited to the feast. "She would make a fine wife for my boy." For the first time for ten years, the house bubbled with joy.

I walked around the garden with the girl Papa dreamed of as a daughter-in-law, a girl who might make his little boy happy. She was pretty, well brought up and very intelligent.

Two months later, the bombshell! "Since you have not been able to provide our central office with a good-conduct certificate from the navy, we regret to inform you that you cannot enter our service."

After the letter came, shattering all his illusions, Papa was sad, saying very little. He was suffering.

Why go on like this? Quick, a suitcase and a few clothes: take advantage of the teachers' meeting at Aubenas and get out.

My grandmother caught me on the stairs. "Where are you going, Henri?"

"I'm going somewhere where they won't ask me for a good-conduct certificate from the navy. I'm going to see one of the men I knew in the disciplinary sections at Calvi, and he'll teach me how to live outside this society I was stupid enough to believe in—a society that knows very well I can expect nothing from it. I'm going to Paris, to Montmartre, Grandmother."

"What are you going to do?"

"I don't know yet, but certainly no good. Good-bye, Grandmother. Give Papa a big kiss from me."

We were getting close to the land, and now we could even see the windows of the houses. I was coming back after a very, very long journey to see my people: to see them after twenty-six years.

For them, I was dead; for their children, I had never existed—my name had never been pronounced. Or perhaps just a few times, when they were alone with Papa. It was only during these last five years that they must gradually have given their kids some idea of Uncle Henri, who lived in Venezuela.

We had corresponded for five years; but even so wouldn't they be afraid of what people might say? Wouldn't they feel rather nervous about meeting an escaped ex-convict at a rendezvous in Spain?

I did not want them to come out of duty; I wanted them to come with their hearts full of genuine feeling for me.

Ah, but if they only knew . . . if they only knew—the coast was coming nearer slowly now, but how it had raced away from me twenty-six years ago—if they only knew how I had been with them all the time during those fourteen years of prison!

If only my sisters could see all the visions of our

childhood I made for myself in the cells and the wild-beast cages of the Réclusion!

If only they knew how I kept myself going with them and with all those who made up our family, drawing from them the strength to beat the unbearable, to find peace in the midst of despair, to forget being a prisoner, to reject suicide—if they only knew how the months, days, hours, minutes and seconds of those years of total solitude and utter silence had been filled to overflowing with the smallest events of our wonderful childhood!

The coast drew nearer and nearer; we saw Barcelona: we were about to enter its harbor. I had a wild desire to cup my hands and shout, with all my strength, "Hey there! I'm coming! Come as fast as you can!" just as I used to call out to them when we were children in the fields of Fabras and I had found a great patch of violets.

"What are you doing here, darling? I've been looking for you this last hour. I even went down to the car."

Without getting up I put my arm round Rita's waist; she bent down and gave me a little kiss on the cheek. Only then did I realize that, although I was going to meet my people full of self-questioning and full of questions to ask as well there in my arms was my own private family that I had founded and that had brought me to this point. I said, "Darling. I was living over the past again as I watched the land come closer, the land that holds my people, the living and the dead."

Barcelona: our gleaming car on the quay with all the baggage neatly in the trunk. We did not stay the night in the great city; we were impatient to drive on through the sunlit countryside toward the French frontier. But after two hours my feelings overcame me so that I had to pull in to the side of the road—I could not go on.

I got out of the car: my eyes were dazzled with looking at this landscape, these plowed fields, huge plane trees, trembling reeds, the thatched or tiled roofs of the farms and cottages, the poplars singing in the wind, the meadows with every possible shade of green, the cows with the bells tinkling as they grazed, the vines—ah, the vines with their leaves that could not hide all the grapes. This piece of Catalonia was exactly the same as all my French gardenlike landscapes: all this was mine and had been mine since I was born; it was among these same colors, these same growing things, these same crops that I had wandered hand in hand with my grandfather; it was through fields like these that I had carried my father's game bag when he went shooting and when we urged our bitch Clara to startle a rabbit or flush a covey of partridges. Even the fences around the farms were the same as they were at home! And the little irrigation canals with their planks set across here and there to guide the water into one field or another; I did not have to go up to them to know there were frogs that I could bring out, as many as I wanted, with a hook baited with a piece of red cloth, as I had done so often as a child.

And I quite forgot that this vast plain was Spanish, so exactly was it like the valley of the Ardèche or the Rhone.

We stopped at the hotel nearest the French frontier. The next day Rita took the train to fetch Tante Ju from Saint-Peray. I should have gone myself, but for the French police I was still a man who had escaped from Guiana. While Rita was away I found a very fine house at Rosas, right on the edge of the beach.

A few more minutes of waiting, Papi, and then you will see Tante Ju step out of the train, the woman who loved your father, and who wrote you such beautiful letters, bringing back to life your memories of those who loved you and whom you loved so much.

It was Rita who got out first. As carefully as a daughter, she helped her tall companion climb down to the platform. And then two big arms enfolded me, two big arms pressed me to her bosom, two big arms conveying the warmth of life and a thousand things that cannot be expressed in words. And it was with one arm around Rita and the other around my second mother that I walked out of the station quite forgetting that suitcases do not come with their owners unless they are carried.

It was eleven in the morning when Rita and Tante Ju arrived, and it was three the next morning when Tante Ju went to her bedroom, worn out by the journey, by her age, by emotion and by sixteen hours of uninterrupted exchange of memories.

I fell into my bed and went straight to sleep, exhausted, without a breath of energy to keep me awake. The outburst of urgent happiness is as shattering as the worst disaster.

My two women were up before me, and it was they who pulled me out of my deep sleep to tell me it was eleven in the morning, that the sun was shining, the sky blue, the sand warm, that breakfast was waiting for me and that I should eat it quickly so as to go to the frontier to fetch my sister and her tribe, who were to be there in two hours. "Rather earlier," said Tante Ju, "because your brother-in-law will have been forced to drive fast, to keep the family from bullying him, they are so eager to see you."

I parked the Lincoln right next to the Spanish frontier post.

Here they were! They were on foot, running—they had abandoned my brother-in-law in his Citroën back there in the line by the French customs.

First came my sister Hélène, her arms out. She ran across the stretch of no-man's-land from the one post to the other, from France to Spain. I went toward her, my guts tied up with emotion. At four yards we stopped to look one another right in the face. Our tear-dimmed eyes said, "It is really her, my childhood Nène" and "It is really him, my little brother Riri from long ago." And we flung ourselves into each other's arms. Strange. For me this fifty-year-old sister was as she had always been. I did not see her aging face; I saw nothing except that the brilliant animation of her eyes was still the same and that for me her features had not altered.

Our embrace lasted so long we forgot all about the others. Rita had already kissed the children. I heard "How pretty you are, Aunt!" and I turned, left my Nène, and thrust Rita into her arms, saying, "Love her dearly, because it is she who has brought me to you all."

My three nieces were splendid and my brother-in-law was in great form. The only one missing was his eldest boy, Jacques, who had been called up for the war in Algeria.

We left for Rosas, the Lincoln in front, with my sister at my side. I shall never forget that first meal, with us all sitting at a round table. There were times when my legs trembled so that I had to take hold of them under the cloth.

1930—1956. So many, many things had happened, both for them and for me. I did not talk about the penal settlement during the meal. I just asked my brother-in-law whether my being found guilty had caused them a great deal of trouble and unpleasantness. He reassured me kindly, but I could feel how much they must have suffered, having a convict as brother and brother-in-law.

No, I said nothing about prison, and I said nothing about my trial. For them and, I sincerely believe, for me, too, my life began the day when, thanks to Rita, I buried my old self, the man on the loose, to bring Henri Charrière back to life, the son of the Ardèche schoolteachers.

That August on the sands of Rosas beach went by too fast. I rediscovered the cries of my childhood, the laughter with no cause the outbursts of joy of my young days on the beach of Palavas, where we used to go with my parents.

One month: thirty days. How long it is in a cell alone with oneself and how terribly short it is with one's own people. I was literally drunk with happiness. Not only had I my sister and my brother-in-law again, but I had also discovered new people to love—my nieces, unknown only the other day, and now almost daughters to me.

Rita was radiant with joy at seeing me so happy. Bringing us together at last, out of reach of the French police, was the finest present she could have given either them or me. I lay on the beach; it was very late—midnight perhaps. Rita was stretched out on the sand, too, with her head against my thigh; I stroked her hair. "They all fly away tomorrow. How quickly it has passed; but how wonderful it was! One must not ask too much, darling, I know; but still I'm sad at having to part from them. God knows when we'll see one another again. A journey like this costs so much."

"Trust in the future: I'm sure we'll see them again one day."

We went with them as far as the frontier. They were taking Tante Ju in their car. A hundred yards from the French border we parted. There were no tears, because I told them of my faith in the future—in a couple of years we should spend not one month of holiday together but two.

"Is it true, what you say, Uncle?"

"Of course, darlings, of course."

A week later my other sister landed at Barcelona airport, by herself. She had not been able to bring her family. Among the forty-odd passengers coming off the plane I recognized her at once, and after she had passed through customs she came straight toward me without the least hesitation.

Three days and three nights—she could spend only a little while with us, so since we did not want to lose a minute, it was three days and three nights of memories almost without a pause. She and Rita liked one another at once, so we could tell one another everything—she her whole life story and me all that could be told.

Two days later Rita's mother arrived from Tangiers. With her two fine, gentle hands on my cheeks she kissed me tirelessly, saying, "My son, I am so happy that you love Rita and that she loves you." Her face shone with a serene beauty in its halo of white hair.

We stayed in Spain too long, our happiness hiding the days that passed. We could not go back by boat—sixteen days was more than we could spare—so we flew (the Lincoln coming later by ship), because our business was waiting.

Still, we did make a little tour of Spain, and there in the hanging gardens of Granada, that wonder of the Arab civilization, I read these words of a poet, cut into the stone at the foot of the Marador tower: *Dale limosna, mujer, que no hay en la vida nada como la pena de ser ciego en Granada;* give him alms, woman, because there is no greater sadness in life than being blind in Granada.

Yes, there is something worse than being blind in Granada, and that is being twenty-four, full of health and trust in life, undisciplined, maybe, and even a little dishonest, but not really corrupt through and through or at least not a killer, and to hear yourself condemned to a life sentence for another man's crime: a sentence that means vanishing forever without appeal, without hope, condemned to rot bodily and mentally, without one chance in a hundred thousand of ever raising your head and being a man again someday.

How many men whom a pitiless justice and an inhuman penitentiary system have crushed and destroyed inch by inch would have preferred to be blind in Granada!

14

The Revolution

The plane we had boarded at Madrid came down gently at Maiquetía, the Caracas airport, and there was our daughter waiting for us, together with some friends. Twenty minutes later we were back home. The dogs welcomed us enthusiastically, and our Indian maid, who was one of the family, never stopped asking, "And how are Henri's people. Señora? And Henri, what did you think of Rita's mama? I was afraid you would never come back, with all those people over there to love you. Thanks be to God, here you are, all in one piece."

The struggle for life went on. We sold the restaurant: I had begun to have enough of steak and french fries, *canard à l'orange* and *coq au vin*. We bought an all-night joint, the Caty-Bar.

In Caracas an all-night bar is a place where the customers are all men, because it has its own girls to keep them company, talk to them and, even more, listen to them, drink with them, and if they are not very thirsty, help them on a little. It's quite a different kind of life from that of the day, much more intense and not in the least peaceful; but it is one where every night you discover something new and interesting.

Senators, deputies, bankers, lawyers, officers and high officials hurried in at night to let off the steam that had piled up during the day, when they had to keep a hold on themselves and maintain an image of perfectly virtuous behavior in their various jobs. And at the Caty-Bar each one showed himself as he really was. It was a bursting out of the social hypocrisy they were forced to observe, a refuge from business or family worries.

For these few hours every single one of them grew young again. With alcohol lending them a hand, they threw off their social chains and started right in on a life that left them free to shout and argue and play the Don Juan with the prettiest girls in the bar. In our place things never went further than that, because Rita ran the bar very strictly and no woman was allowed out during working hours. But all the men enjoyed the presence of these girls who were kind enough to listen when they talked (they loved that) and to fill their hours of freedom with beauty and youth.

How often I have seen them at daybreak, all alone (because the girls left by another door), but nevertheless happy and easier in their minds. One was an important businessman who was always at his desk by nine; he was a regular customer, and I used to walk to his car with him. He would put his hand on my shoulder, and waving the other arm toward the mountains of Caracas, sharp against the early-morning sky, he would say, "The night is over, Enrique, the sun is going to rise behind the Avila. No hope of going anywhere else—everything is shut; and with the daylight we come face to face with our responsibilities. Work, the office, the slavery of every day is waiting for me; but how could we go on without these nights?"

Very soon I had another place, the Madrigal, and then

a third, the Normandy. Together with Gonzalo Durand, a Socialist and an opponent of the régime who was ready night and day to defend the interests of nightclub, bar and restaurant owners, we formed an association for the protection of places of this kind. Some time later I was made president, and we defended our members as well as we could against the abuses of certain officials.

I turned the Madrigal into a Russian joint, calling it the Ninotchka; and by way of adding to the local color I dressed a Spaniard from the Canaries as a Cossack and perched him on a horse I knew was placid because of its great age. The two of them were to act as porters. But the customers started giving the Cossack drinks—he was bored stiff at half a dollar an hour—and, what was worse, they did not slight the horse either. Of course, the horse couldn't knock back glasses of whisky, but it dearly loved sugar dipped in liqueur, particularly kümmel. Result: when the old horse was drunk, and the Cossack tight as a drum, they would tear off down our street, the Avenida Miranda, an important artery crammed with traffic, galloping right and left, the Spaniard shrieking, "Charge! Charge!" You can just imagine the scene: brakes jammed on so hard they almost tore up the asphalt, cars banging into one another, drivers bawling, windows opening and angry voices shouting about the din at that time of night.

To top it all, although I had only a single musician, he was not one of the ordinary kind. He was a German named Kurt Lowendal; he had a boxer's hands and he played the cha-cha on his organ with such zeal that the walls trembled even up to the ninth floor. I could hardly believe it, but the concierge and the owner took me up with them one evening to see, and they weren't exaggerating.

My other joint, the Normandy, was really beautifully

placed—right opposite police headquarters. On one side of the street, terror and grilling, and on the other the gaiety of life. For once I was on the right side. Not that that prevented me from making things tricky for myself: I did the most dangerous thing I could—I acted as a secret post office for the prisoners, both political and criminal.

1958. For some months now things had been on the move in Venezuela: Pérez Jiménez's dictatorship was limping badly. Even the privileged classes were dropping away from him, and the only supporters he had left were the army and the Seguridad Nacional, the terrible political police, who were making more and more arrests.

Meanwhile, in New York, the three most important political leaders, all in exile, had worked out their plan for seizing power. These were Rafael Caldera, Jóvito Villalba and Rómulo Betancourt. On January 1 an air force general, Castro Leon, tried to get his men to revolt, and a small group of pilots dropped a few bombs on Caracas, particularly on Pérez Jiménez's presidential palace. The operation failed, and Castro Leon fled to Colombia.

But at two A.M. on January 23, a plane flew over Caracas. It was Pérez Jiménez going off with his family, his closest associates and part of his fortune—a cargo of such value in people and wealth that the Venezuelans christened the plane *The Holy Cow*. Pérez Jiménez knew he had lost the game—the army had abandoned him, after ten years of dictatorship. His plane flew straight to Santo Domingo, where another dictator, General Trujillo, could only welcome his colleague.

For almost three weeks there were no police in the streets. Of course, there was pillaging and violence, but only against Pérez Jiménez's supporters. A nation was bursting out after being muzzled for ten years. The Seguridad Nacional's headquarters, opposite the Normandy, was attacked, and most of its members killed.

During the three days that followed the departure of Pérez Jiménez I very nearly lost the result of twelve years' work. Several people telephoned to tell me that all the bars, nightclubs, luxury restaurants and places frequented by the top supporters of Pérez Jiménez were being broken into and sacked. We had our apartment on the floor above the Caty-Bar. Our building was a little villa at the bottom of a blind alley, with the bar at street level, then our living quarters and then a flat roof over that.

I was determined to defend my house, my business and my people. I got hold of twenty bottles of gasoline, made them into Molotov cocktails and lined them up neatly on the roof. Rita would not leave me: she was at my side with a lighter in her hand.

Then they came! A crowd of pillagers—more than a hundred of them. Since the Caty-Bar was in a blind alley, anyone who came along it was coming to us.

They came closer and among the shouts I heard, "This is one of the Pérezjiménists' places! Sack it!" They broke into a run, waving iron bars and shovels. I lit the lighter.

Suddenly the crowd halted. Four men with their arms stretched out were strung across the alley: they stopped the overexcited mob. I heard them say, "We are workers, we belong to the people, and we are revolutionaries, too. We've known these people for years. Enrique, the boss, is a Frenchman, and he's a friend of the people—he's proved it to us hundreds of times. Get out, there's nothing for you to do here."

They began to argue, but more quietly, and I heard these splendid men explain why they were defending us. It lasted a good twenty minutes, with Rita and me still on the roof, holding the lighter. The four must have persuaded them to leave us in peace, because the mob withdrew without any threats.

Lord, that was a close one! A close one for a good many of them, too, I may say. None of them ever came back.

These four men of the people, our defenders, worked for the Caracas Water Company. And it so happened that the side door of the Caty-Bar, down at the bottom of the alley, was right next to the entrance to the company's depot, the gate the tankers used when they went to supply places that were short of water. We often gave the men who worked there something to eat, and if they came for a bottle of Coke we said there was nothing to pay. Because of the dictatorship they almost never talked politics, but sometimes, when they had had a drink, a few would let out an incautious word—it was overheard and reported. Then they were either imprisoned or sacked.

Often either Rita or I had been able to get one of our customers to have the culprit let out or given back his job. In any case, among the senators, deputies and officers belonging to the régime, a good many were very kind and obliging. There were few who would not do a favor.

On that day the Water Company's men paid their debt to us, and they paid it with very great courage, because the mob was in no laughing mood. And the most extraordinary thing was that the same miracle happened for our two other places. Not a pane of glass smashed at the Ninotchka. Nothing, absolutely nothing destroyed and nothing stolen at the Normandy, right opposite the terrible Seguridad Nacional, the hottest spot of the whole revolution, with machine guns firing in all directions and revolutionaries burning and pillaging the shops right, left and center all along the Avenida Mejico.

Under Pérez Jiménez, nobody had argued; nobody had done anything but obey. The press was muzzled.

Under his successor, Admiral Larrazábal, everybody danced, sang, disobeyed to his heart's content, spoke or wrote anything that came into his head, drunk with joy at being able to sling bullshit in total freedom, with no inhibitions.

The sailor was a poet into the bargain, an artist at heart, sensitive to the wretched position and poverty of the thousands of people who came flooding into Caracas, wave after wave of them, as soon as the dictator had fallen. He thought up the Emergency Plan, which handed out millions from the national funds to these unfortunate souls.

He promised that there should be elections. More than true to his word, he prepared them very fairly; but although the admiral got in at Caracas, it was Betancourt who won the election. Betancourt had to face up to a tricky situation—not a day went by without some plot's being hatched, not a single day without his having to win a battle against the forces of reaction.

I had just bought the biggest café in Caracas, the Grand Café in the Gran Sabana: over four hundred seats. This was the café where Julot Huignard, the guard of Levy's jewelry shop, had said we should meet when we were in the corridor of the Santé way back in 1931. "Keep your spirits up, Pap! We'll meet at the Grand Café in Caracas." Here I was at the rendezvous, twenty-eight years later, to be sure, but still here—and I owned it. But Huignard had not kept the appointment.

The political state of the country did not make Betancourt's job an easy one. A vile, cowardly attempt on his life suddenly upset the still youthful democracy. Under the remote control of Trujillo, the dictator of Santo Domingo, a car stuffed with explosives went off right by the president as he was driving to an official ceremony. The head of the military household was killed, the chauffeur very badly wounded; General Lopez Henriquez and his wife were horribly burned, and the president himself had his forearms painfully injured by the flames. Twenty-four hours later, with his hands bandaged, he addressed the Venezuelan nation. It seemed so unbelievable that some people claimed the man who spoke was his double.

In such an atmosphere Venezuela, too, though blessed by the gods, began to be attacked by the virus of political passion. There were cops everywhere, and among the officials, there were some who made evil use of their political connections.

Officials belonging to different ministries came and badgered me many times. Inspectors of every kind appeared: inspectors of drinks, of municipal taxes, of this and of that. Most of them had had no training and held the job only because they belonged to some political party or other.

What's more, since the government knew about my past, and since I was inevitably in contact with various crooks who passed through even though I had nothing to do with them in the way of business, and since on top of that I had been granted asylum here while proceedings against me were still in force in France, the pigs took advantage of my position to carry out a kind of blackmail. For example, they dug up the case of a Frenchman murdered two years back, in which the killer had never been found. Did I know anything about it? I knew nothing? Wasn't it in my interest, considering my position, to know a little?

Oh, this was beginning to be a splendid party, this was. I had had about enough of these bastards. It might not be very serious for the moment, but if it went on and I blew up, God only knew what would happen. No, I couldn't blow my stack here, not in this country that had given me my chance of being a free man once more and of making a home for myself.

There was no point in going round and round the mulberry bush: I sold the Grand Café and the other joints, and Rita and I went off to Spain. Maybe I'd be able to start some kind of business there.

But I couldn't get going. The European countries are too well organized. In Madrid, when I had obtained the first thirteen permits to open a business, they kindly told me I needed a fourteenth. It seemed to me that that was just one too many. And Rita, seeing that I was literally incapable of living far from Venezuela and that I missed even the jackasses who badgered me, agreed that although we had sold everything, we should go back there.

15

Camarones

Caracas once more. This was 1961, and sixteen years had passed since El Dorado. Nightlife had changed a great deal in Caracas, and finding a joint as clean, attractive and important as the Grand Café was impossible. A ridiculous new law held that the people who had bars and sold alcoholic drinks corrupted public morals—which meant all kinds of abuses and exploitation on the part of certain officials, and I didn't want to get back into that racket at all.

Something else was needed. I discovered not a mine of diamonds but a mine of very big shrimp, the kind called *camarones* and even bigger ones called *langostinos*. And all this was back at Maracaibo once again.

We settled down in an elegant apartment: I bought a stretch of shore and founded a company called the Capitan Chico, after the district that included my beach. Sole shareholder, Henri Charrière; manager, Henri Charrière; director of operations, Henri Charrière; chief assistant, Rita.

And here we were, launched into an extraordinary adventure. I bought eighteen fishing boats. They were big craft, each with a fifty-horsepower outboard and a net five hundred yards long. A crew of five to each boat. As one fully equipped boat cost twelve thousand five hundred bolívars, eighteen meant a lot of money.

We transformed the little villages around the lake, doing away with poverty and the dislike for work (since the work I gave was well paid) and bringing a new life in place of the old listlessness.

These poor people owned nothing, so without any guarantee from them we gave one full set of fishing gear for each crew of five. They fished as they chose, and their only obligation was to sell me the *langostinos* and *camarones* at the market price less half a bolívar, because I paid for all the equipment and its upkeep.

The business ran at a tremendous pace, and it fascinated me. We had three refrigerated trucks that never stopped hurrying about the beaches to pick up my boats' catch.

I built a pier on the lake about a hundred feet long, and a big covered platform. Here Rita managed a team of between a hundred twenty and a hundred forty women who took off the heads of the *camarones* and *langostinos*. Then, washed and washed again in ice-cold water, the shrimp were sorted for size, according to how many would go to one American pound. There might be ten to fifteen, or twenty to twenty-five, or twenty-five to thirty. The bigger they were, the more they brought. Every week the Americans sent me a green sheet which gave the market price for *camarones* each Tuesday. Every day at least one DC-8 took off for Miami, carrying 24,800 pounds of *camarones*.

I would have made a lot of money, if I had not been such a fool as to take a Yankee partner one day. He had a moon face, and looked worthy, stupid and straight. He spoke neither Spanish nor French, and as I spoke no English we couldn't quarrel.

This Yankee brought in no capital, but he had rented the freezers of a well-known brand of ice that was sold all over Maracaibo and in the neighborhood. As a result, our *camarones* and *langostinos* were perfectly frozen.

I had to oversee the fishing, the boats, the loading of each day's catch into my three refrigerated trucks and the payment of the fishermen: and I had to provide these considerable sums out of my own pocket. Some days I would go down to the beach with thirty thousand bolívars and come home without a cent.

We were well organized, but nothing runs itself without a hitch, and I had a continual war with pirate buyers. As I've said, the fishermen who used my equipment had agreed that I should buy their catch at the market price less half a bolívar a kilo, which was fair. But the pirate buyers risked nothing. They had no boats, just a refrigerated truck. So they could afford to turn up on the beaches and buy *camarones* at the market price from no matter who. A boat carrying eight hundred kilos of *camarones* gained four hundred bolívars by selling a day's catch to the pirate buyers. You would have to be a saint to resist a temptation like that. So whenever they could, my fishermen took the pirates' money. That meant I had to protect my interests almost day and night; but I liked the battle— it gave me intense satisfaction.

When we sent our *camarones* and *langostinos* to the States, the payment was made in the form of a letter of credit, once the bank had seen the shipping papers and a certificate indicating that the quality of the goods and their perfect deepfreezing had been checked. The bank paid 85 percent of the total, and we then received the remaining 15 percent when Miami told Maracaibo that the consignment had arrived and had been found satisfactory.

It often happened that on Saturdays, when there were two planeloads of *camarones*, my partner would go along on one plane to accompany the consignment. On those days the freight cost five hundred dollars more, and as the Miami cargo handlers did not work on Saturdays, someone had to be on the spot to get the consignment out, loaded onto a refrigerated trailer and taken to the buyer's works, either in Miami itself or at Tampa or Jacksonville. As the banks were closed on Saturday there was no way of using the letters of credit; nor was there any way of insuring. But on Monday morning, in the States, the shipment sold for 10 or 15 percent more. It was a sound venture.

Things were running smoothly, and I was delighted with my partner's elegant strokes of business when he flew off at the weekend. Until the day he did not come back.

By stinking bad luck, this happened at the season when there were few *camarones* in the lake. I had hired a big boat at the seaport of Punto Fijo to fetch a whole cargo of splendid crayfish from Los Roques. I'd come back loaded to the gunwales with extra-prime-quality goods; and I'd had their heads taken off ight there. So I had a very valuable shipment, made up entirely of best crayfish tails, weighing from a pound and a half to a pound and three-quarters each.

And that Saturday two DC-8s loaded with my crayfish tails took off with this choirboy and vanished into the clouds.

Monday, no news; none on Tuesday, either. I went to the bank: nothing from Miami. I didn't want to believe it, but I knew already: I had been taken. As it was my partner who dealt with the letters of credit, and as there was no insurance on Saturday, he had sold the whole consignment the moment he got there, and walked quietly away with the dough.

I flew into a terrible rage and went off to look for Moonface in America, with a souvenir for him in my pocket. I had no trouble picking up his train, but at each address I found a woman who said that, though he was her lawful wedded husband, she didn't know where he was. And this three times, in three different towns! I never did find my worthy partner.

There I was, flat broke. We had lost a hundred and fifty thousand dollars. We still had the boats, of course; but they were in poor condition, and so were the outboards. And as this was a business in which you had to have a lot of ready cash to carry on day by day, we could not stand the loss, nor get on our feet again. We were pretty well ruined, and we sold everything. Rita never complained or blamed me for having been so trusting. Our capital, the savings of fourteen years of hard work, more than two years of useless sacrifice and continual effort—everything was lost; or very nearly everything.

With our eyes filled with tears, we left the great family of fishermen and workers we had brought into being. They were appalled, too; they told us how it grieved them to see us go and how grateful they were to us for having brought them a prosperity they had never known before.

16

The Gorilla

There was a knock at the door (the bell was not working)
and I went to open it. It was my buddy, Colonel Bolagno.
He and his family had always called me Papillon; they
were the only people in Venezuela to do so. All the others
called me Enrique or Don Enrique, according to how I
was doing at the moment. The Venezuelans have a feeling for that; they know right away if you are prosperous
or on the rocks.

"Hey there, Papillon. It's three years since we've
met."

"True enough, Francisco: three years."

"Why haven't you been to see me in my new
house?"

"You never asked me."

"You don't ask a friend. He comes when he feels like
it, because if his friend has a house it's his house, too. To
invite him would be an insult."

I made no answer; I knew he was right.

Bolagno embraced Rita. He sat there with his elbows
on the table, looking disturbed and uneasy; he had taken
off his colonel's cap. Rita gave him a cup of coffee, and I
asked, "How did you find my address?"

"That's my business. Why didn't you send it to me?"

"A great deal of work and a great deal of worry."

"You have worries?"

"All I want."

"Then I've come at the wrong moment."

"Why?"

263

"I came to ask you to lend me five thousand bolívars. I'm in a jam."

"Impossible, Francisco."

"We are ruined," said Rita.

"Ah, so you're ruined? You're ruined, Papillon? It's true you're ruined? Is that why you did not come to see me, so as not to let me know about your worries?"

"Yes."

"Well, let me tell you you're an ass. Because when you have a friend, he's there so you *can* tell him your worries and so you can rely on him to do something to get you out of a hole. You're an ass not to have thought of me, your friend, to back you up and give you a hand. I heard about your difficulties from other people, and that's why I'm here to help you."

Rita and I were so moved we scarcely knew where we were; we couldn't say a word, we were so touched. We had never asked anyone for anything, and that was a fact; but there were a good many people I had helped a lot, some who even owed me their jobs, and although they knew we were ruined, not one had come to give us a hand in any way at all. Most were French; some straight, others crooked.

"What do you want me to do for you, Papillon?"

"Setting up a business we could live off would cost too much. Even if you have the money, you couldn't spare it."

"Go and get dressed, Rita. We'll all three of us go and eat at the best French restaurant in town."

By the end of the meal, it was agreed that I should look for a business and tell him how much it would cost to buy. And Bolagno said, "If I have the money, there's no problem; and if I haven't enough, then I'll borrow from my brothers and my brother-in-law. But I give you my word I'll get hold of what you need."

All the rest of that day, Rita and I talked about his

wonderful consideration. "When he was just a corporal at El Dorado," I said, "he gave me his only civilian suit, so that I could leave decently dressed; and now here he is giving us a hand to make a fresh start."

We paid our overdue rent and moved to a pleasant, well-situated café-restaurant in the top avenue of La Delicias, still in the Gran Sabana district. It was called the Bar-Restaurant Gab, and that was where we were at the time of Long Charlie's arrival.

Charles de Gaulle, then president of the republic, came on an official visit, invited by Raúl Leoni, the president of Venezuela.

Caracas and the whole of Venezuela celebrated the occasion. The people, the real people, the ones with horny hands, straw hats and rope-soled shoes, all these open-hearted people without exception were waiting, filled with emotion, to cheer Charles de Gaulle.

The Gab had a charming covered terrace, and I was sitting there quietly drinking anisette with a Frenchman. He explained the mysteries of the processing of fish meal; and in a low voice he also told me about an invention he was just perfecting—one that would bring him millions, once it was accepted. The discovery was cinema in relief; he whispered and looked sideways to seem more confidential and also to tell me how much money I could invest in his researches.

It is always amusing to listen to the line of a guy who is trying to con you, and his spiel was so smooth and so charmed me that I did not notice a neighbor pricking up his ears and leaning over to listen to us—until I unfolded a little note from Rita, who was at the cash desk and had sent the message discreetly by one of the waiters: "I don't know what you are talking about, but there's no doubt your neighbor is very interested in catching what you say. Looks like a foreign pig."

To get rid of the inventor, I strongly advised him to carry on with his researches, and I told him I was so sure he would succeed that I should certainly have come in with him if only I had any savings, which was unfortunately not the case. He went away; I got up, turned around and faced the table behind me.

Sitting there I saw a well-built guy, too well built and too well dressed, with a tie and all, and a steel-blue suit; and there on the table in front of him, an anisette and a pack of Gauloises. No need to ask his trade, or his nationality either.

"Excuse me, are those French cigarettes you are smoking?" I asked in Spanish.

"Yes: I'm a Frenchman."

"Really? I don't know you. Tell me, you wouldn't be one of Long Charlie's gorillas, by any chance?"

The well-built guy stood up and introduced himself. "I'm Commissaire Belion, in charge of the General's security."

"Pleased to meet you."

"And what about you? Are you French?"

"Come off it, Commissaire. You know very well who I am; it's not just by chance you're here on my café terrace."

"But—"

"Don't go on. You put the Gauloises right out on your table so that I should talk to you. Right or wrong?"

"Right."

"Another anisette?"

"Okay. I came to see you because since I'm responsible for the President's security, I'm getting the embassy to draw up a list of people who might have to leave Caracas before the General arrives. The list will be shown to the minister of the interior and he'll take the necessary steps."

"I'm on the list?"

"Not yet."

"What do you know about me?"

"That you have a family and that you are going straight."

"What else?"

"That your sister is Madame X and she lives at such-and-such an address in Paris and that the other one is Madame Y. who lives in Grenoble."

"After that?"

"That proceedings against you lapse next year, in June, 1966."

"Who told you?"

"I knew it before I left Paris, but the consulate here has also been notified."

"Why didn't the consul let me know?"

"Officially he doesn't know your address."

"Well, thanks for the good news. Can I go to the consulate and be told officially?"

"Whenever you like."

"But tell me Commissaire, how come you're sitting on the terrace of my restaurant this morning? It's not just to tell me about the lapse of proceedings, or to let me know my sisters haven't changed their address, eh?"

"Correct. It was to see you. To see Papillon."

"You only know one Papillon. the guy in the Paris police file, a heap of lies. exaggerations and twisted reports. A file that never even described the man I was before, still less the man I have become."

"Quite sincerely I believe you, and I congratulate you."

"So now you've seen me, are you putting me on the list of people to be expelled during De Gaulle's stay?"

"No."

"Well now, do you want me to tell you why you're here, Commissaire?"

"That would be interesting."

"It's because you said to yourself, a guy on the run is always a guy on the lookout for dough; and although Papillon may have become a good citizen, he's still on the loose, he's still an adventurer. He might refuse a considerable sum for doing something against De Gaulle himself; but as for picking up a bundle for just helping to prepare an attack—why, that's something else again, and very possible."

"Go on."

"Well, you've got it dead wrong, dear Commissaire. In the first place, I wouldn't get mixed up with any political crime, not even for a fortune; still less one against De Gaulle. Secondly, who could possibly gain by such a thing in Venezuela?"

"The OAS."

"Right. That's not only very possible but even very probable. They've pulled things off so many times in France that in a country like Venezuela, it's a cinch."

"A cinch? Why?"

"The way they're organized, the OAS men don't have to get into Venezuela by the ordinary ways, the ports or airfields. The land frontiers are enormous—Brazil, Colombia, British Guiana—not to mention a coastline of over a thousand miles. They can come in just when they want, on the day and at the time that suits them, without anyone's being able to do anything about it. That's your first mistake, Commissaire. But there's another, too."

"What's that?" asked Belion, smiling.

"If these OAS guys are as sharp as people say, they've taken great care not to contact the French living here. Because since they know the cops are going straight to the Frenchmen, their very first precaution must be to go nowhere near a single one of them. And don't forget, no evil-intentioned guy is ever going to stay in a hotel. There are hundreds of people here who'll rent a room to no matter who without declaring him. So you see there's no point in looking for people who might make an attempt on De Gaulle's life among the Frenchmen here, crooks or not."

When Belion left he told me to come and see him when I returned to Paris; and he played it straight with me. Unlike some other Frenchmen, I was not expelled from Caracas during De Gaulle's stay—a stay that passed off with no trouble at all.

Like a fool I went along and cheered De Gaulle.

And, like a fool, in the mere presence of this great leader who had saved my country's honor, I forgot that that same country had sent me to the clink for life.

And, like a fool, I would have given one of my fingers to shake his hand or be there at the embassy's reception in his honor: a reception to which I was not invited, of course. But the underworld was able to take an indirect revenge, because some old, retired French whores slipped in: they had turned over a new leaf, as you might say, by making a good marriage, and there they were with their arms full of flowers for De Gaulle's delighted wife.

I went to see the French consul, and he read me out the notification that proceedings against me lapsed the next year. One more year and I'd go to France.

Our situation improved rapidly, and I went back into all-night bars, buying the Scotch Club in Chacaito, in the very middle of Caracas. This was an odd business, because I went into it in the first place to rescue a poor French hairdresser some ugly bastards were trying to fleece. Later this Robin Hood caper paid off very well.

So for several years I was living by night again. The Caracas nightlife was growing more and more vulgar, losing that touch of bohemianism that was its charm. The men who lived it up were no longer the same, and the new customers lacked culture and good manners.

I stayed in the bar as little as possible, living in the

street almost all the time, wandering about the neighboring districts. I came to know the kids of Caracas, the urchins who drifted about all night looking for a few cents, and the wonderful inventiveness of these children whose parents lived in rabbit hutches. Not always model parents, either; for there were a good many who, in their poverty, had no hesitation in exploiting their children.

And these kids bravely launched themselves into the night to bring home the amount required of them. They were any age between five and twelve; some were shoeshine boys, others waited at the door of all-night joints, offering to guard a customer's car as he went in, and others rushed to open the car door ahead of the doorman. A thousand dodges, a thousand clever gimmicks to add bolívar to bolívar until they had ten or thereabouts, so that at five or six in the morning they could go home.

Often, when a customer I knew was just going to get into his big car, I would urge him to be generous, using this formula: "Be handsome, now! Think of the money you've spent in this joint—a hundredth part of what you've splashed about would be a godsend to this poor kid." Nine times out of ten it worked, and the playboy would give the kid a ten- or twenty-bolívar note.

My best friend was named Pablito. He was rather small and thin, but he was tough, and he fought older, bigger boys like a lion. For there were conflicting interests in this struggle for life, and if a customer had not specially pointed out one boy to guard his car, then when the man came out again, the quickest off the mark got the coin. That meant a pitched battle.

My little friend was bright, and he had learned to read from the papers he sold now and then. There was none like him at outstripping all competition when a car drew up; and he was the quickest at running little errands—fetching things the bar was short of, like sandwiches or cigarettes.

Every night my little Pablito carried on the struggle so that he could help his grandmother; she was a very, very old grandmother, it seemed. with white hair, faded blue eyes and rheumatism so bad she couldn't work at all. His mother was in jail for having crowned a neighbor with a bottle when he tried to steal her radio. And he, at nine, was the only breadwinner in the family. He wouldn't let his grandmother, his little brother or his little sister come out into the streets of Caracas, either by day or by night. He was the man of the house, and he had to look after all his people and protect them.

So I helped Pablito when he had had a bad night or in cases of emergency, with money for his grandmother's medicines or for a taxi to take her to see a doctor at the free hospital.

"And she has these bouts of asthma, too, my grandmother. Do you realize what that costs, Enrique?"

And every night Pablito gave me a report on his grandmother's health. One day there was an important request: he needed forty bolívars to buy a secondhand mattress. His grandmother could not lie in a hammock anymore, because of her asthma: the doctor said it compressed her chest.

He often used to sit in my car, and one day the policeman on guard was talking to him, leaning on the door and playing with his revolver: without the least bad intention he put a bullet into Pablito's shoulder. They rushed him to the hospital and operated. I went to see him the next day. I asked where his hut was and how to get to it; he said it was impossible to find it without a guide, and the doctor wouldn't let him get up in that condition.

That night I looked for Pablito's friends, hoping one of them would take me to his grandmother. The terrific solidarity of street urchins: they all said they did not know where he lived. I didn't believe a word of it, because every day a whole gang of them waited for one another to go home together.

I was interested and puzzled, and I asked the nurse to call me when Pablito had a visitor she knew was a member of the family or a neighbor. Two days later she called and I went to the hospital.

"Well, Pablito, and how are you coming along? You look worried."

"No, Enrique; it's only that my back hurts."

"Yet he was laughing only a few minutes ago," said his visitor.

"Are you one of his family, Madame?"

"No. I'm a neighbor."

"How are his grandmother and the little ones?"

"What grandmother?"

"Why, Pablito's grandmother."

"But Pablito hasn't got a grandmother."

I took the woman aside. Yes, he had a little sister, and yes, he had a little brother, but no grandmother. His mother was not in prison; she was a wreck of a woman, very dim-witted.

That wonderful Caracas street kid did not want his friend Enrique to know his mother was half crazy, and he had invented this splendid asthmatic grandmother so that his buddy the Frenchman, giving because of her, might relieve his poor mother's unhappiness and distress.

I went back to my little friend's bed: he was ashamed to look me in the face. Gently I pulled his chin up; his eyes were closed, but when at last he opened them I said, *"Pablito, eres un tronco de hombre."* (You're a real man.)

I slipped him a hundred-bolívar note for his family and walked out, thoroughly proud and pleased with myself for having such a friend.

17

Montmartre—My Trial

By 1967 proceedings against me had lapsed. I left for France by myself; to keep the business running properly you had to have authority and courage and the power of making yourself respected, and only Rita could do that. She said to me, "Go and embrace your people in their own homes; go and pray at your father's grave."

I went back to France by way of Nice. Why Nice? Together with my visa, the French consulate in Caracas had given me a document verifying the lapse of proceedings; but as he handed the papers to me, the consul said, "Wait until I have instructions from France about the conditions under which you can return." They didn't have to spell it out. If I went back to the consul and he had received the reply from Paris, he would tell me I was *forbidden to enter the Département of the Seine* for *life*. But I had every intention of making a trip to Paris.

This way I avoided getting the notification; and since I had neither received nor signed it, I would be committing no offense unless the consul learned that I'd left and told the police at the Paris airport to hand me the notification. Hence my two stops—I should arrive at Nice as though I were coming from Spain.

1930–1967: thirty-seven years had gone by.

Fourteen years of the road down the drain: twenty-two years of freedom, twenty of them with a home, which meant that I could go straight, reintegrated into society.

In 1956, there'd been a month with my people in Spain; then a gap of eleven years, though during these eleven years our many letters had kept me in contact with my family.

In 1967 I saw them all. I went into their homes, I sat at their tables, I had their children on my knee and even their grandchildren. Grenoble, Lyons, Cannes, Saint-Priest and then Saint-Peray, where I found Tante Ju in my father's house, still faithful at her post.

I listened to Tante Ju as she told me why Pap had died before his time. He watered his garden himself and he carried the cans for hours and hours over a distance of more than two hundred yards. "Just imagine that, my dear, at his age! He could have bought a rubber hose, but Lord above, he was as stubborn as a mule. And one day, as he was carrying these watering cans, his heart failed."

I could just see my father lugging those heavy cans all the way to his beds of lettuces, tomatoes and stringbeans. And I could see him obstinately persisting in not getting the hose his wife, Tante Ju, kept begging him to buy. And I could see him, that country schoolmaster, stopping to draw breath and to mop his forehead, advise a neighbor or give a botany lesson to one of his grandsons.

Before going to see his grave in the cemetery, I asked Tante Ju to go with me on his favorite walks. And we went at the same pace he used to go, following the same stony paths lined with rushes, poppies and daisies until a milestone or some bees or the flight of a bird would remind Tante Ju of some little happening long ago that had touched them. Then, quite delighted, she would recall for me how my father had told her about his grandson's being stung by a wasp. "There, Henri, do you see? He was standing just there."

I listened, with my throat constricted, thirsty for more, still more of the smallest details about my father's life. "You know, Ju," my father had said to her, "when my boy was very small, five or six at the most, he was stung by a wasp when we were out for a walk—not once, like my grandson, but twice. Well, he never cried at all; and on top of that, we had the greatest difficulty keeping him from going off to look for the wasps' nest to destroy it. Oh, Riri was so brave!"

I did not travel on into the Ardèche; I went no farther than Saint-Peray. For my return to my village I wanted Rita with me.

I got out of the train at the Gare de Lyon, and put my bags in a locker at the station so as not to have to fill out a registration form at the hotel. And then, once more, there was the asphalt of Paris under my feet.

But this asphalt was not *my* asphalt until I was in my own district, Montmartre. I went there by night, of course. The only sun the Papillon of the Thirties knew was that of the electric lights.

And here it was, Montmartre: the Place Pigalle and the Pierrot Café and the moonlight and the Passage Elysée des Beaux-Arts and the hellbenders whooping it up and the jokers and the whores and the pimps that anyone in the know could recognize right off just by the way they walked, and the joints crammed tight with people at the bar. But all this was just my first impression.

Thirty-seven years had gone by, and nobody took any notice of me. Who was going to look at an old man of sixty? The girls might even ask me upstairs, and the young men might be so disrespectful as to elbow me out of my place at the bar.

Just one more stranger, a possible client, a provincial manufacturer—that's what this well-dressed, tie-wearing gent must be; a middle-class guy, another who had lost his way at this late hour and in this dubious bar. You could see right away he wasn't used to these parts; you could feel he was uneasy.

Sure I was uneasy, and that was understandable. These

were not the same people or the same faces; at the first whiff you could tell that everything was mixed up now. Pigs, lesbians, flits, know-it-alls, squares, blacks and Arabs; there were only a few characters from Marseille or Corsica, speaking with a southern accent, to remind me of the old times. It was a completely different world from the one I had known.

There wasn't even what there had always been in my time—tables with groups of poets, painters or actors, with their long hair that reeked of Bohemia and an avant-garde intellectuality. Now every silly little jerk had long hair.

I wandered from bar to bar like a sleepwalker, and I climbed stairs to see if the pool tables of my youth were still on the second floor, and I civilly refused a guide's offer to show me Montparnasse. But I did ask him, "Do you think that since 1930 Montmartre has lost the soul it had in those days?"

I felt like slapping him down for an answer that insulted my own personal Montmartre: "Oh, but Monsieur, Montmartre is immortal. I've lived here forty years, seeing I came when I was ten, and believe me, Place Pigalle, Place Blanche, Place Clichy and all the streets running off them are just the same and always will be the same forever."

I fled from the dreary bastard and walked along under the trees on the raised part in the middle of the avenue. From here, yes—as long as you didn't see the people clearly, as long as you saw only their shapes—from here, yes, Montmartre was still the same. I went slowly toward the very spot where I was alleged to have shot Roland Lepetit on the night of March 25–26, 1930.

The bench, probably the same bench repainted every year (a public bench might perfectly well last thirty-seven years with wood that thick), the bench was there, and the lamppost, and the bar over the way, and the half-closed shutters on the house opposite, they were still there. They were the first, the only, the true witnesses of the tragedy; they knew very well the man who fired that night was not me. Why didn't they say so?

People went by, unconcerned, never noticing this sixty-year-old man leaning against a tree, the same tree that had been there when the shot was fired.

Twenty-four I was in 1930, when I used to run down the Rue Lepic, that street I can still walk up pretty briskly. The ghost has come back in spite of you all; he's pushed back the gravestone under which you buried him alive. Stop, stop, you half-blind creatures passing by! Stop and have a look at an innocent man who was condemned for a murder on this very ground, before these same trees and these same stones—stop and ask these dumb witnesses, ask them to speak out today. And if you lean close, you will hear them whispering faintly, "No, this man was not here at half past three on the night of twenty-fifth to twenty-sixth March thirty-seven years ago."

"Where was he, then?" the doubters will ask. Simple: I was in the Iris Bar, maybe a hundred yards from here. In the Iris Bar, when a taxi driver burst in, crying, "There was a shot outside just now."

"It wasn't true," said the pigs. "It wasn't true," said the boss and the waiter of the Iris, prompted by the pigs.

Once again I saw the inquiry; I saw the trial: I could not avoid being brought face to face with the past. You want to live through it again, man? Nearly forty years have passed, and you still want to go through that nightmare again? You're not afraid this going back will make you long for a revenge you gave up ages ago?

Sit down there, on this same green bench, the one that saw the killing just opposite the Rue Germain-Pilon, right here on the Boulevard de Clichy, by the Clichy Bar-Tabac, where the tragedy began after the inquiry.

It's the night of March 25–26: half past three in the morning. A man comes into the Clichy and asks for Madame Nini.

"That's me," a tart says.

"Your man's just been shot in the guts. Come on; he's in a taxi."

Nini runs after the unknown guy, together with a girl friend. They get into the taxi, where Roland Lepetit is sitting on the back seat. Nini asks the unknown guy who told her to come, too. He says, "I can't" and disappears.

"Quick, the Lariboisière hospital!"

It was only during the drive that the taxi driver, a Russian, learned that his passenger was wounded: he had not noticed anything before. The moment his fare was unloaded at the hospital he hurried off to tell the police what he knew: he had been hailed by two men arm in arm outside 17, boulevard de Clichy: *only one of them got in*—Roland Lepetit. The other told him to drive to the Clichy Bar and followed on foot. This man went into the bar and came out with two women; then he vanished. The two women told him to drive to the Lariboisière hospital: "It was during the trip that I learned the man was wounded."

The police carefully wrote all this down; they also wrote down Nini's declaration that her boyfriend had played cards all that night in that same bar where she plied her trade, had played cards with an *unknown man;* he'd played dice and had a drink at the bar with some men, still *all of them unknown*; and Roland had left after the others, *alone*. There was nothing in Nini's statement to indicate that anyone had come to fetch him. He'd gone out by himself, after the others, the unknowns, had left.

A commissaire and a cop, Commissaire Gérardin and

Inspector Grimaldi, questioned the dying Roland Lepetit in the presence of his mother. The nurses had told them his condition was hopeless. I quote their report; it's been published in a book written to pull me to pieces, with a preface and therefore a guarantee by a *commissaire divisionnaire*, Paul Romain. Here it is. The two pigs are questioning Lepetit:

> *"Here beside you you have the police commissaire and your mother, the holiest relationship in the world. Tell the truth. Who shot you?"*
> He replied, *"It was Papillon Roger."*
> *We asked him to swear that he had really told the truth. "Yes, Monsieur, I have told you the truth."*
> *We withdrew, leaving the mother beside her son.*

So what happened on the night of March 25, 1930, was clear and straightforward: the man who fired was Papillon *Roger*.

This Roland Lepetit was a pork butcher and a pimp, who put his girl friend Nini out to work for him: he lived with her at 4, rue Elysée des Beaux-Arts. He was not really a member of the underworld, but, like all those who hung around Montmartre and all the genuine crooks, he knew several Papillons. And because he was afraid they might arrest another Papillon instead of the one who had killed him, he was exact about the Christian name. For although he was fond of living outside the law, like all squares he also wanted the police to punish his enemy. A Papillon, sure, but Papillon *Roger*.

Everything came flooding back to me in this accursed place. I must have run through this file in my head a thousand times; I'd learned it by heart in my cell, like a Bible, because my lawyers had given it to me and I'd had time to engrave it on my mind before the trial.

So there was Lepetit's statement before he died; and the declaration of Nini, his girl. Neither of them named me as the killer.

Now four men come upon the stage. On the night of this job they went to the Lariboisière hospital to ask:

(1) if the wounded man was in fact Roland Lepetit;
(2) what condition he was in.

The pigs were told at once, and they began a search. Since these men did not belong to the underworld and were not concealing themselves, they had come on foot and they left on foot. They were picked up as they were walking down the Avenue Rochechouart and kept in custody at the station in the XVIII arrondissement.

They were:

Georges Goldstein, 24; Roger Dorin, 24; Roger Jourmar, 21; Emile Cape, 18.

All the statements they made to the commissaire of the XVIII arrondissement station on the very day of the killing were cut and dried. Goldstein stated that in a gathering of people he had been told that a man called Lepetit had been wounded—shot *three times* with a revolver. Thinking it might be his friend Roland Lepetit, who was often in that district, he walked to the hospital to find out. On the way he met Dorin and then the two others and asked them to go with him. The others knew nothing about the business, and they did not know the victim.

The commissaire asked Goldstein, "Do you know Papillon?"

"Yes, a little. I've met him now and then. He knew Lepetit; *that's all I can tell you.*"

So what of it? What does this Papillon mean? There were five or six of them in Montmartre!

Dorin's statement: Goldstein asked him to go along to

the Lariboisière to inquire after a friend *whose name he did not mention*. Dorin went into the hospital with him; and Goldstein asked if the Lepetit who had been brought in was seriously wounded.

"Do you know Lepetit? Do you remember Papillon Roger?" the commissaire asked.

"I don't know Lepetit, either by name or by sight. I do know a man called Papillon, having seen him in the street. He is very well known and they say he is a terror. I know nothing more."

The third man to be questioned, Jourmar, said that when Goldstein came out of the hospital, having gone in alone with Dorin, he said, "It's certainly my buddy."

So before he went in, he was not sure about it, right?

The commissaire: "Do you know Papillon Roger and a man called Lepetit?"

"I know a man called Papillon who hangs around Pigalle. The last time I saw him was about three months ago."

The same with the fourth thief. He didn't know Lepetit. A Papillon, yes, but only by sight.

In her first statement the mother also confirmed that her son had said Papillon *Roger*.

So far, everything was plain, clear-cut and exact. All the chief witnesses gave their evidence in complete freedom before a local commissaire without being prompted, threatened, or guided.

In short, Roland was in the Clichy Bar before the tragedy, and all the people present were unknown. They may have been playing cards or dice, which meant they were acquaintances of Roland's, but still they were unknown. What was odd, and indeed disturbing, was that they remained unknown until the very end.

Second point: Roland Lepetit was *the last to leave the bar, and he left it by himself;* his own girl said so. Nobody came to fetch him. A very little while after he went out, he

was wounded by a man whom he positively identified on
his deathbed as Papillon *Roger*. The man who came to
tell Nini was another unknown; and he, too, was to remain so. Yet he was the one who helped Lepetit into the
taxi immediately after the shooting—an unknown man
who walked along with the cab as far as the bar where he
was going to warn Nini. And this essential witness was to
remain unknown, although everything he had just done
proved he belonged to the underworld, to Montmartre,
and that he was therefore known to the pigs. Strange.

Third point: Goldstein, who was to be the prosecution's
chief witness, *did not know* who had been wounded and
went to the Lariboisière hospital to find out whether it
was his friend Lepetit.

The only clues as to this Papillon were that he was
called Roger and that he was said to be a terror.

Was I a terror at twenty-four? Was I dangerous? No,
but maybe I was on the way to becoming both. It's certain
that I was a tough guy, an "undesirable" then; but it's also
certain that at only twenty-four I could not have become
set forever as one particular type of man. It's also certain
that at that age, having been only two years in Montmartre, I could not have been either the head of a gang or the
terror of Pigalle. Certainly I disturbed public order; and
certainly I was suspected of having taken part in big jobs,
but nothing had ever been proved against me. Sure, they
had pulled me in several times and grilled me pretty hard
at 36, quai des Orfèvres, but without ever getting anything out of me, either a confession or a name. Sure, after
the tragedy of my childhood, and after my time in the
navy, and after the government had refused me a steady
career, I had made up my mind to live outside that
society of clowns and to let them know it. Sure, every
time I was picked up and grilled at the Quai des Orfèvres
for an important job they thought I was mixed up in, I
insulted my torturers and humiliated them in every pos-

sible way, even telling them that one day I'd be in their place, the shits, and they would be in my power. So of course the pigs, humiliated through and through, might have said to themselves, "This Papillon, we'll have to clip his wings the first chance we have."

But still, I was only twenty-four! My life wasn't just a matter of resentment and rancor against society and the squares who obeyed its damn-fool rules: it was also *life itself,* continually on the move, sending off showers of sparks. It's true I'd pulled some serious nonsense; yes, but it was not wicked nonsense. Besides, when I was taken in there was only one conviction on my file: four months' suspended sentence for receiving stolen goods. Did I deserve to be wiped off the face of the earth just for having humiliated the pigs and just because I might turn dangerous one day?

It all began when the criminal police took the business over. The word went round Montmartre that they were looking for all the Papillons—Little Papillon, Pussini Papillon, Papillon Trompe-la-Mort, Papillon Roger, etc.

As for me, I was just plain Papillon; or sometimes, to avoid confusion, One-Thumb Papillon. But it was no part of my way of life to hobnob with the pigs, and I moved off fast: yes, that was true. I went on the run.

And why did you do that, Papi, since it wasn't you?

You ask that now? Have you forgotten that by the time you were twenty-four you had already been tortured several times at the Quai des Orfèvres? You were never really fond of being knocked about, or of all those exquisite tortures: the way they shoved your head under the water until you were perishing for want of air and you didn't know whether you were dead or alive; the way the pigs would give your balls five or six twists and leave them so swollen you walked like an Argentine gaucho for weeks on end; the way they crushed your nails in a paper press till the blood spurted and the nails came off; the way they beat you with a rubber truncheon that wounded your lungs, so blood poured out of your mouth; and the way those two-hundred-pound bruisers would jump up and down on your belly as if it were a trampoline. Is it your age, Papi, or have you lost your memory? There were a hundred reasons for going on the run right away. It was a break that didn't carry you too far; since you weren't guilty, there was no need to go abroad; just a little hideout near Paris would be enough. Soon they'd pick up the Papillon Roger in question, or at least identify him; and then fine, you'd jump into a taxi and be back in Paris. No more danger for your balls or your nails or all the rest.

Only this Papillon Roger was never identified. There was no culprit.

Then all at once a wanted man was produced like magic. This Papillon Roger? Simple: you just wipe out the Roger and you pick up plain Papillon, the nickname of Henri Charrière. The trick's done: all that's left is to pile up the evidence. It's no longer an honest, impartial inquiry into the truth, but the total fabrication of *a culprit*.

Policemen, don't you see, need *to solve a murder case* to deserve promotion in their very noble, very honest career. Now this Papillon has everything going for him as a culprit. He's young, and there is something of the procurer about him. . . . We'll say his girl's a whore. He's a thief, and he's been in trouble with the police several times; but he's either got off on a dismissed charge or he's been acquitted.

And then into the bargain the guy is a difficult bastard; he curses us to hell when we arrest him, he sneers at us, humiliates us, names his dog after our chief of police, and sometimes he says, "You'd be well advised to grill a little more gently, if you want to reach retirement age." These threats of punishing us one day for our "modern" and "thoroughgoing" methods of interrogation worry us. So go right ahead, man. We're covered on all sides.

That was the sinister beginning of it all, Papi. Twenty-four you were, when those two lousy pigs flushed you out at Saint-Cloud on April 10, while you were eating snails.

Oh, they went right ahead, all right! What drive, what zeal, what steadiness, what passion, what diabolical cunning it took to get you into the dock one day, and for the court to deliver that blow that knocked you out for fourteen years!

It wasn't so easy to turn you into the guilty man, Papi. But the inspector in charge of the job, Mayzaud, a Montmartre specialist, was so eager to send you down that it was open war between him and your lawyers even in the court, with insults, complaints and foul blows; and right beside Mayzaud was the plump little Goldstein, one of those phony bastards who lick the underworld's feet in the hope of being accepted.

Very amenable, this Goldstein! Mayzaud said he met him maybe a hundred times *by chance* during the inquiry. This precious witness stated *on the very day of the killing* that in a crowd of people he had heard someone named Roland had got three bullets in the guts, and he had then gone to the hospital to ask the exact identity of the victim. More than three weeks later, on April 18, after many contacts with Mayzaud, this same Goldstein changed his story: On the night of March 25–26, before the killing, he had met me with two unknown men. I had asked him where Lepetit was. Goldstein: "At the Clichy." As soon as I left him, Goldstein went to warn Lepetit. While he was talking to Lepetit one of Papillon's companions asked Lepetit to come outside. Goldstein himself went out a little later and saw Papillon and Lepetit talking quietly; but he did not linger. Later, coming back to the Place Pigalle, he *once more* met Papillon, who told him he had

just shot Lepetit and asked him to go to the Lariboisière
and see what state Lepetit was in, and to warn him to
keep his mouth shut.

For of course, I, who was described to the court as a
terror, a member of the underworld all the more dangerous because of my intelligence and cunning; of course I
would hang around the Place Pigalle, right on the spot
where I'd shot a guy, until Goldstein came that way
again. Do I stand there like a signpost on some little
Ardèche lane, so that the pigs only have to come strolling
along to ask me how I'm doing?

This Goldstein was not such a fool as all that; the day
after his statement he hightailed it to England.

Meanwhile I stood up for myself stoutly. "Goldstein?
Don't know him. I may have seen him; may even have
exchanged a few words with him, like you do with people
always around the same district, without knowing who
you're talking to." I really could not fit a mug to that
name; so much so that it was only when we were brought
face to face that I succeeded in identifying him. And I
was so taken aback that a little square I didn't know
should make such a detailed charge against me, that I
wondered what crime he could have committed—nothing
much for sure, he was such a dreary runt—for the pigs to
have such a hold on him. I am still wondering; sexual
offenses? Cocaine?

Without him, without his successive statements, which
added new material to the pigs' case *every* time he
opened his trap, without him nothing held together. Nothing.

And now there appeared something that at first sight
looked miraculous but later turned out to be exceedingly
dangerous—indeed fatal. A diabolical police plot, a horrible trap that I and my lawyers fell into headfirst. I
thought it meant safety, but it was disaster. Because there
was nothing solid in the file: Goldstein's successive bits of

evidence were all very improbable. The file had so little body to it that my alleged killing lacked even a motive. Since I had no cause to dislike the victim, and since I was not raving mad, I was as out of place in this job as a hair in the soup; and any jury at all, even one made up of the dullest idiots on earth, could hardly fail to realize it.

So the police invented a motive; and the one who provided it was a pig who had been working Montmartre for the last ten years, Inspector Mazillier.

One of my lawyers, Maître Beffey, liked wandering about Montmartre in his free time; and he met this pig, who told him he knew what had really happened on the night of March 25–26, and that he was prepared to tell—implying that what he had to say would be in my favor. We said to ourselves, either he's motivated by professional honesty or else—which is more likely— there's some rivalry between Mayzaud and him.

And *we* called him as a witness. *We* did.

But what Mazillier had to say was not at all what we had expected. He stated that he knew me well and that I had done him many favors. Then he added, "Thanks to the information provided by Charrière I have been able to carry out several arrests. As for the circumstances in connection with the murder, *I know nothing about them.* But I have heard it said [Lord, how many "I have heard it said"s we had during my trial!] that Charrière was the object of ill will on the part of persons unknown to me who disapproved of his relations with the police."

And there was the reason for the murder! I'd killed Roland Lepetit during a quarrel because he was spreading it around Montmartre that I squealed, that I was an informer.

When was this statement of Inspector Mazillier's made? April 14. And when did Goldstein make his, the one that contradicted his statement on the day of the killing? April 18, *four days after Mazillier's.*

When the court of first instance was presented with this padded, elastic evidence, this mass of rumors, lies and prompted statements, they sensed there was something fishy about the whole thing. Because although you often put them all into the same bag, Papi, as if judges, pigs, jurymen, the law and the prison administration were all part of the same conspiracy, you must admit that there have been some exceedingly honest judges.

As a result, the first court *refused* to send me before the assizes with that phony file, and sent all the evidence back to the investigating magistrate, insisting upon *further inquiry*.

The pigs were utterly infuriated; they found witnesses everywhere—in prison, just about to be let out or just having been let out. But the further inquiry produced nothing, absolutely nothing, not the slightest clue or the least suggestion of new and serious evidence.

In the end, without anything fresh—still a bad bouillabaisse made with all the wrong fish—the file was at last allowed to be sent up to the assizes.

And now came the clap of thunder. Something happened that is almost never seen in the legal world: the public prosecutor, the man whose job it is to protect society by putting as many defendants as possible behind bars—the public prosecutor who had been given the brief to act against me, took it with the tips of his fingers, as though he were holding it with tongs, and put it back on the desk, saying, "I won't act in this case. It smells fishy and prefabricated: give it to someone else."

How splendid he looked, Maître Raymond Hubert, when he came to tell me this extraordinary news at the Conciergerie! "Can you imagine it, Charrière! Your file is so unconvincing, a prosecutor has refused to have anything to do with it and has asked for the brief to be given to someone else!"

*   *   *

. . . It was cool that night on the bench in the Boulevard de Clichy. I walked up and down under the shadow of the trees; I did not want to walk into the light for fear of interrupting the magic lantern as it projected these pictures from thirty-seven years ago. I turned up the collar of my overcoat, and pushed back my hat a little, to air my head. I sat down again, pulled my coat over my legs, and then, with my back to the avenue, I slid my legs over the bench and sat the other way around, my arms leaning on the back as they had leant on the rail of the dock during my first trial in July, 1931.

Because there was not just one trial for me. *There were two*. The first in July, the other in October.

It all went too well, Papi! The court was not blood-red, like a slaughterhouse; it was more like an enormous boudoir. In the flooding light of that marvelous July day, the hangings, the carpets and the judges' robes were almost pale pink. And in this court, a smiling, kindly, rather skeptical presiding judge, so little convinced by what he had read in the file that he opened proceedings like this: "Charrière, Henri, as the indictment does not entirely correspond with what we should have liked to see in it, will you explain your case to the court and the jury yourself?"

The president of an assize court asking the defendant to lay open his case! You remember that sun-filled July assize and those wonderful judges? It was too good to last, Papi. Those judges conducted the proceedings with such impartiality, the president calmly and honestly looking for the truth, asking the pigs embarrassing questions, worrying Goldstein, pointing out his contradictions, and allowing my lawyers and me to ask him awkward questions —it was too splendid; it was sunlit justice, a holiday sitting with the judges in your favor.

The first important witness, already primed by the pigs, was the mother. I don't think it was out of bad faith that she had adopted the pigs' insinuations. She really did so unconsciously.

The mother no longer said that she and the commissaire had heard "Papillon Roger." Now she stated that what she had heard was, "It's Papillon. Goldstein knows him." She had forgotten the Roger and she had added the "Goldstein knows him," words that Commissaire Gérardin and Inspector Grimaldi did not hear. Odd that a commissaire should not write down something as important as that, don't you think?

Maître Gautrat, the lawyer appearing for the family, wanted me to ask the victim's mother to forgive me. I said to her, "Madame, I do not have to ask your forgiveness because I did not kill your son. I express my sorrow for your grief; that is all I can do."

But Commissaire Gérardin and Inspector Grimaldi changed nothing of their first statement: Lepetit had said, "It was Papillon Roger," that was all.

Now the key witness came forward: Goldstein. Using a recording machine at 36, quai des Orfèvres, this witness had made five or six statements, three of which were used. Each one accused me; it did not matter if they were contradictory—each time they brought a fresh piece of wood to the framework the police were building up. Sitting on the bench thirty-six years later, I could see Goldstein as if he were right in front of me. He spoke in a low voice: he scarcely raised his hand when he said, "I swear it."

When he had finished his statement, Maître Beffey went for him. "Goldstein, how many times have you met Inspector Mayzaud 'by chance'? He himself states that he has met you and talked to you about this case 'by chance' several times. It's curious, Goldstein. In your first statement you said you knew nothing about the affair; then you knew Papillon; after that you said you had met him on the night of the crime, before it was committed; then he tells you go to Lariboisière and see how Lepetit is getting on. How do you explain these differing statements?"

Goldstein's only reply was to repeat, "I was afraid, because in Montmartre Papillon is terribly dangerous."

I made a gesture of protest and the president said to me, "Defendant, have you any questions to ask the witness?"

"Yes, Monsieur le Président." I looked straight at Goldstein. "Goldstein, turn this way and look me in the face. What is it that makes you lie and accuse me falsely? What crime of yours does Mayzaud know about? What crime are you paying for with these lying statements?"

The shit trembled as he looked me in the face, but he did manage to bring out the words "I'm telling the truth" quite distinctly.

I could have killed the swine! I turned toward the court. "Gentlemen of the court, gentlemen of the jury, the public prosecutor says I am an intelligent, sharp-witted, knowing character; but the witness's evidence shows me to be a perfect idiot, and I'll prove it to you. Admitting something as important as this, telling a man you don't know at all you've just killed his friend, is the act of a total imbecile. Yet I don't know Goldstein." And turning toward Goldstein I went on, "Goldstein, please name one single person in Paris or in the whole of France who can say he has seen us talking together even once."

"I don't know anyone who could testify to that."

"Right. Please name a bar, restaurant, or eating place in Montmartre, Paris, or anywhere in France where we have eaten or drunk together even once."

"I've never eaten or drunk with you."

"Very well. You say the first time you met me that extraordinary night I had two men with me. Who were they?"

"I don't know them."

"Nor do I. Now say quickly, without hesitating, where I told you to meet me with the answer you were to bring back from the hospital, and say whether you mentioned that place to the men who went with you. And if you did not mention it to them, why not?"

No answer.

"Reply, Goldstein. Why don't you reply?"

"I didn't know where to find you."

Maître Raymond Hubert: "So my client sends you on an errand as important as this—he sends you to find out Roland Lepetit's condition, and you did not know where to give him the answer? It is as absurd as it is unbelievable!"

Yes, it was unbelievable all right; but it was even more unbelievable that the whole indictment had been allowed to be built up on the successive accusations of this dreary jerk who, although carefully coached by the pigs, did not even have wits enough to give a quick answer.

The president: "Charrière, the police claim that you killed Lepetit because he called you an informer. What have you to say to that?"

"I've had dealings with the police six times, and each time I came away with the charge dismissed or an acquittal, except for my four months' suspended sentence. I've never been arrested with another man; I've never had another man arrested. It makes no sense that when I am in the hands of the police I stay mum, and when I'm at liberty I inform on my friends."

"An inspector says you are an informer. Call Inspector Mazillier."

"I state that Charrière was an informer, one who enabled me to arrest several dangerous individuals, and that this was known in Montmartre. As to the Lepetit affair, I know nothing about it."

"What have you to say to that, Charrière?"

"It had been on Maître Beffey's advice that I had

asked for this inspector to be called at the inquiry; Maître Beffey had told me Mazillier knew the truth about the murder of Lepetit. And now I see that both my counsel and I fell into a horrible trap. Inspector Mazillier, when he advised Maître Beffey to call him, said he knew all about the killing; my counsel believed him, and so did I. We imagined that either he was an honest cop or there was some rivalry between him and Mayzaud that led him to give evidence about his crime. But now, as you see yourself, he says he knows nothing about it.

"On the other hand, it's clear that the inspector's statements at last provided the missing motive for my alleged crime. This statement, coming from a policeman, was a godsend: it preserved the framework of the accusation and gave some body to an indictment that just didn't hold together. Because there's no doubt that without the help given by Mazillier, the indictment would have fallen to pieces, in spite of all Inspector Mayzaud's efforts. The dodge is so obvious that it's astonishing the prosecution should ever have used it."

I fought on and I said, "Gentlemen of the court, gentlemen of the jury, if I'd been a police informer, one of two things would have happened: either I wouldn't have killed Roland Lepetit for calling me a squealer—because a character as low as that takes such an insult without batting an eyelid—either I wouldn't have killed him at all, or, if I had shot him, the police would have played the game: they would never have gone after my blood with all this zeal and all this clumsiness, if I'd been so useful to them. More than that, they would have closed their eyes or fixed some gimmick to make it look as though I was acting in legitimate self-defense. Plenty of precedents of that kind could be quoted; but fortunately for me they don't apply. Monsieur le Président, may I ask the witness a question?"

"Yes."

Knowing what I was up to, Maître Raymond Hubert asked the court to free Inspector Mazillier from his professional secrecy, otherwise he would not be able to reply.

The president: "By its discretionary powers, the court releases Inspector Mazillier from his professional secrecy, and requires him, in the interests of truth and justice, to answer the question the defendant is about to put to him."

"Mazillier, name one single man in France, the colonies or abroad whom you have arrested because of my information."

"I cannot reply."

"You're a liar, Inspector! You can't reply because there's never been one!"

"Charrière, moderate your language," said the president.

"Monsieur le Président, I'm defending two things here, my life and my honor."

But the incident went no further. Mazillier withdrew.

And the other witnesses, how they came rolling up! All cut from the same cloth, all the handiwork of the pigs at 36, quai des Orfèvres, Paris.

And your last explanation, Papi, don't you remember that? The last and the most logical of them all. I can still hear it. "Gentlemen, play it straight with me and listen to what I have to say: It is a fact that Lepetit got only one bullet; he was shot once only; he remained on his feet, he walked off alive, he was allowed to take a taxi. That means the man who shot him did not want to kill him; otherwise he'd have fired four, five, six shots the way we do in the underworld. Anyone who knows Montmartre knows that. So suppose it was me, and suppose I confess and say, 'Gentlemen, this man, for such-and-such a reason, right or wrong, had a row with me or accused me of something; he put his hand in his pocket, and as he was an underworld sort like me, I was afraid, so I fired just one shot to defend myself.' If I said that, at the same time I'd be proving I didn't mean to kill him because he went off on his own feet and alive. Then I would end up by saying to you, 'Since an inspector says I'm very useful to the police, I ask you to accept my confession and to treat the business as unintentional homicide.' "

The court listened in silence: thoughtful, it seemed to me. I went on, "Ten times, a hundred times, both Maître Raymond Hubert and Maître Beffey have asked, 'Was it you who fired? If it was you, say so. You'll get five years at the outside, maybe even less. You'll still be very young when you come out.' But, gentlemen of the court and gentlemen of the jury, I can't take that path, not even to save myself from the guillotine or penal servitude, *because I'm innocent and I've been framed by the police.*"

All this in that sunny courtroom where they let me explain things properly. Poor credulous kid, couldn't you see it was too good to last?

For this was the point where Mayzàud quickly thought up a gimmick. Afraid his fifteen months of effort might be reduced to nothing, he did what was forbidden. During a pause in the hearing he came to see me in the room where I was watched by the *Gardes républicains,* and which he had no right to enter. He came up to me and had the nerve to say, "Why don't you say it was Corsican Roger?"

Completely taken aback, I said, "But I don't know any Corsican Roger."

He talked for a moment, walked quickly out, went to the prosecuting counsel and said to him, "Papillon's just confessed to me that it was Corsican Roger."

And now what this accursed Mayzaud wanted to happen did happen. The trial was stopped, in spite of my protests. Yet I still fought on and I said, "For the last eighteen months Inspector Mayzaud has been saying there's only one Papillon in this case and that it's me; Inspector Mayzaud says there's no doubt that I am Lepetit's killer; Inspector Mayzaud says he's brought honest, unanswerable witnesses who prove my guilt without the shadow of a doubt. Since the police have found all the necessary witnesses and proofs against me, why is their whole framework collapsing? So isn't this whole mass of evidence a pack of lies? And is just one new name tossed into the arena enough for it to seem uncertain anymore that Papillon is guilty? Since you say you've got all the proofs of my guilt, is it merely on the existence of some imaginary Corsican Roger that the trial is to be stopped and started all over again? Just because of some imaginary Corsican Roger, thought up by Mayzaud if you believe me, or thought up by me, if you trust him once again? It's impossible: I demand that the proceedings should go on: I demand to be judged. I beg it of you, gentlemen of the jury and Monsieur le Président!"

You'd won, Papi, you'd very nearly won; it was the honesty of the prosecuting counsel that made you lose. Because this man, Cassagnau, stood up and said, "Gentlemen of the jury, gentlemen of the court, I cannot proceed . . . I no longer know . . . the incident must be expunged . . . I ask the court to postpone the trial and order a further inquiry."

Just that, Papi, just those three phrases of Maître Cassagnau prove that you were condemned on a rotten charge. Because if this upright lawyer had had something clear, straight and unanswerable in his hands, he would not have said, "Stop the trial; I can no longer proceed."

He would have said, "Just one more of Charrière's inventions: the defendant wants to lead us astray with his Corsican Roger. We do not believe a word of it, gentlemen; here I have everything that is required to prove Charrière guilty, and I shall not fail to do so."

But he did not say that, and why not? Because in his

conscience he did not fully believe in his brief, and because he must have begun asking himself questions about the honesty of the pigs who had put it together.

The trial was stopped, and they ordered a supplementary inquiry, *the second in this case*.

One of the newspapers said, "Such a lack of conviction is most unusual."

Of course the supplementary inquiry provided *no new facts whatsoever*. Corsican Roger? Of course he was never found. During this further inquiry the *Gardes républicains* played it straight; when they were asked about the incident in July they gave evidence against Mayzaud. In any case, how could a man who proclaimed his innocence, and proved it logically, and felt the court favorably inclined toward him, how could this man throw the whole thing up and suddenly say, "I was there but I wasn't the one who fired; it was Corsican Roger?"

And what about the other trial, Papi? The last, the decisive hearing: there where the dry guillotine began to work, there where at twenty-five your youth and your faith in life received the great hammer blow of a life sentence; where Mayzaud, sure of himself once more, apologized to the prosecuting counsel and admitted having made a mistake in July; where you shouted at him, "I'll rip off your mask, Mayzaud!" . . . do you really want to live through all that again?

Do you really want to see that courtroom again, and that gray, unhappy day? How many times do I have to tell you that thirty-six years have gone by since then? Do you want to feel that savage blow on the jaw again, the swipe that forced you to struggle for thirty-six years to be able to sit on this bench in the Boulevard de Clichy, in your Montmartre? Yes, indeed; I want to go down those first steps of the ladder that took me to the very bottom of the pit of human degradation, I want to go down them one

by one again, so as to have a better notion of the road I
traveled.

How different it was when I entered the second courtroom, a good-looking boy in a perfectly cut double-
breasted suit. In the first place the sky was so low and
rainy they had to light the chandeliers. This time everything was draped in red, blood-red. Carpets, hangings,
judges' robes—as if they had all been dipped in the
basket that holds the heads of guillotined men. This time
the judges were not about to go off for their holidays; they
had just returned from them; it was not the same as
July.

The old hands of the law courts, the attorneys and
magistrates and so on, know better than anyone how the
weather, the time of the year, the character of the presiding judge, his mood that day, the mood of the prosecuting
counsel and the jury, the defendant's and his lawyers'
fitness—their form—can sometimes influence the scales of
justice.

This time the president did not pay me the compliment
of asking me to explain my case myself; he was quite
satisfied with the monotonous voice of the clerk of the
court reading out the indictment.

The twelve bastards who made up the jury had brains
as damp and dreary as the weather; you could see that in
their moist, dull, half-witted eyes. They lapped up the
baloney of the indictment.

There was absolutely nothing human about the prosecuting counsel.

I felt all this the moment I glanced quickly round the
court. And I had sized it up exactly; during the two days
the trial lasted they hardly let me speak at all.

And now came the same statements, the same evidence, as in July. No point in going over it in detail; it
was the same party beginning all over again with the one

difference that, if I felt outraged and if I sometimes burst out, they shut me up at once.

There was only one really new fact, the appearance of the taxi driver Lellu Fernand, the witness for my alibi, who had not had time to give his evidence before the postponement in July—the only witness the pigs had never been able to find: a myth, according to them.

Yet he was an essential witness for me, because he stated that when he went into the Iris Bar saying "There's just been a shot," *I was there.*

They accused him of being a put-up witness.

Here, on the green bench, thirty-six years later, fury seized hold of me again; I felt neither the cold nor the drizzle that had begun to fall.

Once again I saw the boss of the Iris Bar come into the witness box and state that I could not have been in his place when Lellu came in to say there had been a shot outside, because two weeks before he had forbidden me to enter his bar. That meant I was such a bloody fool that in a job as serious as this, with my freedom and perhaps my life at stake, the alibi I gave involved a place where I was not allowed to go! And his waiter confirmed his evidence. Naturally they forgot to add that permission to stay open until five in the morning was a favor granted by the police, and that if they told the truth their closing time would be brought back to two o'clock. The boss was defending his till and the waiter his tips.

Maître Raymond Hubert did all he could, and so did Maître Beffey—a Maître Beffey so disgusted that he reached the point of open war with Mayzaud, who, in confidential police reports, tried to damage his standing as a lawyer by giving details of sexual matters that had nothing to do with the case.

Now it was the end, I was the last to speak. What could I say? "I'm innocent. I've been framed by the police. That's all."

The jury and the court withdrew. An hour later they returned and I stood up while they went back to their places. Then in his turn the president rose: he was about to read the sentence. "Prisoner at the bar, stand up."

And so firmly did I believe I was in the court, there under the trees in the Boulevard de Clichy, that I jumped to my feet, forgetting that my legs were pinned against the back of the bench, which made me fall back on my ass.

So it was sitting, not standing as I ought to have been, that there under the boulevard trees in 1967, I heard the toneless voice of the president who, in October, 1931, pronounced this sentence: "You are condemned to penal servitude for life. Guards, take the prisoner away."

I was just about to hold out my hands; but there was no one to put on the handcuffs; there were no *Gardes républicains* beside me. There was no one except a poor old woman curled up at the far end of the bench, with newspapers on her head to protect her from the cold and the rain.

I untwisted my legs. Standing at last, I let them get over their stiffness and then, lifting the papers, I put a hundred-franc note into the hands of this old woman, sentenced to extreme poverty for life. For me, "life" had lasted only fourteen years.

And still keeping under the trees in the middle of the Boulevard de Clichy, I walked along to Place Blanche, pursued by the last image of that trial--myself standing to receive the unbelievable blow that wiped me out of Montmartre, my Montmartre, for nearly forty years.

I had scarcely reached that wonderful square before the magic lantern went out, and all I saw were a few bums sitting there at the exit from the Métro, squatting with their heads on their knees, asleep.

Quickly I looked round for a cab. There was nothing here to attract me, neither the shadow of the trees that hid the glare of artificial light nor the brilliance of the square, with its Moulin Rouge blazing away for all it was worth. One reminded me too much of my past, and the other proclaimed, "You don't belong here anymore." Everything, yes, everything had changed; get out quick if you don't want to see that the memories of your twenties are dead and buried.

"Hey! Taxi! Gare de Lyon, please."

In the suburban train that took me back to my nephew's, I recalled all the newspaper articles that Maître Raymond Hubert had given me to read after my conviction. Not one of them could avoid speaking of the doubt that had hung over the whole case; *Le Journal* gave it the headline "A Dubious Case."

I looked up these papers later.

An article from *L'Humanité* of October 28 deserves to be quoted at length.

CHARRIÈRE-PAPILLON CONDEMNED
TO PENAL SERVITUDE FOR LIFE

In spite of the persisting doubt as to the identity of the real Papillon, the jury of the Seine convicted Charrière of being the Papillon who is said to have killed Roland Lepetit on the Butte one night in March.

At the beginning of yesterday's hearing, the witness Goldstein, upon whose statements the whole charge rests, gave evidence. This witness, who remained in continual contact with the police and whom Inspector Mayzaud said he had seen more than a hundred times since the tragedy, made his statements on three separate occasions, each deposition being more serious than the last. It is clear that this witness is a loyal helper of the criminal police.

While the witness was uttering his accusations, Charrière listened closely. When Goldstein had fin-

ished, Charrière cried, "I don't understand, I don't understand this Goldstein: I have never done him any harm, and yet he comes here and pours out lies whose only aim is to get me sent to penal servitude."

Inspector Mayzaud was recalled. This time he claimed that Goldstein's evidence was spontaneous. But skeptical smiles were seen in court.

For the prosecution Siramy made a rambling closing speech in which he observed that there were several Papillons in Montmartre and even elsewhere. Nevertheless he asked for a conviction, though without being exact as to the sentence, which he left to the jury.

Maître Gautrat, representing the family, comically held up penal servitude as a school of "moral betterment" and then asked that Charrière should be sent there for his own good, so as to be made an "honest man."

The counsels for the defense, Maîtres Beffey and Raymond Hubert, pleaded innocence. It did not follow that since Corsican Roger, otherwise Papillon, could not be found, Charrière, otherwise Papillon, was therefore guilty.

But after a long retirement the jury came back, bringing in the verdict of guilty, and the court sentenced Henri Charrière to penal servitude for life, awarding the family one franc damages.

For years and years I have asked myself this question: why did the police go all out to screw a little crook who they *themselves* said was one of their best helpers? I have found a single answer, the only logical one: they were covering up for someone else, and this someone else was a *genuine informer.*

*   *   *

The next day, in the sun, I went back to Montmartre. I found my old haunts again, the Rue Tholozé and the Rue Durantin; and the market in the Rue Lepic.

I went into 26, rue Tholozé to see the concierge, pretending to be looking for someone. My concierge had been a big fat woman with a hairy wart on her cheek. She had vanished, and a woman from Brittany had taken her place.

The Montmartre of my youth had not been stolen; no, everything was there, absolutely everything; but it had all changed. The dairy had turned into a laundromat, the local bar into a drugstore, and the fruit shop into an automat.

The Bandevez Bar, at the corner of the Rue Tholozé and the Rue Durantin, used to be the meeting place for women from the post office in the Place des Abbesses; they came and drank their little glass of *blanc-cassis,* and to make them fly off the handle we solemnly reproved them for getting blind drunk while their poor husbands were working. Well, the joint was still there; but the bar had been moved to the other side, and the two tables were no longer in their right place. What's more, the owner of the bar was a *pied noir* from Algeria, and the customers were Arabs or Spaniards or Portuguese. Where can the old boss have vanished to—the fellow from the Auvergne?

I went up the steps that lead from the Rue Tholozé to the Moulin de la Galette. At least the handrail had not changed; it still ended as dangerously as ever. It was here that I had picked up a poor little old man who had fallen on his nose, not seeing well enough to make out that the rail stopped so soon. I stroked the rail: I saw the scene again and I heard the old man thank me: "Young man, you are truly kind and very well brought up. I congratulate you upon it, and I thank you." These simple words so disturbed me that I did not know how to set about picking up the gun I had dropped as I leaned over him; I did not want him to see that the good young man was maybe not as kind as all that.

Yes, my Montmartre was still there all right. It had not been stolen from me—they had just stolen the people.

That evening I went into a rough bar. I chose the oldest of all the old guys there and I said to him, "Excuse me, but do you know So-and-so?"

"Yes."

"Where is he?"

"Inside."

"And So-and-so?"

"Dead."

"And So-and-so?"

"Don't know him. But you ask a lot of questions. Who are you?"

He raised his voice a little on purpose, to attract the others' attention. It never misses. An unknown who just walks into a men's bar like that without introducing himself or having a friend—you have to find out what he's after.

"My name's Henri. I'm from Avignon and I've been in Colombia. That's why you don't know me. Be seeing you."

I did not linger but hurried off to catch my train so I'd be sure to sleep outside the Département of the Seine. At no price did I want them to notify me that I was forbidden to be there.

But I was in Paris. I was there. I went and danced at the little places round the Bastille. At Boucastel's and at the Bal-à-Jo I shoved my hat back and took off my tie. I even had the nerve to ask a skirt to dance just as I used to do when I was twenty, and in the same way. And as we waltzed to the sound of an accordion almost as good as Mimile Vacher's when I was young, the chick asked me what I did for a living and I told her I kept a house in the provinces; so I was looked upon with great respect.

I went and had lunch at La Coupole, and as if I had returned from another world I was simpleminded enough to ask a waiter whether they still bowled on the flat roof. He had been there twenty-five years, but my question absolutely stunned him.

At La Rotonde I looked for the painter Foujiya's corner, but in vain; my eyes gazed hopelessly at the furniture, the layout of the tables and the bar, looking for something that belonged to the past: disgusted at seeing that everything had been turned upside-down and that they had destroyed everything I had known and loved, I walked straight out, forgetting to pay. The waiter grabbed my arm at the entrance to the Vavin Métro just by, and, as manners have been forgotten in France, he bawled the amount of the bill into my face and told me to pay up quick if I didn't want him to call a cop. Of course I paid, but I gave him such a paltry trip that as he left he threw it at me. "You can keep that for your mother-in-law. She must need it more than me!"

But Paris is Paris. As brisk as a young man, I walked right up the Champs-Elysées and then right down again, the Champs-Elysées lit with thousands of lights, with that light of Paris that warms you through and through and casts its wonderful spell, giving you a song in your heart. Ah, life is sweet in Paris!

There was not the least overexcitement in me, not the least longing for violence, as I stood there at the Porte Saint-Denis or in front of the old *L'Auto* office in the Faubourg Montmartre, where Rigoulot, then champion of the world, used to lift a huge roll of newsprint. My heart was quiet as I passed in front of the club where I used to play baccarat with Stavisky; and I went to watch the Lido show alone and perfectly calm. Quietly I mixed in the turmoil of Les Halles for a few hours—they, at least, were more or less the same as before. It was only when I was in Montmartre that bitter words rose in my heart.

I stayed eight days in Paris. Eight times I went back to the scene of that famous murder.

Eight times I stroked the tree and then sat on the bench.

Eight times, with closed eyes, I put together all I knew of the inquiry and my two trials.

Eight times I saw the ugly faces of all those swine who manufactured my conviction.

Eight times I whispered, "This is where it all began, the theft of those fourteen years of your youth."

Eight times I repeated, "You have given up your revenge; that's fine; but never will you be able to forgive."

Eight times I asked God that as a reward for my giving up my revenge the same kind of thing should never happen to anyone else.

Eight times I asked the bench whether the false witness and the shifty pig had cooked up their next statement in this very place.

Eight times I went away, less and less bowed down, so that the last time I walked off as straight and supple as a young man, whispering to myself, "You won after all, man, since you're here, free, fit, beloved and master of your future. Don't go trying to find out what has happened to those others—they belong to your past. You're here, and that's close to a miracle. And you can be sure that of all the people involved in this business, you're the happiest."